UNLEASH

The phenomena of status and weapon dogs

Simon Harding

First published in Great Britain in 2014 by

Policy Press
University of Bristol
6th Floor
Howard House
Queen's Avenue
Clifton
Bristol BS8 1SD
UK
t: +44 (0)117 331 5020
f: +44 (0)117 331 5369
pp-info@bristol.ac.uk
www.policypress.co.uk

North America office:
Policy Press
c/o The University of Chicago Press
1427 East 60th Street
Chicago, IL 60637, USA
t: +1 773 702 7700
f: +1 773-702-9756
sales@press.uchicago.edu
www.press.uchicago.edu

© Policy Press 2014

British Library Cataloguing in Publication Data
A catalogue record for this book is available from the British Library.

Library of Congress Cataloging-in-Publication Data
A catalog record for this book has been requested.

ISBN 978 1 44731 620 6 paperback

The right of Simon Harding to be identified as author of this work has been
asserted by him in accordance with the Copyright, Designs and Patents Act 1988.

Cover design by Soapbox design
Front cover: image kindly supplied by Getty
Printed and bound in Great Britain by CMP, Poole
Policy Press uses environmentally responsible print partners

Contents

List of figures and tables

Figures

Tables

List of abbreviations

ABC	acceptable behaviour contract
ABD	American bulldog
ABH	actual bodily harm
ABM	All 'bout Money (south London gang)
ACPO	Association of Chief Police Officers
ADBA	American Dog Breeders Association
ALHC	Animal Legal and Historical Center at Michigan State University
APBT	American pitbull terrier
ASBO	antisocial behaviour order
BARK	Brent Action for Responsible K9s (or generic Borough Action for Responsible K9s)
BDCH	Battersea Dogs and Cats Home
BSL	breed-specific legislation
CPS	Crown Prosecution Service
CRIS	Crime Reporting and Information System (used by UK police)
CWU	Communication Workers Union
DDA	Dangerous Dogs Act 1991
DD(A)A	Dangerous Dogs (Amendment) Act 1997
Defra	Department for Environment, Food and Rural Affairs
DLO	dog legislation officer
FOI	freedom of information
GBH	grievous bodily harm
GLA	Greater London Authority
HES	Hospital Episode Statistics
HMCS	Her Majesty's Courts Service
HSUS	The Humane Society of the United States
IED	Index of Exempted Dogs
LDDF	London Dangerous Dog Forum
LTOA	London Tree Officers Association
MPS	Metropolitan Police Service
MPS SDU	Metropolitan Police Service Status Dog Unit
NHS	National Health Service
PBT	pitbull terrier
PCSO	police community support officer
RSL	registered social landlord
RSPCA	Royal Society for the Prevention of Cruelty to Animals
SBT	Staffordshire bull terrier
SDU	Status Dog Unit
SNT	Safer Neighbourhood team
SOCA	Serious Organised Crime Agency
YOT	youth offending team

About the author

Simon Harding is a visiting lecturer on community safety at the University of Bedfordshire, UK, where he is currently studying for a Professional Doctorate in Youth Justice at the Vauxhall Centre for the Study of Crime. He has worked in crime and community safety for 25 years, including the Home Office, local authorities and the Audit Commission. He currently works in research, consultancy and training.

Acknowledgments

My thanks are due to many who have assisted with this project since its inception, offering evidence, advice, guidance and support, information, argument, critique and, of course, their valuable time.

Initial thanks goes to Claire Robinson of the RSPCA, who kindly invited me to one of its conferences on status dogs where I was introduced to Dr David Grant of the Harmsworth Memorial Animal Hospital in north London. David, a passionate believer in animal welfare keen to bring this issue to light, has kindly written a foreword for this book.

I am grateful for the advice and assistance of practitioners, particulary officers, managers and workers of organisations such as the RSPCA, MPS, Blue Cross, the Dogs Trust, and the People with Dogs project. I am particularly indebted to those practitioners who provided me with lengthy and extended interviews: Ian McParland (ex-MPS), Inspector Trevor Hughes of the MPS, Sergeant Steve Pennington of the Merseyside Police Service; PC Keith Evans at West Midlands Police; Doug Skinner, MPS Greenwich; Mark Callis at Wandsworth Council; and Russell Taylor at Lambeth MPS.

Thanks also to other writers and researchers, including Gillian Diesel, Rachel Moxon, Jane Healy and Hanna Coate at the Animal Legal and Historical Center, Michigan State University College of Law, and Dr Mary Lou Randour, Director, Department of Human–Animal Relations: Education & Outreach at HSUS. I am also grateful to support from Tracy Chopping at GLA and to Amy Watson, Charlotte Walsh and colleagues at Battersea Dogs and Cats Home.

My gracious thanks also to my interview respondents; I am hugely indebted to them for their time and for the information they provided their time and information. I offer special thanks to the four boys I interviewed in Forster Park, who gave insights into organised dog fighting, and to Carl James Oyston for his insightful and fascinating accounts of the role of dogs in excluded communities. A special mention goes to his faithful old dog, Max.

Thanks are especially due to Professor John Pitts, Dr Tim Bateman and Professor Anthony Goodman for reading early drafts and offering guidance on presentation. Their assistance and their time was very much appreciated.

Lastly I extend my gratitude to staff at Policy Press, particulary editorial assistant Laura Vickers and commissioning editor Karen

Bowler, who had the forsight to recognise that a publication on this topic in the UK was overdue and championed this author and this publication.

My final thanks to my partner Tomai for allowing me to fill the house with books on dogs and for resisting the temptation to get a pet.

Foreword

For the past five years or so it was obvious that there was a problem with certain types of dogs and in particular their owners. A year or so ago, it became worse. In the RSPCA Harmsworth hospital, we were seeing two or three dog fights per day. One weekend, a colleague on duty had to deal with 10 separate fights. All these dogs were Staffordshire bull terrier crosses or pitbull crosses. On the Monday morning, this colleague decided he had had enough and handed in his notice.

The loss of an experienced and valued colleague concentrated my mind and I started to look for answers. To do that, I had first to decide exactly what the problem was and what, if any, were the underlying causes. Only then might it be possible to start considering solutions. From the outset, it seemed obvious to me that the media, politicians, some animal charities and most veterinary surgeons did not really understand the problem and were keen to come up with quick-fix answers. The most obvious example of this is the Dangerous Dogs Act (DDA) 1991, a hasty Act that has achieved nothing.

In terms of the problem there were two separate issues. First, Staffordshire bull terriers and their crosses had over a period of some years become a fashion accessory dog. This had led to some people realising that these dogs could be bred for profit. Puppies, with no pedigrees, were changing hands for £500 each. Bitches were being bred twice yearly until exhausted, netting the 'breeder' (usually living in social housing in poor areas) up to £8,000 in a year. Many people bought the pups, either on a whim or for breeding. This resulted in considerable cruelty by neglect caused by people with no interest in or knowledge of animal welfare. Subsequently, these owners often found they could not afford to keep the dogs, which led to unprecedented abandonment. Even some years later, following much debate and many attempts to educate the public, dog rescue centres are full to overflowing with abandoned dogs.

The second problematical issue was the pitbull or its type. Despite being illegal under the DDA, I was seeing large numbers of such dogs either owned or abandoned. These are the so-called status dogs, or dangerous dogs. From this sector of the problem came most of the headlines in the newspapers. It seemed to me that these dogs were owned predominantly by young, poorly educated, unemployed men. I am not sure that status dog is that useful a term, but it seems to have caught the public's imagination. My experience of dealing with these owners made me realise that they had very little status in society. They were usually in gangs and took pride in the toughness of their dogs. On questioning, they would always say that they loved their dog. But their actions did not support this statement. I would see many fights, attacks on other dogs and attacks on people. The fatal attacks would inevitably cause an outcry and pressure on politicians to act, and do something.

Most such dogs were viewed as protection for the owner. Being a member of a gang seems to me to be inherently dangerous and whereas carrying a knife is protection from rival gangs, this might lead to prosecution. Having a dog as protection is seen as a better strategy and came with the additional advantage of conferring status. Because there was soon a demand for such dogs inevitably the indiscriminate breeding followed, with exactly the same kind of problems associated with the indiscriminate breeding of the Staffordshire bull terrier crosses. In addition to the pit-type dog other large dogs such as the dogue de Bordeaux, bull mastiff, rottweiler, Japanese akita and others became very popular as large protective dogs. None of these dogs in the right hands poses a problem. In the wrong hands, they can be lethal, especially if trained, as many are, to be aggressive.

Apart from protection and, at the extreme end of the cruelty spectrum, the large dogs were used by some individuals to attack people and commission crime such as muggings. From a veterinary perspective I noticed that when any of these dogs were injured or diseased there was frequently an unreasonable delay, days to weeks, before veterinary advice was sought, leading to prosecutions.

My thoughts on the underlying causes of the problem were entirely to do with the owners not the dogs, which exposes the illogicality of trying to ban specific breeds. Indiscriminate breeding of dogs by poorly educated young people for undeclared profit is a major driver of the problem. As this is occurring predominantly in socially deprived areas of major cities such as London, what are social housing providers doing about their properties being used to breed dogs? Do they have tenancy agreements? And are they enforced?

Why are these young people failing our education system? Many of them can hardly read. Why is this? It seems obvious to me that these young people, especially if they are born into poverty, are destined to lead blighted lives from the moment they are born. They are on a conveyor belt of social and educational deprivation from day one. There is plenty of evidence of woefully inadequate parenting. The government is, or should be, well aware of this; ministers need only read the Graham Allen Review,[1] February 2011, which advocates early years intervention. Thus I regard the dangerous/status dog issue as a sign of society's malaise, with breeding being a major contributing factor.

In order to concentrate the minds of politicians, the only people who can actually act to make a difference, lobbying is needed to educate them as to what the problems are. In order to convince politicians of the complexity of the problem, it is no use people like me continually harping on about the scale of the problem, as I think they are aware of it. What is needed now is scientific evidence as to the underlying causes and an assessment as to whether my analysis is correct. This book by Simon Harding, a practitioner and criminologist, is based on careful evidence collection from individuals causing the problem and additional original research. He sources the existing relevant evidence and for the first time collates this in one document. It should be read by anyone who wants to understand the phenomenon of status dogs, to make a difference and to do something about the malaise afflicting certain segments of society. This malaise is leading to blighted lives and animal cruelty, both of which are totally unacceptable in a modern, developed country such as ours.

David Grant
Director, RSPCA Harmsworth Memorial Animal Hospital, London

Note
[1] Labour MP Graham Allen was appointed by the government in 2010 to lead an independent review into early intervention. The report, published by HMSO in January 2011, is entitled *Early intervention: The next steps.*

Introduction

The murder of Seyi Ogunyemi

On the night of 27 April 2009, 16-year-old Seyi Ogunyemi and five friends, associates or members of the ABM (All 'bout Money) gang based in Stockwell Gardens Estate, London SW9, entered Larkhall Park, Lambeth. The park is contested territory between local gang ABM and a rival gang, 031 (pronounced O-tray), whose members are predominately from neighbouring SW8. The two gangs had been rivals for the previous two years or more. Rivalry between the two groups sometimes precipitated a shoot-on-sight policy. In 2007, five young men aged between 15 and 23, each with links to one of these two groups, were murdered in the local area, with a further young man dying in 2008. Deaths were often linked to 'respect' issues, failure to pay debts or 'slippin' ', the name given to a being in the wrong place at the wrong time – it usually refers to gang members or associates being on rival territory.

By 2009, tensions between ABM and 031 were high. A group of around 12 members of the 031 gang were said to be 'patrolling their home turf' of the Larkhall Park Estate off Wandsworth Road. Aged between 15 and 21, they were described by witnesses as being 'on a mission', dressed in dark, hooded tops with bandanas covering their faces. Among the 12-strong group of 031 members were brothers Chrisdian Johnson (22), Shane Johnson (20) and Darcy Menezes (18). Two aggressive dogs accompanied the gang: an adult female brindle Staffordshire bull terrier (called Mia) belonging to Menezes and an adult male Staffordshire bull terrier–bull mastiff cross (called Tyson). Having spotted Seyi and his friends, and recognising them as ABM members, the 031 gang chased the boys across the park. At this stage, Chrisdian Johnson and Menezes unleashed their dogs, with 'devastating consequences'.[1] Seyi and his friends scattered, pursued by the dogs. Seyi, weighing 44kgs, tried to escape by scaling a fence, but was caught by Johnson's dog, Tyson, and pulled to the ground. The other dog caught up with 17-year-old Hurui Hiyabu and attacked him on the ground. Both boys were then attacked by the dogs and bitten on the legs. During this time, the pursuing gang caught up with both boys and began stabbing them repeatedly. Hiyabu was stabbed nine times and survived. Seyi was badly bitten and stabbed six times, with two blows piercing his aorta. Despite emergency surgery at the scene, he died shortly afterwards. Two other friends of Seyi were also bitten and attacked, while one was stabbed in the attack but survived. According to evidence given at the trial 'the dog was still biting (Seyi's) legs while the stabbing was going on'.[2] Other members of the 031 gang were involved in the stabbing, moving actively between the two key victims prostrate on the grass. The 031 gang ran off, although a few minutes later a smaller group returned with one of dogs to watch the events unfold. One of this group was heard to shout out, "You've been shanked" (stabbed), before running away.

Chrisdian Johnson was later arrested near the scene, having removed the top half of his clothing, which was covered in his dog's blood. His dog had apparently been mistakenly stabbed during the incident. Shane Johnson and Darcy Menezes were also arrested and charged with murder and attempted murder. At the Old Bailey trial in 2010, Prosecutor Brian Altman QC described the murder as "an unusual if not unique case", noting that "in the initial stages of the attack both dogs were deployed as weapons". This fact was confirmed by one of the witnesses who heard Johnson command his dog to "get them".[3] The attack was described by one onlooker as 'vicious' and the actions of the gang as 'mirroring the behaviour of a pack of wild animals'. Continuing, Brian Altman QC said the dogs "were unleashed and brought down and savaged their victims, gaining their human an advantage by enabling them to access their victims in order to stab them".

Johnson's injured dog (Tyson) was treated for injuries at the Blue Cross veterinary hospital in Victoria. Tyson had previously been microchipped and insured by Chrisdian Johnson, thus confirming him as owner. It was also established that in September 2008, several months previously, Johnson was issued with a court order under the Dangerous Dogs Act (DDA) 1991, requiring that Tyson be leashed and muzzled at all times in public. The dog was placed on the Index of Exempted Dogs, thus saving it from destruction. The second dog, Mia, had also been involved in a previous attack on an 11-year-old boy in the same park several months earlier, resulting in the boy needing hospital treatment. No action was taken against Mia or the owner at the time.

Dr Robert Ogden, an expert in non-human genetics, gave evidence at the trial that it was Mia who caused the damage to Seyi's clothing.

Crucial to the case was the fact Johnson's dog Tyson had been accidentally stabbed. A 550 metre trail of blood led from the scene where the injured dog had been carried away. Blood samples taken from Johnson were then tested by Dr Ogden and scientists at Edinburgh University on a newly established dog DNA database. While previously only permitting identification of dog breed, this new database also enabled statistical analysis on samples. Johnson had been found to have both Seyi's DNA and non-human DNA on his body. Analysis by Dr Ogden and his team used the dog DNA to establish a one-in-a billion match between Chrisdian Johnson and Seyi Ogunyemi. Saliva found on Hiyabu's clothing also matched the DNA profile of Mia.

Johnson was convicted of murder and attempted murder and was jailed for life with a minimum sentence of 24 years. Judge Moss QC told him, "You used two fearsome weapons, the first was your pitbull cross dog which I have no doubt you had trained to attack and bring down your prey", noting that "you were plainly members of rival London gangs" and adding that "gang-related violence such as this will not be tolerated".[4] Johnson's brother Shane was cleared of murder and attempted murder. Darcey Menezes was cleared of all charges, though acknowledged to have been present at the time.

Detectives claimed this was the first time that it had been proven in court that dogs were used as weapons. This killing was widely reported in London and triggered several police operations to target 'weapon' or 'assault dogs' used either to threaten and intimidate or attack rival gang members or for dog fighting. Some three months after the Larkhall Park murder Lambeth police launched Operation Navarra, a series of raids on properties in the borough known to house aggressive or dangerous dogs.

This event both shocked and intrigued Londoners. How could such a thing happen? Regional media increasingly covered the incident. Regional media began to pick up the story and airwaves and newspaper columns began to fill with the views of anxious dog owners and dog walkers keen to suggest this was an incident waiting to happen. They talked anxiously about rising number of pitbulls and other aggressive dogs regularly seen in parks and open spaces, often used by young men to intimidate their rivals and the general public. There was also, as in this case, a perceived link to violent urban street gangs, a relatively new phenomenon currently evolving in London. As I was already undertaking ethnographic research into such gangs in south London, this tragic incident caught my attention and I too began to ask similar questions: how could this happen here and why did this happen? Thus began a two-and-a-half year investigation into the topic of status dogs.

The new phenomenon of status dogs

A new issue for social policy and community safety has emerged in recent years in the UK and the US. Some dog owners are using certain breeds of dog to convey authority, power and control over other people and places while gaining a sense of what they believe to be elevated image and 'status'. The terms 'status dog', 'trophy dog' and even 'weapon dog' are now used in the public lexicon to describe dogs associated with this phenomenon. They are usually dogs prescribed by the DDA 1991 or considered sufficiently fierce or aggressive to warrant pariah status by the public, for example pitbulls, bull breeds (notably mastiffs), Staffordshire bull terriers and rottweilers. Evidence for this newly emerged issue includes widespread national media coverage, an alarming upsurge of illegal dog fighting in the UK, coupled with a rise in dog attacks against the public, and an increase in irresponsible breeding of both dangerous dogs and aggressive dogs. A similar phenomenon has emerged in the US.

The association between certain dog breeds and status is not a new phenomenon. Dogs' place in society has long been linked to their particular attributes, abilities or associations, for example, corgis as royal lapdogs, greyhounds as racing dogs, and bloodhounds as tracking dogs. What is new, however, is that the qualities of aggression and fierce loyalty often found in dogs such as pitbulls, Staffordshire bull terriers and other bull breeds are now actively sought after by owners who admire such qualities. These dogs are increasingly associated with 'hoodies', criminals and gangs. A sizeable number of owners of these aggressive breeds now empathise with their pariah social status and actively identify and associate themselves with the image of aggression, violence and strength for which these breeds are reputed. For some owners, these canine qualities are then adopted or internalised, as if the very act of ownership or handling and controlling an aggressive dog confers on them the same qualities. For some owners these are qualities to be valued and valorised. And to retain such qualities, even vicariously through ownership of a dog perceived to have these characteristics, is a way of generating respect from others and thus gaining status in their social circle. In short, owning such a dog is believed to convey a certain 'status'. This in turn conveys personal power and authority in certain social settings. This in itself can designate authority or ability to exert control over people, property or places. The breeds that are considered to generate and convey status have been dubbed status dogs by the media and by practitioners.

Since the introduction of the DDA 1991, some dog breeds have been pathologised and demonised in public life, that is, legally classified as dangerous/lethal and subject to legal seizure and euthanasia, and to negative media portrayals and reports. This may in turn become attractive to certain people who believe that owning such a dog equates to being above the law. These breeds now come with a negative PR that is not only embraced and coveted, but is also seductive and impressive to some. For example, amateur and professional dog-fighting enthusiasts often refer to such dogs as being 'the ultimate warriors'. The breed that typifies this image more than any other is the pitbull, although other bull breeds follow close behind.

For many, these dogs are frightening and a threat to public safety. The public, practitioners and the media have branded the dogs a menace and the media has generated debates about the aggressive nature of both the dogs and their owners. These aggressive breeds have entered the public consciousness in many ways and are highly visible on streets, in parks, and in contemporary culture. Indeed, they are eulogised in contemporary rap culture and in television series such as HBO's *The wire*.

In examining this phenomenon, there are several aspects to consider:

- Is the traditional role of dogs, including bull breeds, changing?
- Why is the DDA 1991 contentious and what is the deed or breed debate?
- What is a status dog? Is the issue real or simply a media construction? Why are some breeds favoured as status dogs?
- Who are the owners/breeders of status dogs? What motivates them to use dogs in this way?
- Do owners of status dogs have links to gangs, crime, dog fighting and cruelty?
- What impact does this issue have for the general public?
- Which cultural signifiers and influencers act as a backdrop to this phenomenon?
- What are the responses from the police, criminal justice agencies and government?

The topic of status dogs raises many questions and straddles a strange middle ground at the convergence of sociology, criminology, social policy, animal welfare and human–animal relations. Falling between so many disciplinary stools has probably inhibited the take-up of this issue in term of academic research, and thus it has, until now, largely been addressed at practitioner level.

This book attempts to address these issues by pulling together the disparate strands of this confusing picture.

Structure of the book

The following chapters explore the phenomenon of status dogs and weapon dogs and attempt to answer the questions raised above. The focus is on aggressive bull breed dogs used by young people to convey status and not on the pampered pooches of celebrities.

Chapter One presents the numerous methodological and ethical challenges of researching status dogs and set out the methods used in the author's research study that sought to evidence this phenomenon.

Chapter Two considers how this issue came into being. After looking at the traditional role of dogs in society, it examines the changing fortunes of the pitbull in the US, providing a useful lens for examining the emergence of status dogs. It acknowledges the reputational qualities of dogs as being central to how status dogs are conceptualised, and critiques the DDA in the UK while assessing its impact.

Chapter Three considers the role of the media in the social construction of the status dog and weapon dog. It offers a definition of these terms before assessing the issue from the perspective of cultural criminology. Central to this chapter is a critical discourse analysis of UK media, which offers insight into media portrayals of status dogs. Comparative analysis from the US provides further insights. The chapter also introduces the concept of commodification of animals, and intrinsic and extrinsic ownership, noting that animal cruelty and breeding are central to discussions of status dogs.

Chapter Four considers the sociological perspectives underpinning motivations for gaining status. It examines the reputational brand values of dogs and proposes a motivational typology and spectrum based on the different social fields and functional uses of dogs. A key motivation is the desire for owners to acquire street capital, which permits social advancement. The chapter also considers the role of status dogs within the 'ghetto family', or the 'hood' (neighbourhood) in relation to gang culture, and how some dogs can be used as weapons. The overarching backdrops of hip hop and the valorisation of dogs within this culture is also reviewed.

The evidence obtained from the author's research is presented in Chapter Five using data from a variety of sources. This chapter also presents in detail the findings from the author's primary research into status dogs, including visual observations, qualitative interviews and focus groups. These findings suggest the issue of status dogs is both widespread and recognised by the public. The chapter examines the fact that debate is now focusing on the criminal links of some owners of status dogs, and concludes that some owners do indeed have considerable offending histories.

Chapter Six looks at the topic of dog fighting, and its recent resurgence as a cultural activity in the US and the UK. It examines evidence of its existence, presenting a typology of the different levels of dog fighting and arguing that this typology, developed in the US, fits the current situation in the UK.

The increased prevalence and visibility of status dogs has led to increased visibility and anxiety among members of the public, specifically with regard to their safety in public and open spaces. Chapter Seven considers the implications of the status dog phenomenon for the users of parks and open spaces.

Chapter Eight examines in detail how the police and criminal justice agencies address this issue, navigating a tricky route between public opinion and legislative arrangements that at times appear to militate against effective solutions. Good practice is, however, evident. The second part of the chapter details the policy and project responses currently being implemented and developed by local authorities, animal welfare agencies and local and regional government. The chapter closes with a look at proposed legislative changes.

Finally, the conclusion summaries the key points and offers some observations for possible solutions.

The appendices hold additional factual data pertinent to the discussion but may only appeal to those seeking the detail. In places interpretations are given.

Notes

[1] Brian Altman QC, prosecuting counsel. Regina vs Chrisdian Johnson and Shane Johnson. Old Bailey. Transcript of stenograph notes of Wordwave International Limited. Crown copyright.

[2] Summing-up by His Honour Judge Christopher Moss, QC. Regina vs Chrisdian Johnson and Shane Johnson. Old Bailey. Transcript of stenograph notes of Wordwave International Limited. Crown copyright.

[3] Summing-up by His Honour Judge Christopher Moss, QC. Regina vs Chrisdian Johnson and Shane Johnson. Old Bailey. Transcript of stenograph notes of Wordwave International Limited. Crown copyright.

[4] Summing-up by His Honour Judge Christopher Moss, QC. Regina vs Chrisdian Johnson and Shane Johnson. Old Bailey. Transcript of stenograph notes of Wordwave International Limited. Crown copyright.

ONE

Methodological challenges of researching status dogs

The purpose of this book is to consider the phenomenon of status dogs and to assemble for the first time the evidence that shows that this is in fact an issue of some import at present in the UK. Before setting out the evidence uncovered, it is important to consider the unique challenges of undertaking research into this topic and the difficulty of obtaining quality robust data.

Any exploration of this topic must unearth evidence to prove or disprove the premise that status dogs are a contemporary issue in the UK. The literature review on this topic revealed only a handful of studies and a clear lack of primary data. This is perhaps symptomatic of the methodological challenges of conducting research into this phenomenon. Moreover, it is indicative of the fact 'that animal abuse remains both a marginal and marginalised area for criminological investigation' (Hughes and Lawson, 2011). The tardiness of the sociological focus on the issue of status dogs has also arisen from the fact it is a cross-cutting issue falling across a range of disciplines and making it something of a sociological orphan. To address this fact, I set myself the challenge of conducting some primary research to which we shall turn presently. Where evidence is absent due to the lack of primary data, it is important to build the evidence base from its roots and establish credible accounts from practitioners and professionals working with aggressive and illegal dogs on a daily basis. Essentially, it must place on record the views of young people who are the owners/ handlers of the dogs and posit an interpretation of motivations. To achieve this, a research methodology was devised to capture this data using a variety of different methods to triangulate findings from different sources. In addition, it is important to establish what evidence is already held by existing practitioners and agencies working in this field. This requires undertaking secondary or desk research. This process requires early identification of the agencies involved. This book examines both the primary and secondary research and explores specific research challenges, not least identifying and then selecting a suitable methodology.

In deciding on a suitable methodology, several initial challenges present themselves. The first is to identify the research question and the attendant methods for obtaining the answers, that is, what is it that you are trying to prove/find out? In researching status dogs and weapon dogs (aggressive dogs used to deliberately intimidate or threaten or harm others), it is not viable simply to enquire whether such dogs exist or whether someone owns one. Nor is it possible to enquire through interviewing if an owner uses their dog to give them status. It is only possible to determine whether certain people are attracted to or favour certain breeds and then whether certain breeds are used in specific ways by different individuals.

Where a dog is used as a weapon or is seized under current legislation, it may be possible to identify the owners offending history or links to criminals or gang activity. Suffice to say that this line of enquiry did indeed produce some interesting results.

A further challenge in conducting this research is how to differentiate between ordinary and aggressive dogs, and between family pets and status dogs or weapon dogs? This question suggests that owing or possessing an aggressive dog (or any dog for that matter) has a prime and latent function (see Chapter Four).

Establishing the primary and latent function of ownership is, however, also problematic, as these functions may not always be acknowledged, admitted, recognised or understood by respondents. The obvious route to obtaining primary data is through qualitative interviews with status dog owners, but this is not straightforward. Qualitative interviewing may provide insights into the functional relationships between the owner/handler, but this may require subjective assessment of primary and latent motivational functions. Qualitative interviews with owners/handlers of aggressive breeds may illuminate motivations or reasoning – or it may not. Either way, subsequent coding and analysis will require further subjectivity and so is inherently biased. It is thus only possible to draw broad conclusions from qualitative interviews, for example in general, people with these breeds presented as x, y or z. Such conclusions can be strengthened when combined with participant observation of the dog and the relationship between the owner and the dog in a public situation. This then means conducting interviews in public spaces where people interact with their dogs (a key methodological point missed by Maher and Pierpoint, 2011). Personal profiling details of owners/handlers, such as employment status, may not be obtainable, though on occasions may become evident during the course of the interview.

Ethical issues

A number of serious ethical issues presented regarding conducting research, in particular interviewing people about status or weapon dogs. These issues are discussed in the following section.

Researcher safety

Conducting research into ownership of aggressive dogs that may be used as weapons or to convey status brings implicit safety considerations for any researcher. While most people would be happy to talk about their animals, this is not necessarily the case with owners of aggressive dogs. Several interviews were terminated when it became clear I was not welcome. On three occasions, I had evidently interrupted a drugs transaction and on one occasion a pending confrontation. I often felt as if I had 'cramped the style' of those approached. I was conscious of potential threats, realising that violence could come from either owner or dog. Suffice to say that on a few occasions I felt intimidated and under threat. On one occasion, I was caught between two dogs as they set off against each other. On another, I was knocked to the ground by an 'enthusiastic' pitbull terrier–Staffordshire cross.

Informed consent

Informed consent is another key ethical consideration. This is the provision for respondents to be advised that they are being invited for interview and that they may choose not to participate. This process was adopted over that of covert interviewing, as the latter would have increased the potential risks to me as interviewer. This adopted method did, however, result in a high number of refusals to participate.

Research locations

Sourcing individuals for interview also threw up ethical issues. The research locations chosen may introduce bias to the sample of respondents. Two key locations were selected – outside the Harmsworth Animal Memorial Hospital and in a range of suburban parks. All sites were visited on numerous occasions over a nine-month period in 2010. Interviews on public transport were achieved at random. Interviews on social housing estates took place with residents rather than with dog owners.

Research methodology

Having tackled the ethical challenges, it became clear that only certain types of research methods would prove productive in researching this topic. To fully explore the phenomenon of status dogs, a triangulated research method was established containing the following elements:

- a literature review;
- media, document and internet analysis;
- participant observations in parks;
- qualitative interviews with professionals working with dogs; with professionals, residents and gang-affiliated young people in the London Borough of Lambeth, London; and with owners/handlers of aggressive breeds;
- focus groups.

The study was conducted over a two-year period, from April 2009 to April 2011. For the purposes of this research, aggressive or status dogs were identified as bull breeds (including cross-breeds), mastiffs and legally proscribed dangerous dogs.

Literature review

The starting point for this research was to undertake a literature review of academic writing, books, articles and scholarly papers. Searches were done for both the UK and US. In line with earlier comments as to how sociology and criminology have largely ignored the issue of human–animal relationships, it was found that very little has been written with regard to status dogs. The topic of dog fighting had slightly wider academic coverage but only in the US, with UK studies noticeably absent. Links between aggressive animals and criminal activity is a nascent area of US academic study and is absent in the UK. With academic literature so evidently scarce, the evidence assembled by animal welfare agencies and enforcement agencies (reports, statistical data, behavioural observations, conference papers, media reports) became more important. Although contemporary, any studies, such as they are, have seldom been conducted to rigorous academic standards and may be little more than complied tables of data. Data quality therefore is a central challenge in exploring this phenomenon.

Media, document and internet analysis

Document analysis included the following approaches and sources:

Media discourse analysis

In the absence of numerous academic texts on this topic, and in line with the recent contemporary nature of the phenomenon, I utilised critical discourse analysis (van Dijk, 1993; Fairclough, 1995) to examine the discursive strategies of new media and to identify the media's role in establishing and problematising the issue. This involved using a socio-cognitive analysis (van Dijk, 1998, 2001, 2003) of 12 newspapers randomly selected from 2009 to 2011.

In addition, newspaper cuttings were retained from *The Guardian*, *The Times*, *The Telegraph* and the *South London Press* from April 2009 to December 2011.

Public records analysis

This included analysing the minutes of local authority meetings; the agendas from meetings of Safer Neighbourhood panels, community groups, police consultative groups, and residents' and tenants' groups; and local authority community safety and environmental reports. Each document provided a source of information, often including factual or statistical data. When undertaking such research, consideration was given as to authenticity, accuracy, local political machinations, credibility, representativeness, balance and meaning. A further rich source of data might have been councillors' mailbags, but it was not possible to access them for this study.

In addition, court records were obtained for trials where dogs had been used as weapons, specifically for those transcripts pertaining to the murder of Seyi Ogunyemi.

Internet analysis

Analysing online documents is useful for generalised sourcing and formulating key concepts, however it is less suited for this research as document creation, authenticity, credibility, and representativeness are key issues. Online documents are useful as generalised sources and for formulating key concepts, although they were less suited to this research, where document creation, authenticity, credibility and representativeness were key issues. Moreover, while online searches enable content and semiotic analysis, they are not randomised if undertaken through a search engine. As a result, this technique was only used for referencing cultural imagery.

Agency data

Over the past several years, various agencies, including the police, the RSPCA, dog welfare and kennel agencies, and local authorities, have begun to collate data on status dogs. Data on fighting dogs and illegal dogs have been gathered over a longer period of time by some agencies. These data have never before been collated in one place. Sourcing data required making contact with five animal welfare agencies, 20 hospital departments, five police services, five local authority dog warden services, two animal hospitals and government departments in the Scottish and English government and the Welsh Assembly.

A word on data quality

It is worth repeating that both the term and concept of status dog are subjective. Thus few of the reports use the term and those seeking its verifiable quantification will be disappointed. When examining the evidence, it is important to consider that data had often been gathered for other purposes; that information collected for early studies was often incidental and is therefore potentially unreliable; and that different definitions and boundaries are used by different agencies.

Statistical data accuracy is further compromised in places by the compilation of data across a variety of different administrative systems.[1] In places, it is necessary to rely on media reports available at the time, for example, reports of court proceedings. Subsequent attempts to retrieve the data have not always proven possible. Other data that might have illuminated an issue lie buried in personal files and could only have been retrieved at great expense, for example, the breed type responsible for dog-bite injuries. This type of information retrieval was seldom possible.

In assembling evidence of status and weapon dogs in the UK we have to work with what is available. We also have to collate data from as wide a variety of sources as possible. The information that does exist is therefore not consistent, and may not refer to specifics such as type of breed. Police reports and public complaints of incidents involving status dogs may prove to be useful, but all too often sources of data that might have provided a useful account of how such issues were raised initially – such as letters to local councillors – are unavailable.

Participant observation

Participant observation was used to verify the presence of status dogs in selected London parks. It could also have been used to quantify the number of dogs in public spaces, namely how many dogs were witnessed in this park over this time period. However, as with verification, there are multiple variables at play here: weather; season; park opening and closing times; use of park (informal leisure or organised activities); different areas of the park; park usage patterns; whether parks are patrolled and activities supervised; access (through routes or limited access); nature of the site (established parkland or common heathland; proximity to social housing. This method was therefore only used for verification that dogs were present in the parks.

A sample of field sites (parks) in London was identified across 10 boroughs (see Table 5.1). Of these, 11 were selected as case-study destinations, having been identified in media reports as having problems with aggressive or status dogs. In addition, various other field sites (parks) were selected at random as being in the vicinity of the designated case-study sites or within the same borough. Each field site was visited for one hour at random times of the day between noon and 6pm, including weekdays and weekends. Visits were made from June to August 2010 regardless of the weather.

In total, 40 field sites were visited for 40 hours. Two exercises were carried out at each visit: first, any pitbull terrier (PBT)-type or other aggressive dogs in the park at that time were identified, and second, short interviews were conducted with two randomly selected park users (dog walkers). Park users were asked if they had ever witnessed aggressive or PBT-type dogs in that park (either on or off a leash) at any time in the past three months. All park users were keen to converse and none refused to be interviewed. All talked openly about their dog-walking experiences in the park and their observations regarding other dogs and dog owners and park users.

Visual data

The use of visual data – photographing breeds in open spaces – was considered dangerous and was not adopted in this research, although the author notes that other studies have employed methods such as inviting schoolchildren to draw or represent their experiences of life in their communities. One such exercise conducted with primary schoolchildren on the Aylesbury estate in Southwark in 2011 resulted in 30 colourful drawings, several of which depicted pitbulls on chains and dog-fighting scenes, indicating that these children were regularly exposed to such sights).

Qualitative interviews

To obtain a wide range of views and experiences, and to triangulate accounts, interviews were conducted with several different groups of respondent.

Practitioners and professionals

Qualitative interviews were conducted with 37 professional staff working with dogs on a daily basis. Interviews focused on their professional daily encounters with dogs, different breeds of dog and dog owners/handlers, and specifically on the issue of aggressive/status dogs. Respondents were asked if they believed the phenomenon of status dogs to be an issue in their area; their experience, opinions and views were solicited. These interviews lasted between 30 and 300 minutes each. The longer interviews were recorded and transcribed for analysis. Interviews with informants and police will be used throughout the book.

Interviews were conducted from April 2009 to April 2011 with the following groups:

- police officers from the Status Dog Unit in the Metropolitan Police Service (three);
- police officers from dog/gang units in Bradford, Liverpool, Glasgow and the West Midlands (four);
- police officers from dog/gang units or dog legislation officers from the London Boroughs of Lambeth, Lewisham, Southwark, Greenwich, Ealing and Tower Hamlets (six);
- local authority park officers or dog warden officers from the London Boroughs of Lambeth and Lewisham, and Liverpool City Council (four);
- RSPCA officers (five);
- officers from Guide Dogs, Dogs Trust and Battersea Dogs and Cats Home (six)
- professional court witnesses on dog breeds (two);
- veterinary hospital and clinic practitioners (three);
- park wardens and police community support officers (four).

Interviews conducted in the London Borough of Lambeth

In addition to the interviews with practitioners and professionals, a total of 30 interviews were conducted in Lambeth during doctoral research into gangs in the borough in 2010. In 27 interviews, respondents were asked to comment on status dogs and dog fighting in the borough. The findings from these interviews are included in Table 5.2. These interviews focused largely on the issue of gangs in Lambeth and the role of dogs within the gang. Each interview was audio recorded and transcribed for analysis. Interviews were conducted with the following groups:

- professional gang consultants and gang mediation specialists (three);
- professional officers from the London Probation Service, Lambeth Community Safety Division and Lambeth Youth Service (three);
- police officers (seven);
- local residents (five);
- gang-affiliated young people (nine).

Owners/handlers of aggressive breeds

Given the nature of the research, it was neither effective nor safe to approach people with a clipboard and semi-structured interview schedule. An interview was deemed effective if the core set of questions was completed. The questions covered the following: breed/age of dog; how the dog was acquired; care of dog, for example, whether it had had all its inoculations and whether it had recently visited the vet; whether the dog was used for protection/guarding; whether it was the family pet; whether the respondent was the owner of the dog; the dog's temperament/sociability; what the dog is fed; how often the dog is exercised; whether people move away from the dog when it is being walked; whether the dog gets involved in fights.

To strengthen and validate interviews, observational points were recorded where possible, including: temperament of the dog at the time of interview; whether it was possible to pat the dog; broad age band, ethnicity and gender of owner; interview location; whether the dog was well behaved or agitated, or muzzled, chained or harnessed; whether the owner was in control; the demeanour of the owner (agitated/relaxed); whether the owner was empathetic towards the animal or disinterested; and whether the dog was scarred or damaged in any way, or aggressive to other passing dogs. As people talk, much of this information can be gleaned very quickly.

Locations for interviewing status dog owners included: parks and open spaces; public transport; animal hospitals and veterinary practices; dog-chipping and animal-training events; magistrates' courts; outside schools and other public venues such as pubs, social services agencies, high street shops and youth offending services. Random selection techniques were used and potential respondents approached if it was considered safe to do so.

The interview technique used in this research involved approaching the respondent in the course of open conversation – sometimes facilitated by walking a dog myself – and usually commencing with comments about their dog. After a brief engagement, I informed the respondent I was doing research into why people favoured certain breeds of dog, and enquired whether I could ask them a few questions about their dog.

A total of 138 people were approached, with the following results:

- participant refused to be interviewed (59);
- interview terminated by researcher through fear for personal safety (seven);
- interview terminated by researcher as participant asked for financial incentive (which was refused) (11);
- interview incomplete (often due to the dog distracting attention or misbehaving) (28);
- successful interviews (33, or 24%).

Only 17 of the 33 interviewees agreed to be recorded, while the remaining 16 agreed to take part as long as their responses were written down rather than recorded.

Of the final sample, 16 respondents were white, 13 were black and four were Asian. The sample was predominantly male (male 66%; female 33%).

Coding framework for analysis of qualitative interviews with owners/handlers of large/aggressive breeds

Interview analysis required construction of a coding framework derived from all the qualitative interviews with practitioners, professionals, residents and gang-affiliated young people in Lambeth. Findings from the research were coded using the typology set out in Chapter Four, with indicative motivations or latent function for owning the dog. It was not possible to identify which owners were seeking status motivated by changing fashions in owning dogs. Similarly, when identifying motivations of protection, it was not always clear if the protection was personal or domestic. Again, it was not always possible to determine if seeking status was a central element to this motivation.

Responses were then categorised against these codes. This required a subjective analysis of each interviewee, which was achieved by analysing interview responses, both spontaneous and prompted, and by making an observational assessment of the dog, its owner and the interaction between the two using the following guidelines.

Response analysis

- Reference to the dog's function, for example, for personal or domestic protection.
- References to intentions to breed or expressions of interest in dog fighting.
- Exercise regime and diet (in particular references to building or amplifying muscles by hanging dog from trees, a practice associated with status dogs).
- Personal knowledge and connectivity to the dog, including knowledge of acquisition and length of ownership, used to determine whether the dog is viewed as a domesticated companion.
- References to the dog's nature, and how this is perceived by the respondent (for example, "She's a lovely dog around the house" or "She frightens people" and "that's great").
- Honesty regarding type of breed (whether the respondent openly acknowledges the breed of dog or claims it is something else).

Visual observations of the owner's dog(s)

- Condition of the dog (well groomed or scarred?)
- Temperament of the dog (The interviewee was asked whether the dog could be patted, with both owner's and dog's responses indicative of temperament.)
- Owner–dog relationship (Is the owner in control of the dog? Is the dog responsive to commands?)
- Presentation of the dog (Is the dog on a bull chain and in a harness with studded collars? Is the dog muzzled?)
- Age and presentation of the respondent

It is recognised that such a coding process is subjective. Participant observation of the dog and owner interacting in situ, however, strengthens the findings allowing for greater interpretation. Despite this, some generalised assumptions still underpin the subjective analysis. These assumptions are in part derived from the qualitative interviews with practitioners and professionals, including veterinary surgeons, shelter care staff, dog wardens, police dog handlers, professional judges and expert witnesses on dog breeds, temperament and condition.

The research findings show different groupings indicating the manifest functions/latent functions of the dogs. Where a code could not be wholly allocated to a single function, a joint code was selected, for example, status/protection. This indicates that both functions were equally evident.

Focus groups

One focus group was conducted with a group of four Asian boys aged 16–17, all of whom were involved to some extent in dog fighting.

Analysis of offending behaviour

The research study also sought to examine the offending histories of owners of status dogs to establish whether any owners were involved in criminal activity or whether the dogs were used for criminal purposes. This was achieved through negotiation with several police forces, three of which (the Metropolitan Police Service, Merseyside Police and West Midlands Police) provided details of key policing operations to address status or dangerous dogs. The offending histories of owners who had had their dogs seized were then requested and personal details redacted.

Caveats

For those seeking to undertake their own research into this topic, it is worth noting that each of these methods presents logistical challenges and ethical considerations. On a few occasions, I entered parks with a dog on a leash. This facilitated general conversation but made scant difference to interviewing the key respondents. Using a status dog to achieve such interviews would bring further ethical challenges. Likewise, a full ethnographical experience of immersion into the world of breeding or dog fighting presented ethical challenges and was not pursued.

This chapter sets out the methodological challenges of conducting research into this topic. Alongside the ethical challenges and the considerable caveats regarding data quality, it sets out the research methodology used to undertake both primary and secondary research.

The next chapter considers the traditional role of dogs in the UK before examining the so-called 'pitbull panic' in the US alongside the characteristics of the breeds most favoured as status dogs.

Note

[1] Throughout this exercise, I reviewed a range of statistics that were subsequently excluded because, for example, they were found to be inaccurate when double-checked or when cross-referenced with figures from alternative sources. Every attempt has been made to check the data reported are consistent by viewing subsequent reports. In addition, some data, for example, data from the London ambulance service, were not released for publication.

TWO

Who let the dogs out? The new phenomenon of status dogs

The traditional role of dogs in the UK

Any discussion of human–animal relationships in the UK naturally assumes a western perspective and it is recognised that other cultures have developed different histories and traditions.

The role of dogs in society and in human–animal relations has changed over the years, but the pace of change has been considerably more rapid over the past 100 years. Dogs have been sought throughout history for their ability to befriend and bond with humans. We have looked to dogs for natural canine functions of hunting, tracking, herding, guarding, scenting and protecting.

Although dogs have long been companions for humans, it is only since the introduction of the domesticated family pet that companionship has become their prime function. By contrast, the use of dogs for fighting is a well-established tradition. Over 2,000 years ago, Phoenician traders introduced fighting mastiffs into Britain from the Mediterranean, and in 55BC, Julius Caesar commented on the fierce nature of these animals, which he encountered in his invasion of Britain.

The English medieval 'sport' of bull baiting developed from the ability of the English bulldog to grasp and hold bulls by their noses. Such dogs were then often used by butchers rather than hunters. Their function as 'cattle controllers' ensured that bulldogs were later highly favoured by immigrants travelling to the US in the 18th and 19th century.

Neither is the keeping of a dog to designate status a new phenomenon. The kings of England always retained wolfhounds or mastiffs as pets/guardians. Companionship remained a central theme for establishing relationships with pet animals. However, in western culture 'there has been a consistent linkage between companion animals and social status' (Sanders, 1999: 5). The retention of an animal as ornament or property was at one time only available to the rich. Working-class people traditionally kept dogs as working animals. Jessup (1995) notes four types of dogs prized in history above all others: the greyhound (sight hunter), the hunting hound (scent hunter), the sheepdog (guardian and herder) and the mastiff bulldog (molossus/bullenbeisser). Such functions of course largely relate to the pre-industrial period, although in agriculture working dogs have retained their purpose and function for much longer.

Phineas (1973) suggests that in the post-industrial period pets provided opportunities for mastery and filled a void for the middle classes, who had been largely displaced from control over politics and economy.

The role that pet animals can play in human emotional wellbeing began to be recognised and domesticity brought dogs from their outhouses or kennels into the family home. For many owners, 'canine characteristics' became 'personalities'. Nast (2006) talks of the ease with which humans anthropomorphise dogs to reflect their personalities, noting how this has led to increased commodification of animals and in turn the commercialisation of pet economies.

In addition, over time, humans have modified canine characteristics to suit themselves. More recently, humans have ensured that canine characteristics fit their desired functional requirements, and have improved on them through breeding (Semyonova, 2006). Such human intervention and manipulation led to functional groupings of dogs: shepherding dogs, guard dogs, fighting dogs, hunting dogs, tracking dogs and companion dogs.

Put simply, humans have purposefully chosen the most suitable breed for the tasks required. These qualities, physical or behavioural, have then over centuries developed genetically within the dog. Selective breeding has expedited this. Hybridisation has been often introduced in attempts to create improved characteristics or breeds even more suited to the functional task.

In terms of status dogs, it can be argued that both human intervention and manipulation have played a part, alongside breed selection, in creating large, physically intimidating and behaviourally aggressive dogs. To some owners – particularly young men in deprived or working-class neighbourhoods – the ability of these dogs to intimidate others and generate fear and respect becomes their function. This function should be contrasted with the contemporary trend for celebrities to be seen with 'designer' pooches. Small and often bijoux, these animals appear to have more in common with designer jewellery and toys than dogs.[1]

Again, the dogs chosen to fit this function are physically at the other end of the spectrum from those chosen to be status dogs. So in many cases are the owners. It must be of some import that as young men from deprived and marginalised communities have sought out ever-bigger, larger, aggressive dogs, young women in high-status, high-fashion, exclusive and economically thriving worlds have chosen ever-smaller dogs to fit into their handbags. Recently in the UK, some young women of lesser means and occupying a lower status in the social hierarchy have tried to emulate these high-status fashionistas by obtaining small, bijoux dogs to fit into larger (often fake) designer handbags. Indeed, the UK charity the Dogs Trust has reported a 39% increase in the number of 'toy' dogs handed into its rehoming centres (GfK NOP, 2011) (see also Chapter Eight).

The difference here, of course, is that these miniature dogs are used to suggest that the owner is a caring person capable of giving affection while simultaneously demonstrating their wealth by submitting their pets to expensive pampering procedures.

It is often stated that dogs provide ideal opportunities for building social capital (Putnam, 2000) by allowing owners to engage each other in discussion and conversation about their pets. In this way dogs are often used as functional image projects. I shall examine this in more detail shortly. But what of the bull breeds so actively sought after by owners of status dogs?

Bull breeds and the 'pitbull panic'[2]

In ancient history, the Romans and others used bull mastiffs as 'war dogs' fighting alongside them in battle. Later these dogs were used for 'sport' and entertainment in pits, often fighting bears and wild animals. Mastiffs proved slow in the pit and thus were cross-bred with terriers to make them faster and more agile. The pitbulls we know today arose from cross-breeding in the 18th century. These ferocious but agile and powerful dogs were ideal for the fashionable sports of bull and bear baiting until these were overtaken by dog fighting. These blood sports were exported to the US in the 17th and 18th centuries where they also become fashionable.

In the 18th and 19th century, bulldogs were popular for a variety of purposes, as hunting dogs and farm dogs, and to assist policing and guarding. Although each had a common origin in the old English bulldogge used for bull baiting and fighting in pits, there were actually a variety of different breeds, including the pitbull, the bulldog and the bull terrier. In 1835, public outcry in England led to the sport being banned through the British Humane Act and dog fighting went underground. Dog fighting retained its popularity in the US and in many other areas of the world it was, and remains, a widely accepted cultural practice, for example in Afghanistan, Pakistan and central Russia.

To follow the recent and contemporaneous development of the bull breeds and the pitbull in particular, we have to look to developments as they unfolded in the US. In the 19th century in the US, bulldogs developed a reputation for fearlessness and loyalty and were quickly perceived as hard-working farm and frontier dogs. By 1900, bulldogs and pitbulls were common in apartment houses in growing urban environments. President Roosevelt famously owned a bulldog while occupying the White House from 1901-09. Delise (2007: 69) cites the 1911 Encyclopaedia Britannica definition of the bulldog, which describes how 'their ferocious appearance, and not infrequently the habits of their owners, have given this breed a reputation for ferocity and low intelligence'. While bulldogs are indeed intelligent, it is curious to already find reference to the reputational issues of the owners from 100 years ago.

Karen Delise charts the history of the bulldog breed throughout the 19th and 20th century, noting that by the early 1900s the shift in husbandry of the animal from hard-working labourer and farm hand to urban domesticated dog had resulted in 'substandard' ownership and an increased number of fatal attacks by dogs on humans. Notwithstanding this trend, early media reports were often favourable towards these animals. Media reporting in the first three decades of the 20th century illustrates the often heroic deeds undertaken by bulldogs, such as saving children from burning buildings or from drowning or attack. During the First World War, the bulldog appeared in propaganda posters in military uniform and the pitbull become synonymous with the US in certain brands, films and cultural imagery. The American pitbull terrier was a patriotic hero often depicted draped in the Stars and Stripes of the US flag, later becoming the mascot for the Radio Corporation of America (RCA) (electronics) and Buster Brown (shoes). From 1922 to 1944, a pitbull called Petey became a household name as the comical and loyal member in the Our Gang film series by Hal Roach. In the UK, the British bulldog experienced a similar lionisation, first through films such as *How a British bulldog saved the Union Jack*[3] in 1906 and later through its association with the wartime Prime Minister Winston Churchill on account of both sporting 'Churchillian jowls'.

After the Second World War, pitbulls and bulldogs faded from the public imagination until the mid- to late 1970s. Through the emergence of mass media the US has now developed an increased cultural awareness of dog fighting. Pitbulls were back in the public eye, but their media profile was now much less favourable. In future years, their reputations would deteriorate even further with the media generating open hostility towards them. By the mid-1980s, pitbulls were increasingly associated with gangs and inner-city urban areas. *Rolling Stone* magazine published a graphic article on the practice among teenage youths of chain rolling[4] pitbulls (Sager, 1987). The article described how dogs that lost fights were disposed of on account of them having embarrassed their owners. Following this exposé, both *Sports Illustrated* and *Time Magazine* covered pitbulls and dog fighting in some detail, with *Time Magazine* using the notorious headline 'Time bombs on legs' (Brand et al, 1987). The modern image of the pitbull was now well under construction.

Clifford and colleagues (1990) chart the media coverage of the pitbull throughout the 1970s and 1980s in their book *The pitbull dilemma: The gathering storm*. They note that the number of pitbulls in the US increased from a few hundred in the 1960s to an estimated 500,000 by 1986. They refer to the media dilemma of reporting the dogs as 'gentle, as well as dangerous and unpredictable' (1990: vii–xiv). This conflicted image has come to dominate public, professional and media discussions, and, for many, now characterises the pitbull.

In the 1980s, media coverage began to dissect the pitbull history and in 1989 the Centre for Disease Control in the US released statistics illustrating the increasing role of pitbulls in fatal attacks. By 1990, the negative public image of the pitbull was sealed. During the 1990s, the rottweiler briefly became popular as a guard dog before media coverage denounced it as the 'new super-predator'. Following increasingly sensationalised media coverage that often linked pitbulls with criminal and gang activity, a number of US cities felt compelled to address growing public alarm. In 1989, Denver, Colorado became the first US city to pass a city-wide ordnance banning pitbulls. This was followed shortly by Miami, Cincinnati, Kansas city and by 2000, over 200 administrative districts of the US had enacted breed bans or restrictions on pitbulls or pitbull-type[5] dogs (Delise, 2007: 103).

As Allen (2007: 41-9) notes, it was during the 1980s that the pitbull in particular began 'its transformation into a threatening outsider' or 'ghetto monster'. She continues, 'not only was he guilty by association, but his brute animality also made him the perfect vehicle for the projection of fears about human savagery that had been displaced onto racial-minority males'. Allen's thesis on the pitbull regards its current social pariah status in the US as one of social constructionism and she argues suggestively that the media and then politicians have sought to heighten our fears about pitbulls. This has been done to successfully manipulate media sales, for media entertainment and for political gain. For her, the pitbull has become associated with any oppositional culture and, as a result, any pitbull attack has become symbolic of the threat posed by 'out of control' others. This is a powerful argument, which draws from Becker's (1963) concept of outsiders and othering and also from Cohen's (1972) concept of moral panic theory. Throughout the 1980s[6] and 1990s in the US many headlines appeared that sensationalised stories of pitbulls and increasingly depicted them in negative and stereotypical ways.

In 2001, the death of the young lawyer Diane Whipple in the hallway to her apartment complex in San Francisco reinvigorated the national and local debates on aggressive dogs and the threat they pose to the public. The dogs that savaged her to death were originally identified in the press as pitbulls but were later confirmed as presa canarios. The dogs' owners were subsequently found to be involved with the Aryan Nation and were actively engaged in the home production of methamphetamine. For many, this was proof of the fact that criminals and gangs were regularly using large aggressive dogs to further criminal activity. Increasingly in the US, this image of gang-affiliated 'homies'[7] with dogs, often pitbulls, entered the public imagination. Interestingly, Delise reports an unprecedented demand for this breed of dog from some elements of the public following this tragic event.

By the early 21st century, the pitbull breeds in the US had undergone a wholesale social transfiguration from noble and popular family pet, working dog and cultural icon to demonised negative stereotype associated with criminal gangs and drugs. In short, it had become representative of violent underworlds and cultural 'others'. It is important and probably not coincidental that this cultural transformation is attributed by many – in terms of shifting cultural loci – to a move from white middle-class family ownership to black and Latino ghetto and barrio ownership. As the pitbull's association with these new cultural locations developed, often through rap videos and hip hop music, for many ethnically white observers and commentators in the white-owned media, the cultural 'relegation' of the pitbull breed was now complete. For some, the pitbull was now wholly associated, not only with black and Latino lifestyles, but also with criminal elements of what they perceived to be the 'underclass'. In the US, where racial dividing lines are more prominent and ever-present, this racist perspective and pejorative 'othering' suggested to some white middle-class owners that the animals were now consigned to a lesser social rank.

Over the past 20 years in the US, numerous dog experts, pitbull breeders and enthusiasts have mounted spirited campaigns to defend the American pitbull terrier (APBT). This has led to considerable public confusion as to the reality of the current situation. Whom does the public believe – the media or the pitbull 'experts'? Are the dogs safe or are they unpredictable? What of the links to criminal activity? Is this a reality or simply the result of isolated incidents blown up by the media in order to manipulate the public mood.

These very same debates are now being expressed in the UK, where 'hoodies' replace 'homies' and talk of status and weapon dogs is now commonplace. As in the US, UK experts on dog behaviour and breeding comment on the canine characteristics of large aggressive breeds. In the UK, the general view of academics thus far is that some criminal elements associate with such dogs, but that, by and large, the debate is no more than media-generated panic of little consequence. Writers such as Hallsworth (2011) and Kasperson (2008) denounce any criticism of bull breeds as ill informed and misplaced. It seems that the UK is destined to follow the US narrative, not just in the way pitbulls are now viewed, but also now in the widespread confusion experienced by members of the public as they try to evaluate the information and 'propaganda' disseminated by pitbull advocates and detractors, and attempt to determine whether the dogs pose a threat. How then does the public navigate this complex set of views and address legitimate concerns regarding public safety?

There is, however, a more realist perspective to be aired, one that suggests that for a variety of reasons and motivations many individuals are increasingly now using certain breeds of dog to construct their image or to engage in criminal activity and that this does indeed pose a threat to public safety. It is to this perspective that I subscribe. To understand how and why young men now seek to use dogs in such a way, it is again appropriate to consider the US experience. It is also necessary to tread a fine line between the two opposing arguments often forcibly put forward by advocates and detractors of pitbulls and bull breeds and to rationally consider the role of the media in the social construction of the issue, including aspects of public safety, links to criminality and so on.

Digging deep into some of the US research, the renowned writers and experts on pitbulls do acknowledge that pitbulls in particular have become increasingly associated with irresponsible abusive and criminal elements. Delise (2007: 87), for example, notes that:'far too much of the pitbull population is owned by three types of exceedingly abusive people'. She cites the groups as drug dealers, dog-fighting enthusiasts and inner-city gang members who use animals to intimidate others. This view is echoed by a police officer from the West Midlands:"Many pitbulls are owned by people who, while not necessarily abusive, are guilty of being irresponsible and ignorant – mostly for protection and or fashion" (interview with Keith Evans, West Midlands Police, for this research).

Noting the huge proliferation of pitbulls in the US, she cites the fact that the 12 animal shelters in Los Angeles receive approximately 840 pitbulls a week (Delise, 2007: 86). The Pennsylvania Society for the Prevention of Cruelty to Animals reported that in 1999 over 4,000 pitbulls werefound wandering the streets (PSPCA, 2000).

Such commentary and statistics suggest there is indeed a legitimate concern for the public regarding ownership of pitbulls and bull breeds. This in turn suggests a need to move beyond oppositional standpoints that pitch sensational rhetoric against the defensive positions adopted by animal rights or animal welfare groups; to recognise that this is an issue that encompasses or adjoins social deprivation and criminality but that overwhelmingly requires authoritative responses to legitimate concerns regarding public safety.

The key US writers on pitbulls and fighting or aggressive/dangerous dogs are all in agreement that the bull breeds have been much maligned and discredited by the media, often for political expediency. They share the belief that these breeds display many highly favourable traits, such as exuberance, intelligence and loyalty, but agree they are also now heavily associated with criminality, drugs and gangs, and used as image enhancers by irresponsible owners. These writers unanimously call for greater recognition of the fact that these breeds have been mistreated, abused and subjected to pejorative media reporting. However, today's breeds, as they exist both in the US and the UK, are frequently the results of poor-quality or illegal back-street breeding. This has had the effect of producing the very aggressive breed so maligned in the press and so feared by the public. This in turn has drawn the breed ever closer to the criminal element so often associated with the breed. This then poses a dilemma: how do we reconcile the positive qualities of the breed with the current reality of its social construction and its social position?

Deed or breed?

In both the UK and the US, one central issue in the public debates over status dogs is the level of potential threat posed by these animals to the general public:

- Are they or are they not a danger to the general public?
- Is this danger then increased if they are used for anything other than household pets?

Debates here are again conflicted (for a further exploration of these issues, please see Appendix A on the Dangerous Dogs Act 1991) and once again it is difficult for a layperson to understand the potential level of threat. It is also important to determine how and in what ways this level of threat or danger is a central factor in the choice of such breeds as status or weapon dogs.

One argument frequently tabled on pitbulls and other fighting dogs is that the breeds themselves are not dangerous but are made so by humans. While this is undoubtedly true, there are still some character aspects of large aggressive breeds used as status dogs that give some pause for thought. For many status dog owners, it is these very characteristics that prove attractive. World-renowned authority on fighting dogs (Semencic, 1984) and on pitbulls and tenacious guard dogs (Semencic, 1991), Dr Carl Semencic has critically assessed the best breeds used for guarding and protection. His observations regarding their characteristics and thus their suitability are listed below:

- **Akita** – a fighting and hunting dog – 'is a large, powerful, fearless, game breed that can become a very useful man-stopping dog' (Semencic 1991: 63).
- **Bullmastiff** – a cross between the powerful English mastiff and faster and courageous bulldog. 'One of the best deterrents against crime in the canine world, as the appearance of the breed is downright awesome' (Semencic, 1991: 126). It is 'capable of bring(ing) down and holding a 200 pound man on the run' (p 122).
- **Doberman** – considered to be quick thinking, alert, fast moving and well balanced. It qualifies as retaining a man-stopping ability, but is perceived as not having the willingness to continue an attack. Seminic continues, 'Crazy people who are in search of a crazy dog to complement their personalities have a tendency to select the Doberman as the breed for them' (Semencic, 1991: 153). Cultural misrepresentation is blamed by Semencic for its bad image.
- **Dogo Argentino** – an Argentinean hunting and fighting dog 'capable of taking down a puma single-handedly' (Semencic, 1991: 170).
- **Dogue de Bordeaux** – 'tremendous guard dog and man-stopping ability. Great willingness to defend. Rumours that it is aggressive and of its ability to do harm are often false.' 'The Dogue is now employed primarily as a companion and guard dog, with tremendous man-stopping ability and a great willingness (some criticise that there is often too much willingness) to test its mettle against any man who dares intrude upon its property'. Semencic continues

by noting that,' too many false rumors portray the breed as being dangerous to own, due to its aggressive nature and its ability to do bodily harm' (Semencic 1991: 180).

- **Mastiffs** – can weigh up to 200 pounds. As a result many breeders have chosen to breed a more docile temperament in these dogs. Noting that despite its history as an active combat and hunting dog, many current breeds are more docile, Semencic continues, 'certainly there is good reason for many Mastiff owners to prefer to keep more docile dogs, as a 200-pound Mastiff that was allowed to become very aggressive would be uncontrollable in anyone's hands'. These are not suitable 'apartment dogs' (Semencic 1991: 245-6).
- **Presa canario** – developed as a fighting dog in the Canaries, Semencic notes that, 'Incredibly game, powerful and determined animals were a match for any dog in the world' (Semencic 1991:142)). 'This dog is protective by nature and will not hesitate to attack anyone whom it perceives as a threat to its family or home. Such an attack could only be a hopeless situation for any man involved' (Semencic 1991: 144).
- **Rottweiler** – 'among the finest of all man-stopping guard dogs ... quick-on-the-trigger when a situation arises ... large, agile and powerful ... known to have a hard bite' (Semencic 1991: 265-7).
- **Tosa** – selective breeding has produced a dog that is silent even when angry. These dogs are bred for Japanese dog fights and it is a rule of these fights that the Tosa must fight in silence. 'The Tosa is a very quiet dog. Even when it is angry, it is angry in silence. this is due to the fact that one of the rules of the Japanese dogfight is that the Tosa must fight its battle in silence. Selective breeding of these dogs that comply to Japanese fighting rules has produced this characteristic of the Tosa' (Semencic, 1991: 300).

While such characteristics might indeed make these dogs an attractive purchase for guarding and protection, they clearly also have implications for the general public.

The pitbull

The pitbull is the breed most associated with status dogs in the media. Its man-stopping ability is often cited by owners as a reason for ownership. It is also said by Semencic (1991: 46) to be the 'the gamest and most capable fighting dog known to modern man'. As this dog is smaller than a mastiff, it is often favoured as an apartment dog. It is recognised for its powerful musculature, physical strength and determination with a 'tremendous biting power'.

Beyond these characteristics, it is clear that the pitbull has amassed a certain level of mythology within the media and at street level.

Delise (2007) notes the considerable 'misinformation' circulating about pitbulls that has now reached mythological status, including that pitbulls:

- have a locking jaw;
- have a higher pound-per-square-inch bite power than other dogs;
- are like 'land sharks';
- are impervious to pain and more dangerous during attack;
- attack without warning;
- are unpredictable and unstable.

All recognised writers on pitbulls decry these as myths. There is no doubt that reputational hype and sloppy, lazy journalism has perpetuated such myths, leaving them unchallenged and circulating widely in the public imagination.

Jessup (1995) notes that pitbulls were bred to grasp cattle and hold on until the bull was brought down. This helped create the myth of the locking jaw as well as the reputation for tenacity. However, a well-trained pitbull will release if told to do so. In terms of bite power, the pitbull is the most tenacious breed, but larger breeds such as an akita or rottweiler have greater jaw strength.

Pitbulls are strong and are able to pull up to 1.3 metric tonnes in weight, although its strength will depend on its gameness. Gameness is a quality defined behaviourally as 'the characteristic of not quitting'. In a fighting dog, this is a dog that 'will continue to cross the pit, even on broken and mutilated limbs, in order to finish a fight' (Jessup, 1995: 156). However, gameness is often confused as meaning a desire to fight, when in reality it means a desire to finish/succeed at any given task.

Interestingly, Jessup (1995) calls for dog-aggressive pitbulls to be destroyed immediately, as they are unrepresentative of the breed. All writers also agree that the breed is too often defined by the unrepresentative behaviour of some dogs.

Aggression, breeding and potential damage

So while certain breeds are larger and look more aggressive, are they necessarily more dangerous? In the UK, the RSPCA argues cogently that breed-specific legislation (for a fuller exploration of this issue, see Appendix A) is not required, as bull breeds present no more danger than other breeds and that any dog can be dangerous if provoked. However, this also appears to be oversimplification of an argument that is actually more nuanced. There are in fact some specific items for consideration with regard to bull breeds that do set them apart from other dogs when considering aspects of public safety. These issues are:

- levels of aggression
- breeding issues
- ability to inflict injury or damage.

Pitbulls are often considered to be non-human aggressive. This is because any human aggression made them unsuitable as candidates for organised pit fights. Overtime, human-aggressive dogs have been bred out in favour of dog-aggressive animals. They are also reputedly very loyal to and protective of their owners. Such benign qualities are clearly discretionary. The pitbull will 'oppose any enemy of its family with a ferocity that was unprecedented in the world of dogs' (Seminic, 1991: 51). This docility around humans, yet aggression towards threats to the family or owner, makes the pitbull highly attractive to those that seek them as status dogs or guard dogs.

Pitbulls are, however, often dog-aggressive, having been bred to be so. Here, though, the pitbull experts differ somewhat. Jessup (1995) notes that pitbulls can often be dog-aggressive and are known for this quality, while Sue Sternberg suggests that this behaviour is indicative of an inherent problem: 'an individual Pitbull who does have aggressive tendencies toward other dogs ... are [sic] a liability and a disaster waiting to happen' (Sternberg 2003: 73). This suggests a range of possible outcomes based on spontaneous or uncontrolled aggression. This then puts a question mark over a large number of the pitbull breed (Semyonova, 2006).

Jessup, Director of the Canine Aggression Research Centre in Washington, US, notes that because pitbulls never faced humans as opponents in the fighting pit, they have learned to exhibit traditional warning signs or threat displays when they feel intimidated or threatened, for example, by growling, barking or baring teeth. This implies a Lamarckian[8] view of the inheritance of acquired characteristics. Trained attack dogs will not demonstrate these displays of warning behaviour. Jessup makes clear, however, that not all dogs exhibit a threat display and that some do so in an abbreviated way. This makes such behaviour difficult for some people, especially for young children or those not familiar with reading warning signs by dogs, to recognise. More significantly, Jessup (1995: 147) claims that although pitbulls do give warning signs, 'the ability or desire to make prolonged threat displays has been bred down in many strains of the breed'. This is a result of dogs being bred specifically to get stuck into a fight – 'dogs which minimized their threat display were used for breeding' – ending up with a dog that would rush its opponent immediately in the pit (Jessup, 1995: 147). While this characteristic would give a dog an advantage in the pit, such a trait may prove altogether more dangerous in a local high street. Moreover, irresponsible breeding in the US and the UK that compounds this trait will surely compromise public safety.

Another issue regarding aggression (of any dog) arises where owners have purposefully trained their (status) dog to be aggressive. Eventually, they will find this dog difficult to have at home: 'Unfortunately while cultivating a very aggressive temperament in a dog is a very simple matter, easing an aggressive temperament is a very difficult and often impossible task' (Seminic, 1991: 309). While certain breeds do have genetically aggressive tendencies (Netto and Planta, 1997), some commentators argue that in pitbulls this aggression is usually learned or instilled by humans (Roll and Unshelm, 1997; but compare Semyonova, 2006).

Thus many aggressive dogs may find themselves out on the street, as the owners cannot have them around the house. Having been trained to be aggressive, they are now permanently aggressive and cannot be kept, so they are dumped, killed, sold on to unwitting owners, neglected, abandoned or given away.

Once a dog has attacked, the potential or ability for it to cause injury or damage must also be taken into account when considering whether or not it is a cause for concern to public safety. Thus we arrive at another debate surrounding the pitbull and definitions of danger. It is certainly true that all dogs will bite, but which is the greatest potential threat? Is it the breed that bites 1,000 people a year giving them grazed fingers, or the breed that bites five people, killing one and presenting the others with life-changing injuries? The latter appears to be the case with the pitbull. Here it is not only the damage the dog is capable of doing, but also the damage it is willing to do. In this regard, pitbulls will not only bite, but hold and tear. As with all other breeds of dog, biting is actually a last resort and is done to place distance between the dog and the perceived threat. The pitbull's technique, which is to hold and shake, will result in enormous damage to the deep muscle and bone. Average dog bites include two puncture marks at the top and two at the bottom. A pitbull bite can result in tissue loss, as the dog will shake until whatever it is holding in its mouth comes away. Such knowledge often appeals to young men when choosing status dogs and research conducted with owners of status dogs indicates that such features and characteristics are enthusiastically discussed and among some young men will form the basis of peer-group bragging rights.

Sue Sternberg, a world-renowned expert in shelter adoption, notes that this potential for extreme damage must be considered:

> The problem is that when a Pitbull is bad, he is really bad. An aggressive pit-bull is a formidable dog ... even a small one is athletic and strong. Physically speaking, he is capable of doing more damage than the average Golden Retriever. (Sternberg, 2003: 72)

Add to this the renowned tenacity of the pitbull and the potential for damage when an attack takes place must surely be cause for concern:

> Quitting a battle is an unknown concept to any of the bull-terrier breeds. Considering the speed, agility, overall power and jaw strength of these dogs, one will be hard pressed to destroy a bull terrier before one is seriously injured. (Seminic, 1991: 130)

Another thing that makes pitbulls so attractive as status dogs and thus a potential threat to public safety is their malleability. They have an inherent willingness to be what the owner wishes them to be, rather than being genetically vicious or gentle. 'Raise them to be gentle and they will be gentle. Raise them to be vicious and they will be vicious' (Semencic, 1991: 52). Not all dog experts, however, are in full concord regarding issues of aggression. For example, Semyonova (2006) argues that dogs themselves are genetically predetermined towards violence and aggression. It is precisely this characteristic of aggression that poses current problems of public safety. Again, the issue is mainly one of irresponsible breeding.

While there are clearly some unresolved questions with regard to the genetics of the breed, the concerns surrounding pitbulls stem largely from those who have become attracted to certain negative characteristics of the breed. Purebred pitbulls seldom display these negative qualities, but selective, poor-quality and irresponsible back-street breeding of the pitbull has exacerbated them.

A further example by Jessup (1995) of irresponsible breeding in pitbulls is their loss of recognition of the dominance/submission signal commonly used among dogs. As dogs fight for their hierarchical place in the pecking order, a submissive dog will roll over and act submissively. It will then be allowed to rise by the dominant dog. It appears that man had been responsible for breeding this instinct out of pitbulls:

> Man has twisted the dog's instincts for his pleasure, and produced a few members of the breed that no longer understand the submissive gesture. These dogs will not cease fighting, even after their opponent is dead. It is this one fact alone, that makes a few Pitbulls very dangerous when they are turned against man. (Jessup, 1995: 143)

Sternberg claims that selective breeding has also resulted in an enhanced arousal response in pitbulls. Traditionally, pitbulls have been bred to be tenacious and not to give up in a fight. While allowing for the fact that not all pitbulls are easily aroused or aggressive, Sternberg claims that this combination of arousal and aggression generally means that a pitbull who fights to the death brings to the fight 'over 100 years of selective breeding [which] have enhanced the Pitbull's ability to trigger or "ignite". Many Pitbulls can instantly become aroused, and remain at the peak of arousal, basically until either the Pitbull dies or his opponent dies' (Sternberg, 2003: 72).

Increasingly, then, it appears that issues of irresponsible breeding are central to how the pitbull presents today in contemporary society. Where selective breeding has produced dogs that have aggressive tendencies and high responses there is a marked increase in the potential for danger to the public.

Stahlkuppe (2000) argues that in the US the pitbull is widely associated with 'street thugs', whereas the APBT is a classic thoroughbred and should be considered as a different grouping. He argues that it is thugs who have altered the public mind about the APBT. Acknowledging two different dog-fighting groups – traditionalists and street thugs – he argues that the traditionalists have perfected dog-breeding skills that maintain pedigrees and high standards, while 'street thugs' inbreed their dogs, causing defects and poorly-bred pitbulls:

> The irresponsible street pit-fighter [sic] of today are constantly crossing, re-crossing and cross-crossing to gain some sort of perceived or imagined fighting advantage. Because the key ingredient in any pit dog must be gameness, this resorting to non-game breeds is foolish. Where, in years gone by, the APBTs of actual fighting strains were aggressive

only toward other pit dogs, the mixed pit dogs of today are often aggressive toward dogs and humans. These dogs account for a vast proportion of the terrible dog bites and fatalities that so greatly contribute to the 'pit bull terror' that has seized the American psyche. (Stahlkuppe, 2000: 8)

To summarise, pitbulls are often the breed of choice for those seeking status dogs. Pure-bred dogs usually pose no problem, but dogs bred by irresponsible back-street breeders may do so. This threat could be significantly enhanced if the genetic arguments proposed by Semyonova (2006) (that is, that pitbulls are genetically predisposed to aggression) are accurate. However, it appears that this is a contested issue.

Finally, there is a need to consider the issues of dog-on-dog aggression, malleability of pitbulls and desire (gameness) to continue fighting/attacking without giving up. Couple these features with poor training, inadequate socialisation and indifferent or unsuitable and unhealthy social environments in which dogs are raised and it seems clear that there are legitimate issues regarding public safety and pitbulls. Similar concerns regarding irresponsible breeding can also be levelled at other breeds.

Setting aside the myths surrounding pitbulls, it appears that there are established facts that make them a potential cause for concern regarding public safety. These very facts (as detailed by renowned experts) are also key reasons for these dogs becoming so attractive as status dogs. Having established that the public concern over the perceived threat to public safety caused by pitbulls and bull breeds is legitimate, how have such issues been addressed in the UK?

This chapter has examined the changing fortunes and controversies of bull breeds in the US, setting the scene for the contemporary UK position and the phenomenon of status dogs. The next chapter considers the pertinent debates and issues surrounding this phenomenon.

Notes

[1] Socialite Paris Hilton famously sports a chihauhau, while singer Britney Spears sports a white bichon frize puppy.

[2] 'The pitbull panic' is the title of an article by Judy Cohen and John Richardson (2002) that refers to the media demonisation of the pitbull in the US.

[3] *How a British bulldog saved the Union Jack* (1906) by Walturdaw Company, retained by the British Film Institute (ID 58131).

[4] Chain rolling is the practice of impromptu dog fighting while retaining the dog on the leash. Young men often 'square off' with their dogs in minor matches or 'rolls'.

[5] Pitbull-type dogs are not recognised as a breed (certainly not by the Kennel Club). They are a human-created mixture of various breeds, genetically constructed to create the perfect fighting dog.

[6] These accounts are collated in *The pitbull dilemma: The gathering storm*, by Donald Clifford et al (1990).

[7] 'Homies' is a slang term in American culture. It is an abbreviation of homeboy or homebuddies. It is a popular term in Chicano communities and also in hip hop and gang culture as a way of referring to the people you 'hang out' with.

[8] French biologist Jean-Baptiste Lamarck (1744–1829) derived an evolutionary theory of the heritability of acquired characteristics, that an organism can pass on to its offspring characteristics acquired through its lifecycle.

THREE

Status dogs: myth or menace?

Chapter Two set the scene with an examination of how bull breeds and dangerous dogs are viewed today in the US and the UK. However, this book is chiefly concerned with the phenomenon of status dogs, and this chapter examines more closely how this term came into being and what it means. It reviews the development of the concept in the UK media before considering in more detail how societal attitudes towards dogs have both changed and added to this debate.

The earliest reference I can find to the term 'status dog' is in an RSPCA briefing note (2007: 1), which notes the 'worrying rise in the ownership of "hard" looking dogs such as Pitbulls by teenagers on inner-city estates'. The document notes that such dogs are used as status symbols in antisocial behaviour and for intimidating people.

At this point, it is perhaps best to define the term status dogs as used in this book.

Definition

In early 2009, Paul Dunne from Animal Wardens published a report entitled *The rise of the urban status dog*, in which he referred to the 'urban status dog', summarised as a phenomenon involving 'youths in urban areas with bull breeds'. He also included dangerous dogs as proscribed by the Dangerous Dogs Act (DDA) 1991, large mastiff breeds such as presa canarios, and rottweilers.

In its 2010 public consultation on dangerous dogs, the Department for Environment, Food and Rural Affairs noted:

> The terms 'status dog' describes the ownership of certain types of dogs which are used by individuals to intimidate and harass members of the public. These dogs are traditionally, but not exclusively used, associated with young people on inner city estates and those involved in criminal activity. (Defra, 2010: 4)

Curiously, this definition applies to the owners rather than the dogs. Other articles and reports similarly fail to provide a definition; see, for example, GLA (2009), Lambeth Council (2010), Hallsworth (2011).

Harding (2010: 30) suggested that status dog was 'the label given to those dogs prescribed by the Dangerous Dogs Act (1991) or those considered sufficiently aggressive to warrant pariah status, e.g. Pit Bulls, Staffordshire Terriers, Rottweilers'.

A simplified version of this is now offered: status dog – an aggressive or illegal dangerous dog used to intimidate or convey status or authority. With the corollary that such dogs are often (but not exclusively), bull breeds owned/handled by young men in deprived urban areas: it is to this definition I refer in all future discussion.

This book suggests a simplified version of this definition, namely that a status dog is an aggressive or illegal dangerous dog used to intimidate or convey status or authority, with the corollary that such dogs are often (but not exclusively) bull breeds owned or handled by young men in deprived urban areas. This is the definition used throughout this volume.

For a detailed examination of the DDA 1991 and the controversies surrounding it, see Appendix A.

The role of the media

Any discussion of status dogs inevitably leads to the airing of numerous opinions that are often emotive and seldom informed. The UK media has been saturated with coverage of the topic over the past two or three years. But to what purpose? What do we really know about status dogs and their owners? Probably not a lot beyond the media-constructed images of hoodies with pitbulls struggling on bull chains and leather-studded harnesses. Research into the topic has thus far failed to offer up balanced reasonings or realist perspectives. Both media reporters and some academics are guilty of giving the topic just a glancing analysis, which has led to inflated rhetoric and ideological grandstanding.

In order to understand the phenomenon, it is important to separate out the strands of the debate, find fact from fiction and develop a balanced perspective on why some breeds of dog, notably bull breeds, are used and favoured by young people, mostly young men, to convey status and authority.

The starting place is the source from which this topic first raised its head – the media.

A moral panic?

We have seen how in the US the public view of bull breeds has changed dramatically over the past 20 years. Delise (2002) argues that this is 'caused almost entirely by the people who own these animals', as 'Pitbulls are chosen by people who desire and permit an animal to behave aggressively' (2002: 81-8).

But what of the UK? Hallsworth (2011) and Kasperson (2008) contend that the hype around status dogs, dangerous dogs and breed-specific legislation (BSL) is all media-fuelled moral panic. This argument is considered in more detail before looking further at UK media representation.

Kasperson (2008) briefly reviewed the period 1990/91 prior to the introduction of the DDA 1991 and argues cogently that in relation to discussions about dangerous dogs, all the elements of moral panic theory (Goode and Ben-Yehuda, 1994) operated sequentially.

In what Goode and Ben-Yehuda term the grassroots model, moral panic commences among the general public with concerns over certain behaviours, for example attacks on the public by aggressive dogs. In the model, the threat posed is both widely held and genuine. The media then generates hostility towards the group causing the concern, that is, the owners of dangerous dogs. This element involves labelling and condemnation, but there is also general consensus regarding the problem. Disproportionality is the fourth element in the model. Here the public considers the problem to be larger than it really is and exaggerated figures compound their fears. The final element in the model is that of volatility, namely the sudden unpredictable emergence and then disappearance of the issue.

Kasperson argues that this moral panic unfairly targeted bull breeds, mainly associated with the working class, as opposed to the dangerous breeds of the middle and upper classes (rottweilers, dobermans and even German shepherds[1]). This then introduces class bias into the way people choose their breeds of dog (Lodge and Hood, 2002). Lodge and Hood observe that in the UK, as in Germany,

> the institutions that maintained the canine 'class system' (e.g. kennel clubs etc) worked to impose the most draconian controls (notably forced sterilisation) onto pit bulls, while partially or fully shielding established dog types such as Rottweilers and German Shepherds with attack records that could be argued to be broadly equivalent to the pit bull kill-rate. (Lodge and Hood, 2002: 10)

Lodge and Hood report that in the UK public opinion supported government legislation introducing additional controls on dangerous dogs and in particular pitbulls. Enforcement of the DDA was, however, 'patchy'. They also claim that by 1992 the Metropolitan Police Service (MPS) made a 'conscious decision not to be pro-active in enforcing the Act' and by 1994 'had gone back in effect to the traditional "one-free bite" approach to dangerous dogs which the DDA had ostensibly replaced' (Lodge and Hood, 2002, 11, note 13). If this claim were correct, it would account, in part, for why the DDA did not achieve full success in eradicating pitbulls.

In a further observation on the period 1990/91, Lodge and Hood note how events of that time presented the government with a 'forced choice', essentially obliging it to legislate on the issue. They report similar pressures in Germany where the federal government was compelled into a 'forced choice' to address public concerns about dangerous dogs.

Setting aside the context of the introduction of the DDA, the next question is to determine whether or not there was moral panic in the UK over status dogs. Certainly, according to Stanley Cohen's analysis of media roles in generating moral panic, there are some aspects that lend their weight to the affirmative: media labelling of hoodies and gangsters; exaggeration and distortion of events using melodramatic language; and symbolism of dogs as part of 'gangsta lifestyle' (Cohen, 1972/2002).

However, moral panics are considered both volatile and temporal, that is, they arrive suddenly and dissipate as attention drifts away. The UK status dog issue surfaced in the late 2000s and remains high on the public agenda, although it tends to make headline news in the local rather than the national press.

There is no doubt that certain cultural signifiers, notably hip hop, urban music and gangsta rap, have situated pitbulls and bull breeds in the domain of deviancy and delinquency, certainly in the US and increasingly in the UK. This has, it seems, compounded the public's negative social reaction.

This also appears to fit Cohen's theory of 'deviancy amplification' (1980: 199). In this model, the initial problem (the structural and cultural position of the working class) requires a solution (the acquisition of status achieved through the acquisition of a large aggressive dog, which also reaffirms masculinity).

Societal reaction involves misperception of the issue through distorted media presentation. This in turn leads to public sensitisation, dramatisation and proposed control mechanisms. This then creates further stereotypes (weapon dogs), leading to increased polarisation and ultimately the confirmation of stereotypes.

On paper, the theoretical proposition of a moral panic appears to fit and it is plausible that moral panics themselves act effectively as mechanisms for simultaneously strengthening and redrawing society's moral boundaries (Ben Yehuda, 1986). It is also possible to analyse these issues from a social constructionist perspective and identify the vested interests of the actors involved through their rhetoric and use of language. This is examined in more detail later in the chapter.

Notwithstanding this, a more detailed interpretation suggests that the exact nature of the deviancy is unclear (Jewkes, 2004). There may indeed be several different strands of deviant activity taking place. Indeed, there may be no consensus as to what these deviant acts are and a lack of clarity over who is offended by them. For example, does the objection to status dogs relate to:

- the acquisition of large aggressive dogs;
- the use of dogs to intimidate;
- the visual parading of dogs and the taking over of public space;
- cruel training of dogs to be aggressive;
- allowing the dogs to fight;
- culpability in fatal attacks; or
- class judgements on the owners and their 'questionable' consumer choices?

It is therefore difficult to disentangle the precise moral element to which the moral panic might attach. Similarly, moral panic theory inherently assumes that the cause of the 'panic' is in fact ungrounded and unworthy of media attention (Jewkes, 2004). As the following chapters show, this is not the case. There are and continue to be legitimate public concerns over the threat posed to public safety from an increased proliferation of bull breeds and large aggressive dogs.

The issue of how these dogs are used to convey status is presently supposed rather than confirmed through research, as is the correlation between the dogs and the criminal activity of their owners. Both these issues are addressed in the coming chapters.

Space prohibits a full exploration of all aspects of moral panic theory. It appears that on paper the theory can be applied to the issues leading to the rapidly assembled DDA in 1991. The emergence, some 20 years later, of the new public policy issue of status and weapon dogs clearly indicates media involvement. Despite such involvement the case for moral panic theory in this aspect remains I think, unproven.

A cultural criminology perspective

A further perspective to air in determining whether moral panic theory has explanatory value in disentangling the multiple facets of the phenomenon of status dogs is that of cultural criminology. Ferrell and colleagues (2008) propose three additional dimensions worthy of consideration.

First, they suggest that there are multiple narratives involved, each of which requires exploration, each targeting a different audience. The action/reaction of all participants in the debate therefore needs to be 'explored symmetrically' or mapped and interpreted to illuminate cultural position and purpose.

Second, citing the contribution of Cohen and Young (1973), they acknowledge the media feeds recognised that the media feeds off the moral indignation of the public. This includes the energy released by all participants in the debates. In relation to status dogs, this energy includes the owners of status dogs who pose and parade with their animals because they want to be seen, and indeed they thrive on this. Some also thrive on the media opprobrium and subsequent designation as 'bad boys', living on the edge of the law.

Third, both Cohen (1972) and Ferrell and colleagues (2008) stress that there is usually an underlying reason for the panic, albeit not the focus of the media attention. That is to say, moral panics do not develop out of nowhere; they may be indicative of a wider issue beyond the media hype and verbiage. These deeper, often hidden, underlying reasons might include a displacement of other fears, or a fear of social change. In this context moral panics, such as they are, may act as a weathervane or looking glass.

Media hype may also cloud issues in mediated fog. Beneath the surface of sensational headlines – the increased use of large aggressive dogs by young men to imply status – lies the real issue with real significance. In this way, moral panic may predict social change. If this is the case, status dogs may act as a totemic symbol of the increased visibility of the underclass, now 'tooled up' with dogs purposefully bred for aggression; an inverted symbol of what the British public holds most dear – the domestic family pet; or a symbol of a society that no longer cares or nurtures (either animals or people) and has become atavistic and primordial or even post-apocalyptic. In this analysis, moral panic displaces other fears and obscures deeper threats. So the emergence of status dogs weapon dogs may herald a possible fracturing of the dominant cultural values, exposing the fault lines of inclusion/exclusion and bringing to reality a fear of the emergence – and the acceptability of – subterranean values (Ferrell et al, 2008).

The nature of UK media reporting

Any exploration of the phenomenon of status dogs must consider how the issue is presented in the UK press. We know that editorial policy determines the content of media publications and that newspapers in particular are selective in what they publish and are subject to errors and distortion. They are also the principle form for mediating news to the public and thus play a key role in any social construction of the issue of status dogs in the public mind.

This is now examined through the analytic paradigm of critical discourse analysis (CDA) (van Dijk, 1993; Fairclough, 1995). As van Dijk informs us, 'CDA focuses on the way discourse structures enact, confirm, legitimate, reproduce or challenge relations of power and dominance in society' (van Dijk, 2001: 2). Both van Dijk and Fairclough view language as a mechanism for social construction and claim that by unpacking language in detail we can identify the often hidden ideology within it, thus revealing the social meaning. One way social construction is achieved is by dominant power groups reinforcing their views and perspectives and 'othering' those with weaker power. In relation to status dogs, this might mean, for example, stigmatising the owners of bull breeds as belonging to the feckless underclass.

To undertake the analysis for the purposes of this chapter, the discursive strategies of three groups of news media were examined – national 'broadsheets' (despite recent resizing including the Berliner format), national tabloids and local press. Using a socio-cognitive approach (van Dijk, 2001), 12 newspapers were analysed, four from each of the three groups, randomly selected from 2009 to 2011.

Table 3.1 illustrates the key criteria used. Genres includes four feature articles with eight news stories, each situated as core articles within the paper. Dramatic dialogue was not identified in the lead opening of any article, but has been identified in other articles not used for this analysis.

The findings of the analysis as shown in Table 3.1 indicate a range of lexical and structural techniques that have been employed throughout the news stories. Without doubt these discursive strategies are used to manipulate our perceptions regarding how we view the breeds involved and their owners.

Table 3.1: Critical discourse analysis of the coverage of status dogs in UK news media

Criterion	Analysis of findings
Headings	These centre on victims' experience or authoritative demands, for example, 'Demands grow for "weapon dogs" to be brought to heel', *The Independent*, 10 November 2009. Transitive verbs, for example, 'savaged', introduce high emotive content. Article headings often assume previous knowledge and tap into previous 'understandings'. Frameworks of danger are often highlighted. Some sensationalising evident.
Lead	Hospitalisation or treatment resulting from attack is common. Problematising of issue and use of dramatic rhetoric and language, for example, 'A hero dad smashed down the door of a flat to save a 7-year-old boy from a frenzied pitbull', *Daily Star*, 27 January 2011. Dramatic use of contrast evident. Ideological positions and values evident. Motif of violence is used by lexical choice in headlines.
Perpetrators	Othering takes place reinforcing the 'us' and 'them' dichotomy, for example, 'Dangerous; alienated generation', *The Observer*, 14 March 2010. Owners are generally irresponsible and often criminal (thugs).
Lexical style	The lexical style is used to reinforce a positive presentation of 'us' (decent, law-abiding, responsible citizens) while deriding those deemed as 'other' by presenting derogatory characteristics (irresponsible, potential law breakers). Themes include man versus nature (mother versus brute); sensationalising (eg, horror, shock); randomness ('ran amok'), unpredictability ('went berserk'); lack of trust; assignation of danger ('rampage'); use of dramatic contrast and language (for example, 'devil dogs', 'danger dogs', 'horrific', 'filthy living room', 'cocaine', 'firearms', 'knives', 'weapon', for example, 'Armed to the teeth: the problem with pitbulls', *The Telegraph*, 15 April 2010
Photos and imagery	Images of snarling pitbulls, often juxtaposed with victims.
Actors quoted	Several different actors are illustrated: innocents (children), families (often mothers), heroes, veterinarians, police, authority figures.

Newspapers have clearly been a powerful locale for the dominant media perspectives that:

- the breeds concerned are dangerous and unpredictable;
- it is 'us' (reasonable and trusted families and responsible dog owners) versus 'them' (irresponsible, uncaring, young, usually working-class and often criminal owners);
- the menace posed by such dogs and owners? the menace posed by such dogs and owners.

While only a sample of newspapers were analysed, clearly key stories appeared in multiple papers. Some newspapers have run a national campaign (*Daily Mirror*) or a localised campaign (*Liverpool Echo*) to tackle 'danger dogs'. UK media coverage, including in newspapers and on talk radio, newscasts and broadcast documentaries, has undoubtedly echoed these discursive strategies. This has acted to reinforce the framework of danger associated with media representation of status dogs and the use of pejorative imaging. The 'them' and 'us' dichotomy identified as a central tent of CDA is evident. Ideological bias is also evident in textual print but less so in other forms of media coverage.

Similar findings have been reported in the US in the work of Cohen and Richardson (2002: 228), which reported that news coverage of pitbulls suffered from distorted headlines, second-hand accounts and journalistic laziness, leading to inaccuracy and distortion.

Allen (2007) in her news analysis of the *San Francisco Chronicle* (1990 to 2001) looks specifically at the media coverage of pitbulls. She notes that volume coverage creates a pattern of artificial understanding, building fear among the public through the use of hyperbole. Arguing cogently that the media has created a 'media monster', she contends that the pitbull problem is a 'newly emergent cultural construction', with the pitbull 'now part of the sign system that is used to announce a potentially threatening situation ... otherness' (Allen, 2007: 65).

Allen's US analysis places her firmly in the camp of moral panic theorists, alongside Hallsworth in the UK, who similarly denies the existence of any 'problem' regarding aggressive or dangerous dogs. For Allen, the issue is one of media 'hyperbole'; for Hallsworth, it is one of media 'myth'. However, both appear locked into a binary offering a false choice: on the one hand, a real problem exists, and on the other, it is all media constructed hyperbole or myth. My analysis suggests there is indeed a real problem that lends itself to hyperbole and media misrepresentation.

Allen further contends that pitbulls and their owners are now represented in the media as being situated at the bottom of the social ladder. Having thus situated them, media discursive practices then support existing power hierarchies that enact repressive legislation to maintain the status quo. This perspective is echoed in the UK by Hallsworth, who claims that:

> By continually posing the many real problems posed by dog ownership in terms such as 'weapon dogs' so a discursive space is created where totally disproportionate responses come to appear justified, while more measured and responsible approaches to what remain real problems get sidelined. (2011: 399)

These measures, he argues, include the 'British state's desire to liquidate the Pitbull as a breed ... that provoked the UK's descent into mass dog killing' (2011: 391). It is 'colourful inflated rhetoric' about 'weapon dogs' and lack of research that ensure 'fantasies about dangerous dogs come to prevail' (2011: 398).

For Hallsworth, it is both media discourse and politicians who are responsible for the criminalisation and destruction of pitbulls and other illegal dogs in the UK. In this regard, his analysis is undiluted grassroots moral panic theory. Arguing that there is no evidence to support this criminalisation, Hallsworth states that 'their construction as a public enemy owes more to an array of populist fantasies whipped up by an irresponsible media and by law and order politicians than to any commitment to evidence' (2011: 392). Here it seems that evidence is either blithely disregarded or wilfully ignored in pursuit of idealist position.

It is clear that although media reporting in the UK and US has been unbalanced, sensationalist and most likely biased, concerns over public safety persist in both countries and still need to be addressed. They cannot be dismissed as 'populist fantasies'. Furthermore, to conclude that the issue of status dogs is one of media panic only suggests an economic interpretation of moral panic theory that also leans towards idealism. Despite the evident media-generated pejorative imagery and inflated rhetoric, one cannot conclude that everything is myth and fantasy. There begins a sociological imperative to find and collate the evidence and then understand the nuances of the issue.

The media 'othering' of owners of specific breeds notwithstanding, it is clear that the media has generated multiple narratives in response to a range of different issues, including:

- personal accounts of dog attack incidents;
- increased visibility of certain breeds in public spaces;
- increased public anxiety over safety;
- well-meaning attempts to raise the topic as a new issue for public and social policy;
- the emergence of the urban street gang;
- concerns over issues of inclusion/exclusion;
- a change in human–animal relationships that can be best summarised as the commodification of dogs.

At times the media has foregrounded one or other of these narratives, failing to group them together and often fostering confusion. Central narratives have become obfuscated and then disordered in presentations themselves often light on facts. The expeditious nature of some journalism has led to contrary and controversial perspectives in the debate, exacerbated by the political slants of newspapers. In this mediated space where convenience trumps context, hyperbole thrives. Over time this has made a confusing issue convoluted but not conflated. Given this position, it is understandable that many people, including some academics, are disorientated. Cultural criminology and moral panic theory both offer useful analytical tools in questioning the phenomenon of status dogs. They also potentially further muddy the already cloudy water.

To cut through any potential misunderstanding, let me clarify my position. I believe that the increase in the use of dogs to convey status is a real problem. I also argue that the media has stayed true to form and reported the issue in often sensationalist ways, using hyperbole and inflated rhetoric. While reporting significant increases in dog attacks on humans and discussing the increased prevalence of pitbulls and Staffordshire bull terriers in the UK, the British media has confused and alarmed, yet apparently struck a chord with the British public. This has simultaneously tapped into the real experience of the public as they use public spaces. It has also unearthed a broader discourse in relation to a growing rift between certain elements of society and for many, illuminates the emergence of the violent street gang or the existence of an underclass. Media representation has usually settled on one or other of these perspectives, while on the ground, police officers, park rangers and the dog-walking public realise the true experience the reality of the phenomenon. So while the phenomenon of status dogs needs something more than classic moral panic theory in order to fully explain its complex nature, media discourse analysis does nonetheless reveal the real significance of the public fear of emerging subterranean values.

Moving on from media analysis and moral panic theory, the chapter now consider the issues from the perspective of human–animal relationships. This includes the commodification of dogs; changes in human–pet relationships and functions; cruelty and welfare; and breeding. It is hoped that an analysis of these issues will provide insight into the cultural changes in the role of dogs and how they have come to be used as objects that convey status.

Commodification

Over the past 20 years, aspects of human–animal relations have emerged as topics of research and exploration in their own right. In many ways, these relations are being reconceptualised, moving on from cultural histories to situating animals within the human experience.[2]

Heidi Nast argues that not only have 'pet-animals (become) increasingly central to notions of sociability, family, companionship and love' but they have 'become invariably positioned screens onto which all kinds of needs and desires are projected' (Nast, 2006). In a post-industrial world, dogs are anthropomorphised and commodified. This is certainly true in relation to status dogs, as this chapter later shows.

Emma Power (2008) continues this analysis of commodification, noting that humans project behavioural and personality expectations on to dogs to ensure that they fit within the family domain – an argument relevant to both domesticated pets and status dogs. Setting aside the role as domesticated pet and focusing on the role as a status dog, it is clear that for some owners the values, behaviours and personalities they seek to instil in their dog replicate atavistic violence and aggression. Certain breeds, such as bull breeds, will often provide an easy match for those seeking an animal that represents the physical embodiment of their own values – a canine 'mini-me'.

In some cases, this has meant a fundamental shift in social values in relation to certain breeds of dog. While arguably a process that has taken place over time, it may be summarised as a shift from viewing the dog empathetically as a sentient being, companion and family member to treating it as an adjunctive commodity that can be traded up, traded in or traded down. While it could be claimed that the proliferation of dog shows such as Crufts and the existence of so-called 'poodle parlours' are indicative of commodification, the emergence of status dogs most likely represents a qualitative shift in any development of this tendency. It is also a shift at the domestic level, where the dog is no longer man's best friend, but man's best chance of making money, winning a bet, building a reputation or getting away with intimidation. This is an important subtext to this topic of status dogs and one that has often gone unstated. It nonetheless remains an unarticulated fear – that these are new values that are the antithesis of recognised UK values towards dogs. Again, we return to fears over the emergence of new societal or subterranean values. While it is likely that those owners seeking to use their dogs as commodities to convey status are relatively small in number given the overall dog-owning population of the UK, they are nonetheless visible. Some commentators have viewed this as a societal shift or a structural change.

If it exists at all, this shift manifests itself in the 'othering' of the owners using their dogs in this way and the 'othering' of breeds involved. For some people, the fault lies at both end of the leash. What is clear in the numerous articles on the subject, however, is that this 'othering' of owners has become an argument situated in a discourse of class, poverty and deprivation, and in media images of hoodies on estates that evoke Cassandra-like warnings over the emergence of a feckless underclass and their feral dogs.

For some, the reports of dog attacks involving hooded owners represent a breakdown in social order and symbolise the rising disorder of inner cities (Allen, 2007). Pitbulls then become the embodiment of a threatening culture.

Staffordshire bull terriers

The media has failed to suitably establish a distinction between owners with 'commodification values' and those with 'traditional values'. The central locale for this foggy middle ground has been the Staffordshire bull terrier (SBT). While pitbulls have quickly become associated in the public mind with 'chavs' and gangsters, SBTs have long been respectable family pets and their owners are therefore not as easy to pigeonhole. In recent media-driven debates, much offence has been generated by sweeping generalisations that all bull breeds, including SBTs, are status dogs and ergo their owners must be vilified. It is certainly possible for young men to train or breed SBTs to be aggressive status dogs, but more often they are average domesticated pets. Dr David Grant, Director of the RSPCA Harmsworth Memorial Animal Hospital, believes that most cases presenting at the hospital involving SBTs relate to ignorance and neglect from owners rather than purposeful intent to create vicious dogs. Those average family owners who have well-socialised SBTs as household pets often feel criticised and caught up in a widening net of antipathy towards all bull breeds and status dogs.

This is understandable, as these are owners with traditional pet-loving values who have chosen to care for a bull breed, often an SBT. They seek to distance themselves from the 'other' owners – young men in hoodies on estates. The radio airwaves and newspapers are full of owners with 'traditional' values who decry the fact that their dogs (and they themselves) are now much maligned. Clearly, there are divergent sets of values in play here, discussed in more detail later in the chapter.

Owners who are aware of the growing stigma surrounding bull breeds often try to minimise the negative attention their dogs attract. Twining (2000: 25), in her study of stigma management of those owners with 'traditional' values, lists a series of techniques employed to minimise association with the 'other' owners and thus avoid stigma:

- passing their dogs off as other breeds;
- denying that their dog is badly bred;
- using humour;
- decrying the negative media coverage;
- emphasising their dog's non-stereotypical behaviour;
- taking preventative measures, for example not using parks or open spaces at specific times;
- avoiding walking their dogs in harnesses and leather chains;
- becoming breed ambassadors.

It should be noted, however, that any consumer who has invested in a loved brand that has developed negative connotations could react in a similar way. Interestingly, many of these points were raised during the research study interviews with owners of status dogs who passed off their dogs as other breeds (see Chapter Five). Where the dog was evidently a pitbull, this was most likely a chosen strategy to minimise police intervention. That said, depending on the owner and their values, expectations and motivations, an SBT can be either a domesticated household pet or a status dog. Some research respondents claimed it was the 'poor man's pitbull', sought after by those who do not feel ready to go for 'the real thing'.

Ownership of the Staffordshire bull terrier was the subject of recent research by Diesel (2008), who completed 549 interviews with dog owners at locations in Manchester, Leeds, Liverpool and London.[3] A large proportion of dogs seen at each location were SBTs:[4] London, 40%; Leeds and Liverpool, 20%; and Manchester, 16%.[5] In London, the sample comprised a higher proportion of male dogs. In all locations,

SBTs aged over six months were less likely than older SBTs to have been neutered, possibly indicating a desire to breed. Some respondents expressed their desire for an 'intact' male dog, adding that a neutered male dog did not 'have the same status'. SBT dogs in London were also more likely to be six months or younger compared with the non-SBT group and locations in the study. In London, Manchester and Liverpool, SBT owners were significantly more likely to have acquired the dog from a friend as opposed to the non-SBT group. In all locations SBT owners were more likely to be younger than other dog owners.

Diesel (2008) found that in London 'image' was much more likely to be given as a reason for obtaining the dog by SBT owners. 'High availability' of the breed was also frequently nominated. Owners were asked if dog type 'said anything about its owner'. In London, where 'image' was the dominant reason for ownership, SBT owners were also more likely to say that dog type 'did not say anything about the owner'. Diesel does not speculate the significance of this finding; however, it is entirely possible that media coverage of status dogs in London was higher than in provincial towns, possibly leading respondents to be circumspect about admitting their reasons for obtaining the dog. Alternatively, it might be the case that status dogs in London are so common that owners no longer consider it worthy of comment. SBT owners also commented on the importance they placed on the dog being 'tough', 'strong', big' and 'scary'. Some boasted about the dog's strength, while others noted its role in personal protection. Some young male SBT owners in London said that having an SBT was "better than carrying a knife". While the research notes that ownership of SBTs for 'image' or status was not yet a problem in the other study locations, it was evidently a growing problem in London.

This research acknowledges an emergent issue in London in 2008 and confirms the growing trend of young men in urban areas using their dog to convey status or to strengthen their image. The research also highlights, and confirms, that not all SBT owners are motivated by such issues. This finding indicates a difference in ownership and ownership motivations, with SBTs on the one hand being used as family pets and domesticated household animals and on the other being used by some young men to convey status, toughness and aggression. These findings corroborate my own.

These and other findings indicate a need for greater clarity as what appears to be a spectrum of ownership, breeds and motivations for ownership. At one end of this spectrum are those with well-socialised domesticated pets and at the other those for whom certain breeds of dog are used as commodities conferring status. This is discussed in more detail in Chapter Four.

Pet relationships and functions

Recent research into human–pet relations provides useful insights into why some people use dogs to convey status. Belk (1996), in his study of metaphoric relationships with pets, contends that two groups of owners exist: those who view their pet as 'a being' and those who view their pet as 'a possession'. The latter often leads to 'owner-projected attributes' that in turn can lead to a 'dark side of pet ownership'.

Beverland and colleagues (2008) develops this concept by further identifying relationships between ownership motives and consumption patterns in relation to dogs, for example, breed choice, animal appearance, responsibilities of ownership and selection and acquisition of pet-marketed products. Beverland and colleagues designate two ownership motivations: 'intrinsic' and 'extrinsic'. Intrinsic ownership sees pets valued as individual sentient beings. For these owners, the relationships are equally giving, empathetic and compassionate, with consumerism, as and when required, being primarily linked to the health of the animal. Extrinsic ownership on the other hand focuses on the status the pet brings to the owner. Here, the dog is used to fit a 'pre-conceived role in the owner's lives resulting in different human–pet interactions' (Beverland et al 2008:492). This results in the dominance of appearance-related criteria in pet selection. Here breeds become brands and canine attributes are preassessed to ensure they are 'fit for purpose'. Belk and Beverland and colleagues are largely discussing owners who treat their pets as material objects or toys. Owners may infantilise dogs and dress them up in a range of branded or designer 'doggie wear', controlling their behaviour and imposing personal desires. The parallel with owners utilising their dogs for status, or as a personal identity project, is clear, not least in Beverland and colleagues' statement that 'owners motivated by a desire for control, domination, and status are more likely to treat their pets as objects for their own pleasure' (Beverland et al 2008:494).

If conferring status is a function of the dog, it must be asked of each owner whether it is a manifest or latent function (Parsons, 1937). Research on this issue remains to be undertaken. It is, however, the dog's latent function that is identified by the media and professionals as conveying status on the owner. To some extent, the public revulsion over status dogs is the result of these latent functions becoming manifestly transparent. This in turn has unveiled the fact that many people have only a functional relationship with their pets. While this may also be true of the owners of 'purse pooches', the public believes that those animals are pampered and therefore loved. Status dogs, by contrast, suggest an unbalanced human–animal power dynamic that is abusive, controlling, manipulative and ultimately deceptive with regard to the bonds of trust and unconditional love. The general public often finds this disconcerting and unappealing. In some ways, this is perhaps a glance backwards to a time when dogs were functional and not fully domesticated – when dogs earned their keep rather than held our empathy. This prospect holds no comfort, as it again suggests a certain atavisim that only reinforces the pejorative public perception of both the owners and the dogs. It also confirms the estrangement of bull breeds in the eyes of the public, suggesting a human–animal relationship that is somehow moving into reverse mode, becoming increasingly estranged rather than increasingly loving and nurturing. This confirms for many the dynamic potential of estrangement – exclusion. Here again, in the eyes of the public, the argument comes full circle – in other words - the excluded dogs are the exclusive preference of the excluded – and thus the perfect match. Restated, for much of the public, bull breeds and their owners are a perfect match.

This is a public debate that rumbles on. It is worth noting how status dogs provide a range of potential functions to an owner, encouraging the owner to exercise their rights as consumers to purchase the goods that match their requirements. Increased demand for certain breeds then creates a market that breeders try to supply.

The question, then, is why are so many consumers now in the market for a dog that will provide them with status? The motivations for this are considered in more detail in Chapter Five, but include fashion and protection. Notwithstanding the range of motivations, it is clear that more and more young people feel the need to purchase an object (a dog) that will convey status in their community or to their peer group. Similarly the dog becomes the template for the owners on to which they project their own attributes and values – in the case of status dogs, violence and aggression.

Cruelty and welfare

It could be strongly argued that status dogs are acquired as functional possessions, with the consumer placing emphasis on appearance and reputation. While acquisitional motivations are addressed in more detail in Chapter Four, it is clear that a key function of the status dog is to act as a foil for the attributes of the owner and vice versa. The dominant object for consideration is therefore the owner, rather than the dog.

As the dog is being acquired for the purpose of becoming an 'extrinsic' functional template, the marketplace is different and often this reflects and mirrors the future expectant relationships with the dog and the reasons behind the acquisition often dictate the owner's expectations about their future relationship with the dog. A dog purchased for its 'intrinsic' reasons with the intention of becoming a family pet is often purchased through pet shops or recognised agencies and kennel clubs. Dogs acquired for 'extrinsic' purposes are often acquired via the internet or are bought on a whim.

Status dogs are thus often acquired through different means than dogs serving other purposes (see Beverland et al, 2008). A higher proportion may be purchased via internet websites or newspaper columns as opposed to pet shops, meaning that dogs may be acquired quickly, easily and on the spur of the moment. Those acquiring the dogs may have little or no previous knowledge of animal welfare, standards of care or discipline techniques. This may lead to animal cruelty and welfare issues.

Dr David Grant, Director of RSPCA Harmsworth Memorial Animal Hospital since 1987, has witnessed the trend for bull breed dogs and from a veterinary perspective has classified different levels of cruelty that became associated with the acquisition of status dogs (RSPCA, 2007). He developed the three-point classification of levels of cruelty shown in Table 3.2.

Breeding

Breeding is another factor when considering animal–human relations. While arguments rumble on about deed or breed and where responsibility lies, dog experts are unanimous in decrying the actions of irresponsible owners who have 'willingly encouraged (aggressive) behaviour or have allowed this behaviour to be expressed genetically' (Delise, 2002: 53).

Dog expert Delise notes that 'there will always be a certain type of person that will obtain a dog as an extension of their own aggressive tendencies', adding that 'dogs can be encouraged and manipulated to act aggressively' (2002: 26-8). Behaviour or temperament is a product of both genetics and social environment. Where irresponsible owners acquire dogs with strength and stamina and 'mould' them to become aggressive, the results can produce a dog that is potentially dangerous. In effect, this means that it is the human managers of dogs who are responsible not only for training dogs to become aggressive but also

Table 3.2: Causes of animal cruelty among owners of status dogs

Level 1 cruelty – associated with the fashion for SBTs, PBTs, and crosses – often relates to ignorance of animal welfare and responsibilities	Acquisition on a whim can lead to 'traditional cruelty' Puppies may receive inadequate care, for example, failure to vaccinate potentially leading to disease, inappropriate feeding, little or no training, failure to socialise the animal Limited economic provision or failure to realise the incurred costs may delay or inhibit owners seeking veterinary advice Failure to exercise the dog on the leash can lead to road traffic accidents Inability to feed, exercise or care for the dog and lack of interest can lead to neglect or abandonment
Level 2 cruelty – associated with indiscriminate breeding of these dogs	Indiscriminate breeding by entrepreneurs seeking profit but with little interest in the dog's welfare. This can be up to £500 per puppy Inadequate prenatal care including cramped and unhygienic conditions Poor postnatal care, emaciation and mastitis Diseases such as atopy (an incurable allergy), generalised demodicosis and congenital abnormalities are common, often leading to abandonment Exhaustion through multiple pregnancies
Level 3 cruelty – associated with antisocial behaviour, gang culture and crime	Cases at the extreme end of animal cruelty which are often picked up by the press Dog fighting, resulting in severe wounding and injuries Delay in seeking veterinary advice Dogs being used to intimidate people or assist in committing a crime Owners using dogs to protect themselves or criminal assets Violence and beatings through training regimes, discipline or 'toughening up', including stabbing and scalding

for breeding dogs to become aggressive. This is a particular factor for status dogs and bull breeds in particular. As Delise notes, 'Allowing a dog to behave aggressively and allowing aggressive animals to breed, will ultimately produce a breed that exhibits increased levels of aggression against humans' (2002: 53). This suggests that these elements first become a characteristic of the breed, then a reputational factor associated with the breed. Reputation then becomes a factor in consumer selection, alongside canine characteristics and appearance (Beverland et al, 2008).

So begins the vicious circle whereby aggressive dogs are bred for aggression, develop a reputation for aggression and thus become attractive for their aggressive reputation; see Figure 3.1.

Figure 3.1: Vicious circle of demand and supply of status dogs

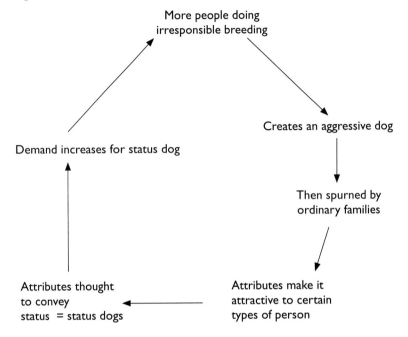

More people doing irresponsible breeding

Creates an aggressive dog

Demand increases for status dog

Then spurned by ordinary families

Attributes thought to convey status = status dogs

Attributes make it attractive to certain types of person

The role and function allocated to the dog by status dog owners then further embeds the tendency for aggression. As Delise points out, 'dogs obtained to protect, guard, fight or enhance an image of danger are obliged or in essence, duty-bound to behave aggressively' (2002: 26). There are three types of breeding practice identified by Delise (2002: 32–3) that can potentially produce dogs with behavioural problems:

- battery farm breeding of puppies as livestock;
- back-street breeding, where breeders are interested in profit rather than health, breeding quality or stable temperament;
- intentional breeding of fractious or aggressive animals, for example for dog fighting.

In dogs that host inherent aggressive tendencies (for example, rottweilers), irresponsible breeding will create a situation whereby aggressive tendencies are selected for breeding. These then become exhibited with increased frequency and rising levels of unpredictability.

This process will become faster and more widespread if the breed is already popular and the marketplace fills with back-street breeders using similar techniques. Through such processes it is possible to develop a ratcheting effect of escalating aggression, with these characteristics embedded in the dog from birth. The RSPCA reports that this situation is now pertinent to bull breeds in the UK. Characteristics such as aggressiveness and unpredictability are thus found in bull breeds and status dogs through genetic breeding as well as through irresponsible ownership and training. This has implications for public safety as one respondent in the current research makes clear:

> 'All the pitbulls are now interbred. You'll never get one now with 100% pure genes. They are all interbred. Now they are all mongrel mixes basically. It can make 'em more aggressive but if you treat 'em badly then it also makes 'em aggressive.' (Professional dog fighter)

The commodification of dogs in general also affects the breeding of aggressive and status dogs. This makes them a commodity in a market economy subject to the vagaries of supply and demand. The RSPCA confirms an increase in back-street breeding as entrepreneurs seek to respond to an increased demand for large aggressive bull breeds. Over the past 20 years in the UK, it has become clear that:

- there has been a significant increase in demand for aggressive bull breeds;
- traditional, recognised or registered breeders have not been able to meet the rise in demand;
- the dogs bred or made available by registered breeders do not fully match the demanded requirements for aggression, physicality and size;
- some types of desired breeds have now been proscribed as illegal;
- cross-breeding with illegal dogs has led to dogs similar to those that were banned, but which may be sufficiently different to subsequently pass as legal;
- the new market is unregulated and open for all to enter, with considerable money to be made;
- there is money to be made in breeding quickly and to order.

This new marketplace has had the following effects:

- demand has been met with increased supply of large aggressive bull breeds, leading in places to market saturation, as is the case with SBTs;
- supply has been met through importation, sale and purchase of dogs via the internet, leading to more irresponsible breeding;
- the circular movement of the market is perpetuating and increasing opportunities for profit and irresponsible breeding;
- the proliferation of bull breeds is increasing with 'scatter-breeding' and random hybridisation;
- there are more health problems for dogs and further social problems for humans.

Conclusion

Having established a definition for status dog, this chapter set out to determine the role and influence of the UK media in the social construction of the term. Moral panic theory is in itself an unsatisfactory explanatory device for the phenomenon of status dogs. The device of critical discourse analysis when applied to recent UK media suggests that elements of the theory are evident in media reporting. However, as often with moral panic theory, it is difficult to disentangle what exactly the moral panic is about. Simply acknowledging that the media has indulged in reporting suggestive of moral panic theory automatically suggests that the issues raised are falsely inflamed and unworthy of media attention. This is not the case. Concerns are legitimate and would benefit from a more informative and balanced journalistic perspective. But perhaps that is too optimistic.

Cultural criminology may offer a more subtle but accurate interpretation of moral panic by suggesting that it indicates and predicts social change, in this case, the emergence of a totemic symbol of the newly visible underclass that subverts established social norms and exposes 'subterranean values'. This argument is supported by the acknowledgment of transformative human–animal relationships, whereby dogs are increasingly commodified as functional acquisitions, with selection based on reputational brand values. Irresponsible breeding is then undertaken to create animals that match the consumer demand for aggressive animals.

The next chapter considers in more detail the motivations of owners seeking to acquire status through their dogs, noting how the reputational characteristics of the dogs are used to match the functional needs of the owners.

Notes

[1] Said by Kasperson (2008: 213) to be the breed most responsible for dog bites. As Kasperson cites, 'In different studies in different countries the German Shepherd is the most commonly biting breed (Roll and Unshelm, 1997)'.

[2] For example, *Animal geographies* by Wolch and Emel (1998) or *Animal spaces* by Philo and Wilbert (2000).

[3] The study targeted those communities that used the services of the RSPCA and PDSA in four specific locations and therefore the results cannot be generalised to apply to all areas or socioeconomic backgrounds.

[4] Includes SBT crosses.

[5] The non-SBT dogs include English bull terriers, bull mastiffs, pitbulls and American bulldogs.

FOUR

Motivations and characteristics of owners

A key question for me as I began investigating the phenomenon of status dogs was why is this occurring? What motivates young men to obtain aggressive dogs, or to obtain a placid puppy and train it to be deliberately aggressive? This chapter considers the motivations of owners by first establishing a typology of motivations. Second, it draws on sociological and criminological theories to help us understand why some people feel the need to boost their status and why dogs may fit this purpose – for example, for use as gang dogs (dogs used by one or more gang members exclusively within the context of the gang or weapons dogs. Finally, it considers the characteristics of owners and the general influence of cultural imagery.

Chapter Five sets out the extensive primary research that underpins these arguments, but suffice to say for the moment that extensive interviews permitted identification of some common groupings. Analysis of these interviews permitted construction of a broad typology of motivations for ownership of aggressive breeds (working dogs, for example, farm dogs, were not included). The typology of motivations for ownership is shown in Table 4.1. The motivational details of those owning dogs as pets or family companions are not further investigated here and the focus is rather on the motivations for owning status dogs.

What this typology tells us is that owners acquire and use aggressive breeds for a variety of reasons. This suggests a spectrum of ownership, where owners use dogs for different functional purposes in different situations (even among those using dogs to convey status).

A motivational spectrum suggests the operation of different social domains or social fields; for example, using a dog to acquire status is probably more relevant to gang-affiliated young men than to a family of five in a leafy suburb. So just what are these different social domains/ fields and why and how is status achieved or acquired? These issues are examined before establishing how and why aggressive dogs fit into this picture, by employing the theoretical perspectives of French sociologist Pierre Bourdieu (1986; 1991).

Table 4.1: Typology of motivations for ownership of aggressive or illegal dogs

Motivation	Comment
Pet/family companion	"Staffies are really gentle dogs and are often mostly pets. But they can be made to fight. They are really the victim of their owners in that regard." (Dr David Grant, Director, RSPCA, Harmsworth Memorial Animal Hospital, London)
Status – fashion	"Staffies have largely become a fashion accessory, bought on a whim, copycatting. Owners don't think it through and then when they become too much, they abandon them. Eighty per cent of issues with them relate to ignorance or neglect." (Dr David Grant, Director, RSPCA, Harmsworth Memorial Animal Hospital, London)
Status – protection	"Often people want a tough-looking dog as a guard dog, really." (Female status dog owner, London)
Status – entrepreneurial (including breeding and dog fighting on professional circuit)	"You do get many of these dogs used in criminal activities." (MPS Police Officer) "Breeding is done for profit and this can often lead to diseased animals." (Dr David Grant, Director, RSPCA, Harmsworth Memorial Animal Hospital, London)
Status – image and identity (including dog fighting by chain rolling)	"These large aggressive dogs can be owned by different people but mostly by people who want to use the dog to boost their image or status." (Merseyside Police Officer) "There are also some who are largely part of the criminal fraternity and unemployed, but now they have these dogs. Often these people are known to the police." (Dr David Grant, Director, RSPCA, Harmsworth Memorial Animal Hospital, London)

Different social fields

Bourdieu developed a theory of practice by considering the relationships formed between individuals and society (Bourdieu, 1990). He argued that social groups or domains (fields) sit in a broad social landscape where relative positions are a function of class and power. Social groupings, be they gangs, artists or academics, seek social distinction from other groupings while simultaneously striving to develop their identity by opposing other social groups. Within each social grouping or field, participants (actors) struggle to achieve distinction and access scarce resources. In this sense, the field becomes 'a structured arena of social conflict' (Bourdieu and Wacquant, 1992). In the social field of a deprived urban neighbourhood, employment opportunities may be limited and low educational attainment may hinder advancement. Thus many local residents may struggle to acquire scarce economic capital.

Bourdieu's theoretical perspective also considers the types of capital available within social fields. In social fields, knowledge, goods and services are acquired by participants seeking to 'accumulate and monopolise different kinds of capital' (Swartz, 1997: 117). In the social field of the urban street gang, the struggle is over money, respect, reputation and status, (Harding, 2012). Such resources are limited and constitute their own form of unevenly distributed capital. Within any field, actors who are lower down the hierarchy struggle to reach the top, for example, poor families trying to achieve financial independence or young gang members aspiring to be the gang leader.

By applying the concept of different social fields to the above typology, it becomes clear that debates about irresponsible use of aggressive bull breeds has in fact been about different social fields. In other words, the public debate has wrongly conflated different social groupings with different social values and norms and bound them together into one homogenous group. Clearly, this misrepresents how dogs fit into different social fields/groupings. It is thus possible to identify three different social fields pertinent to the debate about status dogs and why people own them:

- average families (with pet/companion dogs);
- young people (with status dogs);
- gangs (with status dogs used for criminal activity).

We can see that there are three different social groups of owners rather than one, and that each group operates differently, with different motivations for their relationship with aggressive dogs. This concept is important, as it allows us to move the argument forward, and in this case, to narrow the focus of study to young people.

This finding also helps put into context the public debate about the Staffordshire bull terrier (SBT), and how it is viewed by some as an aggressive status dog and by others as a sociable family pet.[1] The former accusation is met with a chorus of angry riposte by a majority claiming to be the responsible owners of a much-loved domesticated pet. What is clear is that these angry responses emanate from a different social field, namely one where dogs are not used to convey status.

How a dog is used within a social field is determined by the function the dog can bring to the social field and the motivation of the owner. In the social field of a mature middle-aged couple, that function is most likely to be companionship. The social norms operating within this social field dictate the social values – the ability to share one's home with a companion animal is emblematic of a tolerant caring household. Different values and social norms operate in different social fields. In one, the SBT is a well-socialised family member; in another, it's an aggressive, poorly socialised dog where the owners purposefully increase its musculature to make it appear bigger and fiercer. The function of the dog thus changes depending on both social field and owner's requirements. In the second example, the motivation is to use the dog as a utility vehicle for acquiring status. Although ordinary family homes can also mistreat dogs or fail to socialise them responsibly, the dogs themselves are seldom used to convey status per se. In this sense, then, it is possible for an SBT to be either a sociable domesticated pet or a beefed-up aggressive status dog, depending on the social field and the motivations of the owner.

This research study identified different motivations for ownership of status dogs depending on the social field of the owner. This is best illustrated visually as a spectrum. Figure 4.2 merges discussions on social fields with that of motivational categories.

Figure 4.2: Spectrum of status dogs and social fields

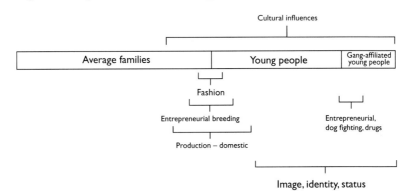

The figure indicates the four motivational categories identified through the research study and maps these against the three relevant social fields indicating the approximate size and coverage of each category. The visual representation seeks to illustrate that:

- fewer young people owning a status dog are motivated by fashion trends than by entrepreneurial factors (making money from breeding/dog fighting and criminal activities);
- breeding is split into professional breeding for the value of the stock and commercial breeding for gain;
- owners using dogs for domestic protection form a similar proportion to that of owners of status dogs. This group, which is largely or disproportionately female, is split across two social fields, average families and young people;
- owners who are motivated by image, identity and personal status form the largest proportion of status dog owners and are found overwhelmingly (though not exclusively) in the social fields of young people and gang-affiliated young people.

Cultural influences are felt most across the social fields for young people and gang-affiliated young people, and less so for average families.

This process represents a first attempt to map these broad categories of motivation to the social groups involved. Naturally, there will be exceptions regarding personal relationships with dogs. The boundaries of the social fields, as with all social fields, are not fixed, but dependent on relationships (Bourdieu, 1987). The motivations of fashion, entrepreneurship and protection are all manifest functions (Parsons, 1937). This differs from image and identity enhancement, which is a latent function.

Brand values

Each group, regardless of their motivation, chooses a status dog because of the strong brand and reputational values associated with large aggressive bull breeds. Each dog comes with its own reputational branding. In the case of bull breeds, this is a reputation that is widely recognised (although it can be stereotypical or generalised). This reputation then corresponds to its commercial brand values or unique selling points. For bull breeds these are aggression, stamina, loyalty, trust, viciousness, 'gameness', 'uncontrollability' and so on. Young men buy into these brand values, which they then seek to adopt to fit their own personalities, or they craft their own personality around these values.

It is these brand values that make bull breeds and mastiffs the 'dogs of choice' as status dogs. They fulfil the function required of the social field, namely providing strong brand and reputational values that boost the owner's image, conveying and enhancing status. Breed characteristics, qualities and attributes are central in this function, for example pitbulls are reputedly aggressive, loyal and trusting. These qualities are equally attractive to owners.

The malleability of pitbulls, which permits owners to stamp their imprint on the dog's character and mould its temperament, is equally attractive. For many, it is this unique brand value that makes the pitbull the perfect fit for their function; for a young man, it is a dog with a fearsome reputation for aggression (whether or not justified) that he then uses to convey a similar reputation for himself.

These brand values of status dogs are used by owners to match the functional requirements that underpin the reason or motivation for obtaining the dog. Whatever the motivational reasons for having the dog, the owner expects the dog to perform these functional requirements in its role. Failure to perform this duty effectively may lead to the dog being abandoned or traded up. Table 4.2 illustrates functional requirements in relation to motivations.

Table 4.2: Functional requirements for status dogs

Motivation	Functional requirements for the dog (roles)
Entrepreneurial	Bouncer, minder, bodyguard, security, guarantor, commercial asset, visual branding or marketable breeding stock, gameness or fighting ability
Protection	Personal guardian – attack dog, defender, fear generator, confidence giver Domestic protection – home guardian, protector, defender
Fashion	Unique or rare, symbol of urban counter-culture, embodies 'frontier' or anti-state values
Image and identity enhancement	Symbolic of power, aggression, violence, volatility; confidence giver, image amplifier, masculinity enhancer; spatial controller, demander of respect, unpredictable, violent

Motivations for owning a status dog

The chapter now examines each of the typologies relating to status dogs:

- entrepreneurship
- protection
- fashion
- image and identity.

The motivation or impetus for owning a status dog varies depending on the owner's functional requirements, and the dog's attributes and manifest/latent function; as well as on the intended perceptional outcome sought by the owner, the social advantage or actual/perceived benefit for the owner, and the level of reputational deficit of the owner.

The type of dog chosen will depend on the reputation of the breed and the ability of the breed to match these requirements. In short, it must be the right dog for the right purpose.

It should also be noted that the first three elements of the typology relate to the dog and its reputational values. The use of a dog to boost the image and identity of the owner relates to the reputational deficit experienced by the owner and this is most likely a latent function of ownership, that is, owners will not say they obtained their dog to boost their image, but will offer others functional motivations. The overarching backdrop to much of this is, of course, cultural influences. The chapter concludes with a summary of how status dogs are viewed within the cultural landscape and the influence this has on young people.

Entrepreneurship

This category may be split into a number of different elements:
- income generation from breeding, either professional breeding to create professional stock or back-street breeding for profit;
- dog fighting (professional circuit);
- use of dogs in crime.

Breeding

A key form of entrepreneurial motivation is using the dog to generate income from breeding. RSPCA officials advise that two distinct groups operate – professional breeders and 'home-grown breeders'. While space prohibits detailed discussion of professional breeders, it is useful to give an overview by way of distinguishing the characteristics of professional breeding from non-professional breeding.

Professional breeders are motivated by developing professional breeding stock, sourcing and building pedigree bloodlines and focusing on the quality, health and history of the animals. They will not breed dogs without documentation of pedigree (working papers) and are hugely knowledgeable about the breeds. The ancestry and wellbeing of the dog is paramount and only dogs meeting breed standards are used. Dogs with genetic defects are not bred and only those with stable temperaments are selected. Breeders are mostly registered and highly professional, presenting quality dogs in shows or trials with valid competing certificates. Dogs are never traded on impulse and prospective buyers are introduced, interviewed, vetted and added to waiting lists. Purchasers who are deemed unfit as owners are often rejected. Dogs are well raised with consideration given to diet, health and socialisation before being sold with health guarantees and associated paperwork. Professional breeders are highly cognisant of potential defects and strive to ensure defects are not perpetuated. Frequently breeding is not undertaken for profit but for improvement of the animal. These breeders are recognised members of professional dog clubs and organisations with good links into professional trainers and veterinarians. There is also a middle ground of semi-professional breeders operating local kennels and mostly declaring taxable income from breeding.

At the other end of the spectrum are the decidedly non-professional breeders, often referred to as back-street -or underground breeders. Here breeding provides an opportunity to make money.

In order to better understand these motivations we need to look more closely at changing fortunes of working class men in the UK. In the UK, the established macro structures that provided traditional bases for male identity and behaviour, such as employment and education, have largely gone (Winlow, 2001). Many working-class young people have seen their neighbourhoods transformed over the past 20 years. By 1997, 25% of the UK's children and young people lived in communities characterised by youth unemployment, low household incomes, high crime, low or limited educational opportunities and few if any employment prospects (Pitts, 2003, 2008). For some young people, these reduced life prospects have been replaced by a more entrepreneurial approach to earning money via personal networks, providing opportunities for legitimate trades but also in the 'shadow economy'. These quasi-underground economics are 'an established fact of working-class life in England' (Robins, 1992: 89; see also Hobbs, 1988; Foster, 1990). Entrepreneurial activity provides an opportunity of escaping this 'concentration of disadvantage' (Pitts, 2008).

Entrepreneurial opportunities can be found in deprived neighbourhoods, allowing young men to make money by, for example, buying and selling stolen goods or breeding dogs. Such people 'innovate' (Merton, 1938), employing unconventional means (such as illegal dog breeding) to acquire conventional goals (money). Here the status dog becomes a commercially viable asset to be bought and sold. As noted by one police officer in this study, "Irresponsible breeding is the real cancer behind society's problem with dogs at the moment."

Back-street breeding both drives the market and responds to demand. It requires acknowledged skills, a network of contacts and the impetus to make money. A Staffordshire bull terrier pup from good stock retailed at £250-£300 in 2009. A litter of six can bring in over £1,000 twice a year as untaxed income, although prices have dropped since due to market saturation. Prices and type of dog for sale vary regionally. A review of the *South Wales Echo* on Monday 2 August 2010 identified several different breeds of status dog for sale: dogue de Bordeaux, £795 per pup; bulldog pups, £1,200 each; and French bulldogs, £1,500 each. In 2011, a top-quality blue-nosed pitbull pup could retail for £800.

However, not everyone can employ entrepreneurial skills and their adoption 'varies according to the skill and dexterity of individuals' (Giddens, 1976: 112). As such, some activities are more 'home-grown'.

Such home-grown breeders operate quite differently from professional or even semi-professional breeders. The dogs sold or traded are usually substandard and a back-street breeder is often unaware of genetic defects. Breeding is done on an ad hoc basis as opposed to through a breeding plan – mating dogs are not researched and 'papers' are non-existent or fabricated. Breeding is frequent, undertaken at any age and repeated for convenience. Dogs with poor temperament, poor socialisation or aggression are not sifted out and rejected – indeed they may be actively desired. Canine health is overlooked, as the goal is not improvement of the dog, but income generation. Dogs may therefore be warehoused and kept in yards or outhouses with poor-quality, cheap food and little exercise. Selling is frequently on a first-come, first-served basis or through advertisements in newspaper columns and on the internet. Transactions are usually in cash and undeclared for tax. The purchaser is not vetted and dogs are sold on regardless of the destination and with no contracts or guarantees. The objective of many of these breeders is to establish a high-volume, high-turnover 'kitchen business'. This in turn can lead to numerous dogs being kennelled in spare rooms in social housing under quite unsuitable conditions as one of the survey respondents describes

> [We had a case in Northolt] a black American man had 25 to 30 pitbulls which he was breeding to sell. He had them all in cages and in bedroom wardrobes. He was supplying them big time.' (Police officer, Ealing, London)[2]

Under such conditions health and socialisation are seldom addressed:

'I've had to deal at the hospital with emaciated bitches being used as breeding machines. Money drives this for young people as she could have a litter of eight twice a year.' (Dr David Grant, RSPCA Harmsworth Memorial Animal Hospital)

Breeding for profit often leads to disease in the animals, including mange, allergies and skin diseases. The diseased animals are then often bred further, compounding their health problems.

The seizure of illegal breeding dogs is expensive for the authorities. Multiple dogs are seized at once as raids tend to result in several dogs being seized at the same time leading to high kennelling costs. In one incident, 12 dogs seized in a raid were kennelled at a cost of £38,000 until the case reached court.[3]

Dogs will even be bred purely to circumvent current legislation:

'What some people have realised recently is that if you cross-breed with an American bulldog then you create this thing that might not fall under the Act. There is a lot of hybrid cross-breeding going on. They like the aggression and the physique of a pitbull but they will tinker with it a bit so it doesn't fall within the legislation.' (Metropolitan Police Service Status Dog Unit officer)

'People will try and move away from the confirmation standard slightly, just enough to almost find a loop-hole in the law.' (Police officer, West Midlands)

Under such circumstances, expert witnesses and judges may seek independent verification of breed/type from organisations such as the Kennel Club.

After the introduction of the Dangerous Dogs Act (DDA) 1991, there was a demand for status dogs that circumvented the legislation, often resulting in dogs exchanging hands at extortionate prices. The dogue de Bordeaux originally entered the UK as a rare breed from the continent, with pups being sold for £2,000 each. During this time, some less professional continental kennels seized an opportunity to get rid of less good stock.

Dogs are also purposefully cross-bred to increase fierceness and aggression. STBs may be cross-bred with American pitbull terriers that weigh up to 120lbs. Such hybridisation effectively creates a new generation of dangerous dog.

'Some of the sort of breeds of Staffs that are coming out now are truly frightening.' (Jan Eachus, Group Chief Inspector, RSPCA)[4]

In these cases, the canine attributes of strength or aggression are purposefully enhanced by the owner to increase the dog's market value. Dogs may be created or 'tailor-made' to be aggressive and are particularly sought after as fighting dogs. These may be particularly sought after by those seeking a fighting dog. To meet the required level of aggression, dogs may be sourced from outside the UK:

'A lot of the pitbull bloodlines are coming over from Ireland. Even the sperm is imported to bypass the searches.' (Police officer, West Midlands)

Dog fighting

Dogs are also bred specifically for dog fighting and such dogs will be required to demonstrate high levels of aggression and 'gameness'. Dog fighting is addressed in more detail in Chapter Six.

Criminal activity

Another key aspect of entrepreneurial motivation is the use of dogs in criminal activity, for example, as protection during illegal business transactions or as 'security' during on-street drug dealing. Dogs are used as a 'heavy' while the owners collect debts from gambling, drug deals, loan-sharking or protection money. Here the reputational value of the status dog suggests a 'credible threat of violence' (Daly and Wilson, 1988), a form of commercial branding and a kite-mark guarantee of violence to come. In street drug deals, the dog creates a palpable sense of menace that recalibrates the odds of engagement and its presence acts as a gesture as well as silently articulating intent.

If contemporary professional criminals are 'adaptive entrepreneurs' (Hobbs, 1995), using a dog as a weapon is a further adaptation (see Chapter Six). In the illegal drugs economy of gang culture, 'violence can be used as an "instrument of commercial control"' and also as 'a way of generating cultural authority' (Hobbs, 1994: 120). The reputational branding of bull breeds generates cultural authority and provides any necessary violence. In this regard, the dog performs a key utilitarian function. Pitbulls in particular are now frequently used by gangs to protect hydroponic cultivation of cannabis in garages, lock-ups, warehouses and even domestic homes. Dogs can be left for long periods to roam free within the premises as a deterrent.

In addition to the groups described above, Traveller communities are also often associated with dogs, dog breeding and dog fighting. In the Traveller community, dogs are multiutilitarian, as this interviewee confirms:

> 'Pitbulls are big in the Travellers' community. It's fighting, and to make money, you've always got to make money. But it's tradition, you've got to have a dog, to protect you or the pitch. But a pit will bring in the money, travellers also breed 'em.' (Professional dog fighter)

They are also used for different entrepreneurial purposes:

> 'In the Traveller community you get a good dog, you always want to have a pitbull. However you may have someone who is doing a bit of poaching, then you'd breed it with a whippet or a ridgeback or wolfhound to get big legs. Them dogs are up for it. You get two of them and a van and you are up for making money – hunting, breeding, fighting, poaching. You can make money.' (Professional UK dog fighter)

As shown in Table 4.2, the functions of the status dog include bouncer, minder, bodyguard, security guard, guarantor, commercial asset, visual branding or marketable breeding stock.

The entrepreneurial activities associated with professional dog fighting and the use of dogs in criminal activity are covered in more detail in Chapter Six.

Protection

The second motivation identified in the typology for owning a dog is protection – either domestic or personal. Owners using dogs for domestic protection will advertise the dog's presence on door stickers and garden gates. Such notices, usually accompanied with warnings, display images of the dogs as aggressive and snarling. These images build on the reputational characteristics of the breeds. Owners in this category purchase a status dog largely out of fear, as a reactionary response to perceived or real local threats. Victims believe they will reduce the likelihood of repeat victimisation by purchasing a guard dog. Unlike a building alarm, the dog is essentially 'portable'. The reputation of the status dog as aggressive and fierce becomes a key attribute.

The motivational impetus here is fear of being attacked or burgled. In deprived neighbourhoods, there is a higher likelihood of being victimised (Hope, 2001) and such fears may be well founded. For some, acquiring a status dog is an empowering process of regaining control following victimisation.

The potential for a status dog to generate fear becomes a potent quality in its purchase or selection. Alsatians have long been used for security or increasing the security of a target so as to reduce the likelihood of victimsation, but the status dog represents something additional – a visual representation to potential offenders that this victim has taken control and will not allow further victimisation. Thus the dog becomes a visual signifier of control. The dog also offers the potential for pre-emptive attack, making owners more confident. As they require much training, exercise, nourishment, attention and financial upkeep, they may be subject to neglect or abandonment.

An unforeseen consequence of acquiring a dog for protection may be that it encourages others to do the same, in a faddish display of target hardening – 'I need one of those' – while yet others seek to 'upgrade' their current dog to something with more 'bite power'.

While owners in this category often provide good canine care, they may fail to understand the financial and physical commitments required for responsible dog ownership. This may lead them to acquire a status dog on the spur of the moment, a decision later reversed or regretted. This interviewee was familiar with dogs that had been abandoned in these circumstances:

> 'A woman single parent may have had a labrador before – so now she's going for a something different. The dog will be walked and cared for, etc. However, it can lead to neglect because of financial implications. Birmingham Dogs Home will be full of those dogs. I recognise this grouping definitely.' (Police officer, West Midlands)

It is also a common narrative for dogs ostensibly acquired for protection to be used as a means of improving the owner's reputational status. In this sense, it could be argued that the dog prevents the owner's low reputational status from falling any further. The dog in effect acts as guarantor, offering protection and security as a 'minder':

'I got him for protection for me. I live on a tough estate and a lot of boys wanna fight with you.' (Boy, aged 17)

'You see, she's my insurance policy, know what I mean?' (Boy, aged 17)

The functional qualities of the dog in this category are different again: it is both pet and guardian, and may also be trained to attack. It counters fear of victimisation by generating instinctual fear of violence and gives the owner confidence.

Fashion

The next typology is that of fashion. Owners in this category are likely to view themselves as willing and able to 'play outside the rules'. Three types of individuals are identified in this category: high-fashion owners, anti-fashion owners and fashion followers.

High-fashion individuals seek rare, high-value, unique or exotic pets rather than traditional domestic pets. Such animals may be used as talking points or to make a statement about the owner's character. The owners are often trendsetters and early adopters and may only collect rare breeds and breeding pairs. They may obtain their animals through elaborate means, and may typically take advantage of questionable circumstances surrounding the introduction of unusual breeds, such as occurred with the dogue de Bordeaux mentioned earlier.

Anti-fashion individuals may be viewed as belonging to the 'fuck you' society. They may be loners in urban, suburban or rural settings or belong to 'individualistic groupings' with counter-culture aspirations, for example, motorbike gangs, survivalists or fascist affiliates. While motorbiking was the epitomy of counter-culture in the 1950s, ownership of status dogs may be viewed in the same way today.

Others see a disparity between the desires of young working-class men and what is ultimately available to them, which may lead to 'intense status frustration' and encourage them to explore 'non-conformist alternatives' (Merton, 1938; Cohen, 1955; Cloward and Ohlin, 1960). In this scenario, the status dog, already a ubiquitous commodity, becomes a signifier of the non-conformist lifestyle. These owners can have a sense of living outside the rules. Dogs may create a sense of danger and rule breaking. Dogs are selected or purchased for what they represent – aggressiveness, strength, fighting ability, uniqueness, ugliness and so on. To these owners, the dogs may represent a reaction to losing power – either to commercialism or to homogeneity.

Fashion followers are those who latch on to the latest trend and aim to have a status dog as a talking point among friends. They are influenced by peer-group conversations, popular culture including music, video games and symbols that are 'trending'. Others may acquire dogs because 'everyone has one' or 'they are easily available'. These owners may also use their dogs for domestic protection, and are often responsive to educational input regarding responsible dog ownership.

Fashion followers acquire dogs for their entertainment value, equating them with other commercial commodities desired by impressionable young people. Status dogs retain the elusive commodity of 'cool' for many young people in urban street culture. Owning something with the 'cool' factor will raise a young person's status only for a limited period of time, so the dog may be used for other functions that transcend the temporal nature of 'cool'. Those chasing 'cool' must acquire the latest item, be it a pair of trainers or a video game. This can become an imperative for some young people, as 'street culture' places huge importance on 'fetishised consumption of personal, nonessential, status-enhancing items' that 'knight them members of a mythic street aristocracy' (Jacobs and Wright, 1999: 56). For these owners, status dogs are 'bling with bite'. Ultimately, the trend or fashion will move on, at which time dogs may be traded up, abandoned or neglected because they are no longer 'cool'.

Associated with 'entertainment' is the need for young people to engage in thrill seeking. Owning a status dog allows the young person to 'get a rush', with the dog used as the basis for a set of 'thrills' viewed by many as 'antisocial'. Katz (1988) says criminal activity can be motivated by such thrills (vandalism), whereby young people seek to transform their emotional state. Crime therefore becomes 'an act of transgression' with a 'transcendent quality'. This may be a motivational impetus for some young people, for example where dogs are used to 'square off' or hold an 'impromptu' dog fight.

Presdee (2000: 9) supports Katz's theory, suggesting that young people can find crime to be 'seductive, stimulating and exciting. Committing crime helps people transcend the 'banality of everyday life.' Owning a status dog may allow a young person to change how they feel about themselves, using the dog to inject excitement and supply an adrenaline rush in much the same way as joyriding or car theft. Such thrills are often fashion-led, however, and fade before long. Again, dogs acquired for these purposes may then be abandoned or neglected.

The reputational functions of the dogs in this category become their unique qualities, appealing to followers of both fashion (embracing contemporary culture) and anti-fashion (embracing counter-culture).

Here ownership often says more about what you are not than what you are.

Image and identity

As shown in Table 4.1, the motivational category that applied to most respondents in the survey was image and identity. This category belies a complex web of different motivations relating to issues of masculinity: the structural and gender roles of young men; a struggle to construct a self-image; what it is to be male and 'macho'; building a reputational identity among one's peer group; building respect that is recognised and valid; and ultimately gaining reputational advantage and status. Reputational advantage can be constructed using status dogs to generate respect, enhance physicality and exert control over public space.

Masculinity and self-image

Issues of masculinity and self-image are central to the issue of status dogs. For many working-class men, masculine self-image is defined by work. Work, particularly labouring, was masculinity affirming and image enhancing. Work was assumed by many to be 'a major basis of identity, and of what it means to be a man' (Morgan, 1992: 76). Sociologists documenting the decline of the traditional employment and skilled trades for working class men argue that such structural movements are paralleled by a crisis in their self-image (Winlow, 2001).

For working-class men experiencing long-term unemployment and limited future prospects, the traditional life trajectory is not only difficult to attain but 'will be unrecognisable' (Morgan, 1992). In deprived neighbourhoods, this new urban environment can be witnessed in shifts in cultural and traditional gender roles, for example, women are now often the breadwinners in many working-class households. This has provoked a crisis for male identity, resulting in a 'defensive insecurity amongst men' (Tolson, 1977). To counterbalance this, men may seek violent or illegal activities, such as dog fighting, that re-establish their male identity.

Marginalised young men are 'typically denied masculine status in education and employment' (Messerschmidt, 1993: 111). This in turn creates a backdrop for a more enhanced and often public display of masculine aggression, through gangs, for example. This identity crisis over masculinity leads some lower class men to 'redefine their masculinity as they go' (Winlow, 2001: 98), seeking out new ways of defining themselves as men. However, as familiar local working-class traditions are increasingly eroded, new global influences, such as hip hop and 'gangsta culture' are identified, and then adopted, as suitable, widely understood replacements.

Masculinity becomes a behavioural response that is highly situational, that is, men undertake certain activities or practices, such as crime, to demonstrate that they are 'manly'. These practices vary widely and are essentially employed or 'done' by men and 'done' differently depending on the social circumstances at the time (Messerschmidt, 1993).

In addition to this is the phenomenon of 'hegemonic' or leadership masculinity, often gained through family relationships, church-related activities or employment (Connell, 1987, 1990). This all-encompassing form of masculine dominance is so universally embraced it results in very clear male power relations and hierarchies, often built into the social fabric of society through a dominance of women. This masculine superiority generates widespread cultural authority, enabling men to adopt controlling and oppressive behaviours in their dealings with women and authority. These men are often highly competitive and individualistic, aggressive and violent.

Within this context, status dogs become a powerful facilitator for men 'doing' masculinity. They also become totemic and symbolic of the masculinity ideal being sought – an alpha-male image.

> 'It's about trying to be seen by people when you are walking down the road with a pitbull. It makes you look harder.'
> (Professional dog-fighter)

Status dogs provide opportunities to stand above the crowd, to gain recognition, to be photographed and talked about. They confer superior status on the owner, providing a reward for masculinity, thus solving any gender problem of accountability (Messerschmidt, 1993). They provide advantage in the fight for reputational supremacy against other marginalised street groups. In a competitive arena, a status dog provides a new reputational baseline and raises the benchmark in proving oneself a man among men. Status dogs become a way of expressing 'hegemonic masculinity' as much as dress, speech, physicality or offending history.

Violence and aggression are tools available to young men for them to display their masculinity. When the 'concentration of disadvantage' (Pitts, 2008) highlights their lack of status or success, they use the resources of violence, intimidation and aggression to both display and construct their masculine identity.

For some young men, bonding in gangs may reinforce this male identity. Often powerless both economically and racially, these young men adapt to their situation by competing for status with their closest rivals – those of the same gender, ethnicity and class (Messerschmidt, 1993: 116). The street then becomes the arena for this struggle for personal power, and the locale for 'constructing a viable masculinity' (Messerschmidt, 1993: 116). As paid employment is not a viable option for many, dominating a street or neighbourhood as a member of the 'street elite' is a viable option (Katz, 1988: 114-63).

To dominate a neighbourhood, physical presence is a key requisite. People must be able to identify, and if necessary avoid, the new cultural authority or at least be intimidated by its presence. Status dogs therefore become an important resource in maintaining personal, physical and reputational dominance of streets or neighbourhoods. This is achieved through establishing a reputational identity, building street capital and thus gaining respect.

Status, habitus and respect

According to Bourdieu's theory of practice (Bourdieu, 1991), the amount of power a person has within a neighbourhood or a social field depends on their place within the hierarchy of the field and the amount of capital they possess. For example, junior gang members are ranked low in gang hierarchies, have little money (economic capital), networked connections (social capital) or prestige, status and authority (symbolic capital).

To advance in any social field, one must accumulate different forms of capital; for example, investing in social networks brings improved connections or career prospects. The social fields of young people, or gangs, have complex social networks within which anyone seeking a higher status (distinction) must actively build and then maintain their reputation (Putnam, 2000: 136). Through reputation, people acquire kudos and respect, and thus elevate their status. A diminished reputation brings diminished status, lack of respect and possible victimisation. Thus it becomes an imperative for young people (whether gang-affiliated or not) to build their own reputations among their peer groups, to generate respect and then maintain it.

People employ different strategies to improve their reputation and status within a social field, for example, by being violent or daring. Which strategies are effective naturally differs across different social fields. In areas of multiple deprivation, high reputational value is allocated to those with reputations for criminal associations, for not 'grassing', for being violent or for fencing stolen goods (Winlow, 2001). A strategy of building a reputation by being violent is unlikely to succeed in the social field of a university. For working–class families in deprived neighbourhoods, practical knowledge of how to survive on 'the street' may be elevated above educational achievement (Bourdieu, 1986; Winlow, 2001). Indeed, the social norms of the social field determine what is suitable as a strategy; for example, the golden rule of not grassing or the ability to speak 'street talk' are both considered valuable forms of cultural capital in some social fields (Anderson, 1999).

While reputation and respect are important to us all, to some young people (especially those affiliated to gangs) they are of paramount importance. In their social fields, it can be difficult to build a reputation from scratch.

As young people decide how to build their reputations, they are guided not only by social norms, but also by what is socially learnt; Bourdieu terms this the habitus. The habitus is a way of describing the learned experiences of habit, history and tradition of someone's social conditions that over time become deeply internalised into mental and bodily dispositions (Swartz, 1997: 101). Habitus is the acquired physical and social characteristics of the human body. It relates to how we each take on attributes of walking, talking, moving and being within our social environments. Thus it is evident in how we present and exhibit ourselves, in eating, dressing, talking and thinking. Thus habitus acts as an 'internal blueprint' that guides people's actions. In addition, those sharing similar social conditions and opportunities in life will share the same habitus, giving them similar outlooks on life or limited aspirations for themselves or their children. The habitus is always evolving, allowing people to incorporate into their life's newly learned behaviours or habits as long as it fits with their overall blueprint or existing pattern of behaviour (Bourdieu, 1990). In deprived working-class neighbourhoods, young men gain respect by having a muscular physique, aggressive swagger or posture. Such bodily dispositions are an expression of the habitus. For young people, habitus can also be seen in ways of walking, and in street fashion and language, all of which demonstrate an understanding of the symbols, actions and ways of being that are most effective within their peer group or social field. In short, they will bring you respect among peers in your social field. Thus wearing the 'right' trainers, talking in the 'right' way or having the 'right' dog earns you status as one interviewee observed:

> 'Them boys in tower blocks who chain roll dogs, it's a reputation thing and protection thing, you can't do nuffink to me, 'cos I got a big dog. The main reason to have a pitbull is to make money from it. The boys in tower blocks are not

making money, it's just for reputation and status really. To make sure no-one goes near 'em. But the dogs often end up starving or abandoned.' (Professional UK dog fighter)

In addition, in the social field of young people, especially gang-affiliated young people, there is an imperative to build 'street capital'. I use this term to signify an aggregate of cultural capital (street knowledge and skills), habitus, local history, family connections, social capital, symbolic capital and reputation (Harding, 2012). For those 'on the street', in gangs or on their periphery, and for increasing numbers of young people, street capital is the premium capital. Each individual has their own stock of street capital and one's accumulated street capital counts towards one's overall status in street life.

Street capital is enhanced by committing acts of violence, knowing the right gangsters, having done time in prison, having connections, never 'grassing' or snitching, always having quality drugs, never welching on a debt or agreement, backing up your mates, being 'up for it' and getting involved, and being aggressive and afraid of no-one. Having an aggressive dog further enhances this status, providing additional street capital and multiple opportunities for engaging with peers in numerous potential scenarios, such as committing acts of violence. Each event brings bragging rights for the participant and places the individual at the centre of future discussions, all of which boost and elevate status among peers. The closer a pitbull is brought into the peer group or gang, allowing members to develop a bond or to interact with it, the closer and more revered the dog will become, and by association its owner will be held in higher regard.

Violence

The scarce resources available in deprived communities are the subject of social competition and for many working-class males, this becomes a matter not only of defining their masculinity, but also of survival. Young men with limited life prospects have 'good reason to escalate their tactics of social competition and become violent' (Daly and Wilson, 1988: 287). Fragile masculinities, social competition and status advancement converge neatly in concepts of honour, violence and respect. In the street world, violence or the threat of violence is omnipresent – it is something to be faced down and addressed or employed.

In street situations where young men are hyper-vigilant regarding their status and male identity, all interactions are quickly assessed as potential confrontations, for example, overstaring may attract a threat of retaliation. In such scenarios, the odds of success are calibrated quickly. Other young males, potential adversaries or compatriots are 'silently ranked as to potential threat or propensity for violence/success through violence', Winlow (2001: 44) refers to this as 'a subliminal hierarchy'. For working-class men in such neighbourhoods, social competition is essentially internal competition, among and between themselves. Violence becomes a highly prized commodity and a quick route to advancement. Status dogs are thus accessorised to enhance this commodity and recalibrate the odds of success.

Violence, reputation and honour have strong cultural importance among active criminals and perceptions of honour are often greatest among those who view themselves from an external perspective (Bourdieu, 1979: 115). Status dogs provide this reputation through a widely recognised pedigree of violence. Owning a status dog thus provides this reputation by association. Being in control of a status dog indicates that you are in control of unleashing potential violence. This unspoken contract is understood by all concerned.

Respect

An individual's level of street capital is measured by the amount of 'respect' they generate (Harding, 2012). In the overarching context of heterosexuality and masculinity, the issue of maintaining respect 'on the streets' is thus uniquely important (Matza and Sykes, 1961; Anderson 1999; Messerschmidt, 2000). Failure to acknowledge this is considered to be disrespectful. In considering respect on the streets, a wider social context has to be taken into account. As Daly and Wilson (1988: 128) note:

> A seemingly minor affront is not merely a stimulus to action, isolated in time and space. It must be understood within a larger social context of reputation, face, relative social status and enduring relationships.

On the street, a status dog can be used to maintain an element of control over any potential disrespect, thus reducing the need for casual violence to 'save face'. Investment in a status dog is an investment of social capital that pays community dividends.

A rival may show disrepect merely by 'cussing' or 'dissing', and such challenges to 'status', 'reputation' and 'manhood' (Sanders, 2005: 123) must be addressed quickly. One response is to fight, which enables young people to exhibit masculine qualities, such as 'bravado, hardness and physical courage'. Such attributes may also be projected on to status dogs. Thus dogs may be used to resolve disputes over respect as a form of 'street jousting' by proxy. Dogs are squared up and let loose on each other even though they may be dramatically mismatched.

Anderson (1999) suggests that fighting may be a 'campaign for respect'. Illegal dog fighting or 'street jousting' may then be viewed in much the same way. In disorganised neighbourhoods and in street culture where violence is normalised, urban dog fighting can be viewed as an extenuation of this culture. Matza and Sykes (1961), Anderson (1999) and Messerschmidt (2000) all found violence to be acceptable under certain circumstances. A similar rationale is employed by owners of status dogs and those who participate in illegal dog fighting.

In a neighbourhood or culture where body language can be readily imbued with meaning, interpreted or misinterpreted or thought to convey respect or disrespect (Winlow, 2001), the body language of owning/holding a status dog can be unequivocal. It demands respect. It also suggests a willingness for a fight – not flight. It hints at an ability to react quickly and not be taken for granted. These social attributes are well recognised and acknowledged by working-class adults and young people. Under such circumstances, owning an aggressive status dog or involving the dog in illegal dog fighting can be both rationalised and normalised.

Body image and physicality

Traditional working-class neighbourhoods have long been characterised or even defined by masculine violence. Central to this is the gendered role of men, masculinity and physicality. Physicality is an easily controlled and modified variable. In working-class neighbourhoods, a strict 'gender regime' operates where a man is ready, willing and able to fight (Connell, 1995). Physicality is a valued attribute for many working-class men, easily achievable through hard manual labour. This ability and readiness to fight can easily be visually communicated via pumped up musculature or an accentuated physique. Having muscles is 'manhood-generating and manhood affirming' for these young men (Wacquant, 1998).

As well as increasing masculine identity, an enhanced physicality is a form of personal advertising, a type of PR for attracting sexual partners. Where male identity is undermined by unemployment, or where male power is diluted by an inability to provide for families or to demonstrate outward signs of success, some men turn to physical body enhancement to build muscles and 'crude bodily capital' (Wacquant, 1998).

The status dog becomes an embodiment of this enhanced physicality. The dog projects and secures a masculine image of 'a virile individual' while repairing a damaged identity. Owning or breeding status dogs amplifies this further by implication – your alpha-male status allows you to control a breed of animal reputed for its violence, virility and strength. By demonstrating that you can control this beast, this in turn offers vicarious or implied virility, violence and strength. This is further amplified if the dog is designated by law as dangerous or illegal. For some owners, tough training regimes or even steroids will enhance the physicality of the dog and ensure a visibly accentuated physique – an alpha dog. This further enhances the owner's 'cool pose' (Majors and Billson, 1992).

Spatial control and territory

Young men also use status dogs to exert control over their personal space, public space and gang 'territory'. Controlling and expanding personal space, often through violence, allows young men to 'save face' and achieve a slight advancement in status (Goffman, 1967, 1971). Status dogs assist in the definition and maintenance of personal body space. Those entering uninvited into this personal body or cultural space may find themselves 'bounced' out of it. Status dogs are sometimes referred to as 'four-legged bouncers'.

In his book *Badfellas* and his depiction of the male identity of bouncers, Winlow (2001) unintentionally draws on similarities between bouncing and status dogs. He says that bouncing 'allows for an elaborate display of the masculine self … and the potentially beguiling prospect of subtle status advancement as your peers recognize the violent potential that is encapsulated within the individual' (2001: 162). Substituting 'dog' for 'individual' indicates the similar potential for the status dog. Winlow acknowledges the 'sign value' of body language used by bouncers to control space and how their facial expressions and demeanour signify danger. Trained status dogs may provide a similar sign value.

One aspect of spatial control of environments is the use of status dogs to control public open space. This is addressed in more detail in Chapter Seven. Gang 'territory' provides a further locale for spatial control using status dogs. Dogs are used in the context of territorial violence as defenders or attackers, for protecting or controlling areas and for incursions into rival territory. Status dogs become active players by providing the teeth for the new 'cultural authority' (Hobbs, 1995) of the neighbourhood gang.

Urban street gangs

Notwithstanding these points, in the social field of the urban street gang, arrangements for building street capital, status and reputation are even more complex, urgent and extreme. Status dogs enhance street capital by establishing and building reputation, but they also permit owners to engage in gambling and other transgressive activities, and they permit members to demonstrate an understanding and commitment to 'the game' (gang culture and life). The physical and behavioural characteristics of the pitbull and some other bull breeds meet specific requirements of gang life and its violent world – primarily toughness, aggression, tenacity alongside concepts of being hard, potentially lethal and having no master. Dogs thus have multiple uses and functionality – protection, projection of authority, menace, ability to intimidate, and potential to make money and generate group social activity.

Furthermore, dogs provide implicit meanings or associations by conveying concepts of animalism, loyalty, alpha–male superiority, unpredictability, determination, illegality, being unleashed, sexual prowess and aggression – all attributes that are appealing and enduring in gang mythology. Such associations are coveted, desired or acted out. Dogs are often elevated within gang hierarchies and referred to as full members through the sobriquet 'family' or 'blood'. Their loyalty to their owners, and to the gang, is rewarded through their adornment with diamond-studded collars secured by improbably thick chains.

Stigmatised dogs, such as American pitbulls, also fit with stigmatised communities and subcultures. They perhaps offer a symbolic reflection or an image of themselves – an avatar. From this perspective, they can be viewed as a visual expression of 'otherness', social exclusion and machismo.

In gang life, dogs also offer owners the rarefied commodity of loyalty and trust. Maher and Pierpoint (2011) also acknowledge that gang members will protect the dog and that the owners gain the trust and loyalty of the other gang members. Gang members may also provide young dogs to young potential recruits to instigate gang affiliation and build loyalty or an expectant future reciprocal favour. It may also be a way of simple indoctrination into the 'sport' of dog fighting.

In summary, status dogs are used by gangs for:

- entrepreneurial motivations – dog-fighting;
- entrepreneurial – protecting drug-dealing and drug-cultivation businesses;
- image and identity, leading to intimidation.

All of these scenarios include the possibility of training the dog to attack other humans, a subject that is considered more fully in the next section, along with gangs as a locus for dog fighting in the US and UK.

Gangs and dogs in the US

As in the UK, until recently most US research into status dogs has been approached from the angle of animal welfare. Evidence linking US gangs, bull breeds, fighting and criminal activity is only now emerging, having been hampered by inconsistent reporting of 'gang-related' offences by different agencies and by considerable variations in procedures from state to state. Similar methodological challenges are faced by those tracking animal cruelty and dog fighting. Despite this, American law enforcement agents now recognise that animal fighting is closely associated with the activity of gangs (Randour and Hardiman, 2007).

It could be argued that traditional (professional) circuit dog fighting fits with theories of delinquent subcultures (Cohen, 1955; Cloward and Ohlin, 1960; Spergel, 1964). However, Solomon (2008) argues that urban street dog fighting occurring in gangland is different. He notes that 'dogmen' (professional dog fighters) almost always share a similar habitus and similar behaviour patterns: 'Dogmen are deliberate and unmistakeable in their habitus. Dogmen have a presence, especially around dogs, that commands respect if not outright fear' (Solomon, 2008: 76). Demanding loyalty and conviction to the 'sport' through the acceptance of the hierarchies of knowledge and status which sustain it. This powerful social field provides opportunities for distinction while the habitus locks people into this form of deviance. In dog-fighting communities ('clusters'), apprentice dogmen ('prospects') will copy and mimic elder dogmen to be accepted and to learn the game. This aspect has clear similarities with the social field of the urban street gang where 'youngers' learn from 'olders' and 'elders' and require their trust and approval in order to advance (Harding, 2012). For a more detailed examination of why people fight dogs, see Chapter Six.

The Chicago Police Department (CPD) now reports direct connections between dog fighting, gang violence, narcotics and weapons. In a review of offender arrests from July 2001-04, the CPD Animal Crimes Unit notes that:

> When compared to offenders arrested for non animal related offences, persons acting violently toward animals are much more likely to carry/use guns in the commission of other crimes, and are involved in the illegal narcotics trade. Further, a strikingly large percentage is members of criminal street gangs. (Degenhardt, 2005: 1)

The CPD analysed the arrest profile data for those charged with crimes against animals from July 2001 to July 2004. The findings revealed that 86% of animal offenders had already experienced multiple arrests (70% had previous arrests for felonies and 70% had previous arrests for drugs). In addition, approximately two thirds had previous arrests for domestic violence or assault. Over half of those profiled were gang-affiliated (Randour and Hardiman, 2007).

Within violent gangs, failing to fight your dogs when challenged can be dangerous and even fatal. In 2006, 26-year-old Julius Birdine in Englewood, Chicago was challenged to fight his pitbulls. He was shot dead when he refused.[5]

In the US, dog fighting is high-profit big business, with large money pots gambled at each match. As John Goodwin, Deputy Manager of Animal Fighting Issues for the Humane Soceity of the United States (HSUS), says:

> 'Dog-fighting doesn't take place in a vacuum. When you have violent people betting large sums of money then you will have problems. Dog-fighting is heavily linked to gambling, drugs, prostitution, gangs and guns.'

A similar observation was made by Cmdr Gerard Simon of the Organsied Crime and Gangs Division in Detroit, commenting on a six-month investigation that resulted in a major dog-fighting raid in Detroit in 2003:'Drugs, gangs, dope, dogs ... they all go together' (cited in Gibson, 2005:18).

Many gangs engage in dog fighting as a way of raising revenue. Some matches can raise more cash than an average armed robbery. With thousands of dollars staked on one dog fight, guns are used to provide personal protection. Large winnings invariably attract the attention

---

of gangs leading to violent robberies. In 2006, one dog fighter and regular gambler, Thomas Wegner, won $100,000 at a dog fight near Texas. He was later tracked down and murdered in front of his family.[6] Investigators arriving at the scene found that $500,000 in winnings had been taken by the assailants, but the assailants had ignored Wegner's 285 pitbulls valued at over $1 million dollars (Ortiz, 2010: 58).

HSUS estimates that the 40,000 US citizens involved in organised dog fights use approximately 250,000 dogs each year and report that pitbulls are now so prolific in the US that over a million are euthanised each year.[7] In addition, there may be a further 100,000 people or dogs involved in street fights. The prevalence of dog fighting in the US causes considerable problems for the authorities. The Pennsylvania Society for the prevention of Cruelty to Animals recorded 1,177 incidents of dog fighting in 2010 in Philadelphia alone.[8]

In research for the Animal Legal and Historical Center (ALHC) at the Michigan State University College of Law, author Hanna Gibson comments that:

> Within the gang community, fighting dogs compete with firearms as the weapon of choice; indeed their versatile utility arguably surpasses that of a loaded firearm in the criminal underworld. To the gang members, the dogs are an extension of each member's status; the fights are championship matches that aggrandize the gang leaders' supremacy and intimidate younger members. It is extremely easy for urban criminals to acquire fighting dogs. (Gibson, 2005: 4-7)

The ALHC reports that until recently few law enforcement or government agencies understood the 'scope or gravity of dog fighting' (Gibson, 2005: 4-7) or the volume of criminal activity it attracted. The ALHC has developed a criminal profile database of the typical urban dog fighter[9] illustrating an overwhelming correlation between dog fighting and criminality. This is now used to prod authorities into more focused action. Now police raids on dog fights result in mass arrests for multiple offences, including the relatively easy apprehension of individuals described as serious hardened criminals. In just eight raids on dog fights in 2004, a total of 165 arrests were made, 372 dogs seized, 20 vehicles impounded, 30 guns and explosives seized, over $300,000 in cash confiscated and several kilos of drugs seized, including, marijuana, cocaine and PCP (phencyclidine or Angel Dust).[10]

Following this work, the Los Angeles Police Department established an innovative new programme to address urban gangs and dog fighting. Entitled Regional Animal-fighting Investigations Division (RAID), the programme was supervised by Chief Bill Bratton and city attorney Rocky Delgadillo. Initiated in 2004-05, it aimed to intervene in gang activity by:

- raiding dog fights to identify, track and apprehend gang members;
- using gang injunctions;
- creating a database of dog fighters;
- tracking and responding to dog-fighting complaints;
- using research to formally establish correlation between dog fighting and criminal activity;
- using high-visibility policing in dog-fighting areas;
- training detectives to deal with dog fighting; and
- making forceful prosecutions.

The HSUS and other criminal justice agencies such as the City Attorney's Office in Los Angeles have initiatives to target gang members who use aggressive dogs to intimidate and harass people (see Chapter Six).

Gangs and dogs in the UK

Evidencing the link between aggressive dogs and gangs in the UK presupposes that gangs exist in the UK and have the same type of relationship with dogs as that outlined in the previous section. Since the millennium, the UK has witnessed the emergence of the violent urban street gang (Palmer and Pitts, 2006; Toy, 2008; Pitts, 2010) in deprived communities from whom executive authorities have largely disengaged (Hagedorn, 2008; Pitts, 2010). These gangs are increasingly involved in drugs and violence (Bullock and Tilley, 2002). Despite such evidence, some UK academics claim the terminology of 'gang' is misattributed and that 'control agents' have a vested interest in 'talking up' the 'gang myth' (Hallsworth and Young, 2008, 2010). There is further debate as to the level of organisation within the UK, with some arguing that gangs are well organised (Harding, 2012) and others arguing that they are less so (Aldridge and Medina, 2007).

The UK street gang is evolving and increasingly embedded in areas of multiple deprivation (Pitts, 2010; Harding, 2012). It is also different from popular conceptions of US gangs as portrayed in popular culture, being home-grown, smaller and more compact. While UK street gangs are violent, violence is mostly contained within the social field of the gang.

Given that the UK has its own emergent and evolving gang problem in deprived neighbourhoods, the question is, to what extent are similar problems regarding dogs situated within the UK gang context? The answer is that these issues are also emergent, again not necessarily imported from the US, but home-grown. The status dog provides the same utility and function for working-class young men in the UK as it does in the barrios of Los Angeles or the public housing projects of Chicago, or for that matter the favelas of Rio. The pitbull is now part of the habitus of these deprived communities, where young men actively seek to acquire street capital through building reputation and status. A large aggressive dog, a bull breed, will provide this opportunity and multiple functionality in London just as it does in Cuba, Philadelphia or Cape Town. This is further confirmed by its cultural emergence in the world of hip hop.

As in the US, UK gang research, sociology and criminology have largely overlooked the links between gangs and dogs (Harding, 2010) and the evidence is only now beginning to emerge (Maher and Pierpoint, 2011; Harding, 2012).

Table 5.2 illustrates the links between gang and status dogs in the London Borough of Lambeth (see Chapter Five). Interviews with police, practitioners and animal welfare agencies confirm this relationship as the words of this interviewee reveal. For example, in an interview for the current research with Bill Morris of Liverpool Citysafe, it was believed that the issue of aggressive dogs it is an issue for the city and for gangs:

> 'One of the guys involved in the murder of Rhys Jones was in a local gang. We ASBO'd him and one of the conditions was that he was not allowed to control/own/have a dog.'[11]

Further evidence is provided in the next section, which considers how gangs use status dogs.

In the UK, the relationship between gangs and dogs is presently dependent on individuals within the gangs. This relationship is situationally determined and based on the utility provided by the dog and that required by the owner, for example, gambling, conveying status or providing protection during a drugs deal. Not all those in a gang will have a status dog or be involved with them, but they will accept dogs as part of the gang habitus. The visibility of such dogs is normalised on social housing estates and within the gang. Similarly, not all gang members are involved in dog fighting, but again its existence as a valid activity is fully accepted. Of course it should be acknowledged that gang involvement does not include all young people. Similarly, aggressive dogs and bull breeds may be owned by those who do not affiliate to gangs. For those who do affiliate to gangs, the close and normalised relationships between gang members and dogs permit differentiation of roles for the dogs: protection, drug dealing, gambling, fighting, breeding, training. Some members will gain further status and kudos by specialising in one of these aspects:

> 'You do get some real gangsters though who know all about dog[s], how to train pits and make 'em hard – to fight. You don't fuck around with 'em, mate. They've got these two dogs and they'd kill you, these dogs.' (Professional UK dog fighter)

Dogs may be owned by individual gang members or by the whole gang, having been jointly acquired (as payment of a bet, for example) or purchased jointly. Gang members may agree to house other members' dogs for convenience, for example, if younger members experience difficulty keeping the dog at their parent's home (Maher and Pierpoint, 2011). Research for this study found similar results, for example, Asian youths in Tower Hamlets, east London, commonly moved individual dogs around their group, with the dog staying a few days with each gang member. This has a negative effect on the socialisation of the dog, as it experiences multiple social environments, different styles of feeding, training, diet, etc. It is a commonly held belief among gang members that joint ownership makes the dog more difficult to trace, but moving the dog around means that it will suffer a lack consistency in environment, feeding and training, which in turn will have a negative effect on its socialisation. Another common problem with joint ownership is that interest in the dog eventually wanes and a single member is left with the responsibility.

Using dogs as weapons[12]

In addition to being used to convey status, aggressive dogs may be used as a weapon by owners to intimidate or purposefully attack other humans. This is what is meant by the term 'assault dog' or 'weapon dog'. Some sociologists contest this view, notably Hallsworth and Duffy (2010), who seek a 'less sensational interpretation', arguing that 'to date there is no evidence to substantiate claims that dogs are being bred to be aggressive to humans or that gang members in fact desire such animals' (pp 16-17). Invoking moral panic theory, they note that 'without in-depth rigorous research into the relationship between dogs and gangs, current anecdotal and subjective evidence can only be viewed as producing false-positive findings of a causal correlation between illegal breeds and gang ownership' (Hallsworth and Duffy (2010: 17). However, emerging US and UK academic research indicates that there is increasing evidence of the link between bull breeds, gangs and criminality.

Professor Frank Ascione, a respected academic on the links between animal abuse and violence, notes that:

> Animals are abused if they become instruments of aggression. Training dogs to engage in dog-fights or using a dog to purposely attack another person essentially converts an animal into a weapon. The animal becomes an extension of the antisocial behaviour of its owner. (Ascione, 2005: 55)

Attacks where dogs are used as weapons and where the dog acts on instruction or orders of the owners include:

- proactive attacks, for example, for revenge, (planned or spontaneous), to demonstrate superiority and status or to provide benefit or advantage;
- reactive attacks, in defence of the owner;
- sentinel attacks, where a dog is used to guard illegal activity (as opposed to guarding legitimate business or property).

Attacks where dogs are not used as weapons include:

- unprompted attacks, where the dog is not used as weapon but is trained to be aggressive and reacts to signs of aggression because it is pre-programmed to get involved;
- animal attacks, which may be reactive or accidental.

Accidental dog attacks on humans and other animals are considered in Chapter Seven.

If an owner deliberately sets a dog on someone, the owner can be arrested for assault and the dog seized for evidence as the weapon. Alternatively, if deliberate intent is unclear or there is no evidence of intent, the police may use section 3 ('Dog dangerously out of control') of the DDA 1991.

In the UK, practitioners and agencies claim that young people are switching to dogs as weapons because of a police crackdown on knives and guns and because possession of a dog is less likely to result in prosecution. Some reports claim that gang-affiliated young people 'are arming themselves with dogs' (Briggs, 2009).[13] Solomon reports a similar situation in the US (Solomon, 2008: 23).

In 2008, the Metropolitan Police Service (MPS) launched Operation Blunt 2, to tackle the problem of young people carrying knives in London. The operation has been extensive,[14] with over 18,000 arrests made and half a million stop-and-searches undertaken. Indeed, many of the police and professionals interviewed for this study believed that young people were using dogs as weapons because of Operation Blunt 2:

> 'Operation Blunt [2] and knife arches have reduced knives
> so dogs are now used as potential weapons.' (Police officer,
> Greenwich)

Although there was no evidence to support this claim, Operation Blunt 2 was acknowledged by many of the young people interviewed through referring to it mainly in the context of stop-and-search activity.

The choice of weapon – gun, knife or dog – usually depends on the situation at the time; how the individual wants to be perceived; his ease and familiarity with the potential weapon; and what image he wants to display to others.

In addition to the murder of Seyi Ogunyemi, described in the Introduction, there have been other incidents in London and beyond where dogs have been used as weapons of attack.

Before the Ogunyemi incident, where ABM gang members were the victims, the gang had itself used a pitbull in a planned attack at a school in Battersea, south London. On 24 April 2008 at 3.15 pm, as pupils exited Salesian College, approximately 10 gang members (aged 14 to 18) entered the playground with a pitbull looking for a member of a rival gang. As the dog was unleashed into the busy playground, the owner swung the dog's metal chain leash at youngsters. One 16-year-old youngster who intervened (Darcey Menezes) was then attacked by the gang and stabbed six times. The dog was put back on its chain and the gang fled. In November 2008, six gang members were sentenced at Inner London Crown Court. It could not be proven who carried out the stabbing and all the members received lesser convictions for violent disorder and provocation of violence.

In another incident in March 2007, Kodjo Yenga (aged 16) was approached by the MDP gang in Hammersmith, west London, while walking his dog with his girlfriend. The 10 MDP members tried to fight him and take his dog, then pursued him and set their dog on him. Kodjo was then stabbed to death. Two gang members were sentenced to life for murder; three others were convicted of manslaughter. One defendant, aged 13, was found to have used his dog to attack Kodjo. At the Old Bailey trial in 2008, Judge Christopher Moss QC acknowledged that the defendants were gang members, adding:

> 'I'm quite satisfied that you ... deliberately set loose your Staffordshire Bull Terrier dog with the intention that it would join in the attack'. The defendant had previous convictions for car theft, attempted robbery, and assault of a police officer. (Judge Christopher Moss QC, Old Bailey, 2008)[15]

These incidents show dogs being used purposefully to attack on command, or being purposefully unleashed in expectation of attack. Dogs may also be trained to attack on 'secret' command, where the command is 'hidden' within an otherwise ordinary sentence. This allows the assailant to later deny giving an explicit order to 'attack' or 'kill', and thereby claim the dog attacked under its own volition. In 2010, a police officer in Kennington, Lambeth was attacked and badly injured by a pitbull terrier (PBT) in such circumstances.

Proactive attacks

Proactive attacks where dogs are used as weapons take different forms, as the following examples show:

Dogs openly commanded to attack

- In September 2009 two police officers were attacked by PBT dogs in Wood Green, north London. Appearing in Wood Green Crown Court in April 2010, two men aged 19 and 20 admitted that they encouraged their PBT dogs to attack by saying, 'I'm going to get my dog to kill you'. PC Tiffin suffered severe injuries to his leg, chest and arms. Both defendants were banned from owning a dog for ten years and were jailed for five years. Both animals were destroyed. Judge Carr noted,

  > 'This is one of those cases receiving much attention at the moment where young men get large, powerful and aggressive dogs that make them feel bigger and more important than they actually are.'[16]

- In May 2008 two members of MDP gang, west London, were each sentenced to five years in prison at Isleworth Crown Court for using their SBT to attack a fellow gang member who wished to leave the gang and failed to repay a drug debt. The gang members stripped the victim naked and placed him in the lift car with the dog. The offenders were charged with GBH, conspiring to supply Class A drugs and being in charge of a dog that was out of control and causing injury.[17]
- A 41-year-old man and his family remonstrated with the owner of three unleashed pitbulls running wild in Northbrook Park, Lewisham on July 9th 2010. The owner then attacked the parents before setting his dogs on the father. The man required hospital treatment. No arrest was made.[18]
- In October 2010, a gang of four young people were denied entry to the lobby of a block of flats in Islington. On gaining entry they set two large Boxers on two students. The students escaped and were chased down again as one of the owners instructed the dogs to 'Get them'. Both students were injured, one seriously.[19]
- In January 2011 a 26-year-old man was jailed for three and half years at Liverpool Crown court for GBH, ABH and owning a dog dangerously out of control in a public place. The owner had unleashed his American pitbull on two men in a prolonged attack. The owner of the dog also attacked one of the men with the metal dog chain and stamped on his head. The 39-year-old victim died in hospital six days later.[20]

Some dogs are trained specially to avenge any attack made on the dog's owner, as one study participant described:

> 'I had one dog called Max – a real dog. I got him from a Jamaican Yardie gangster who was covered in scars. The dog was trained to go for guns. It was a lovely dog but the police put it down. It had won a lot of fights. When the bloke went to prison he gave it me. It was one year old. It was trained to go for anything you had in your hand, guns, knives. If you pointed anything, the dog would jump up and grab you by the hand and pull you down.' (Professional UK dog fighter)

Dog attack where owner failed to prevent attack

• In March 2010 during a fight between two men at a retail park in Aberdeen, one of the men allowed his dog, an SBT to attack the other for several minutes. The dog inflicted severe injury to a 19-year-old man. The dog stopped attacking immediately on command. The owner of the dog paid to have the dog destroyed shortly after the attack. The attacker was jailed for three years at Aberdeen Sherriff court in February 2011. Sherriff Buchanan said,

> 'this is an extremely disturbing case because what you effectively did was use your dog as a weapon. It was a very serious and savage attack ... it was clear that you had the power to call off this dog at any point and you did not do so.'[21]

According to one interviewee, similar attacks have occurred against police officers:

> 'One of our PCs got attacked while following up outstanding warrants. The owner had two pitbulls, but he had cut their vocal chords so they made no noise in the house and when they attacked. The police raid the house, the dogs panic and run out the back door to the PC waiting out the back. He doesn't hear them coming. He got attacked and armed cops had to come and shoot the dog. This was August 2010.' (Police officer, Greenwich)

• In Stretford in September 2008 a 21-year-old man was attacked by two thugs in an unprovoked attack. The pitbull-type dog with the two men then attacked the young man causing multiple injuries. The two teenage attackers then calmly walked off.[22]

Dog trained to attack on 'unknown' command

• In September 2010, PC Jim Russell and a colleague visited an address in Paddington, west London following reports of men fighting their dogs nearby. While at the address a 25-year-old male arrived with a pitbull. After several minutes the man was advised his dog was to be seized at which point he issued a secret command to the pitbull which attacked the police officer causing a deep bite to his arm, which required surgery. In March 2011 at the Old Bailey the 25-year-old man was sentenced to five and half years.[23]

It is thought to take considerable training to get a dog to attack on command, as one interviewee confirmed:

> 'It takes a lot of training to get a dog to go on somebody. You can use a couple of words to get the dog to react, or an unusual word. My mate uses an unusual word and the dog goes mad. To get the dog to do that you have to show the dog loyalty. But you can't have it mix with people. You lock it in the garden, through the winter in a kennel, don't let anyone see it or feed it or have any contact. Once you have done that for a year and half, the dog won't go near anyone else, but once you socialise it, it goes soft.' (Professional UK dog fighter)

- In May 2010 a 32-year-old Liverpool woman was handed a two year ASBO regarding her behaviour, including training her SBT cross to be used as a weapon and to attack anyone wearing fluorescent clothing, including the police.[24]

Dog attack to assist acquisitive crime

- In March 2011, a 25-year-old man in Tottenham Hale, north London was chased and attacked by two men. The men unleashed their PBT dog that then attacked the victim causing injuries. He dropped his mobile phone. According to Haringey Police, the men used a dog to inflict injuries to the victim in order to obtain a piece of property.[25]
- In November 2008, an 18-year-old man set his American pitbull dog on a 17-year-old student in south London during an attempt to rob him of his MP3 player. In June 2009 the attacked was ordered to pay compensation to the victim.

Some young people interviewed for this study thought it quite commonplace for dogs to be used for acquisitive crime:

> 'Boys also try to set the dog upon you, to rob you. It happened to me. I was coming home from Tesco and actually had just bought some fly-spray. It was three boys and a Staffie–pit cross. They said, "Have you got a pound for me?", I said, "No." They said, "Right, we'll set the dog

on you." So they did. I sprayed it in the face. They kept it on the chain and it jumped all over me. I was lucky I had the spray really.' (Professional UK dog fighter).

While not all of the above incidents occurred within the context of urban street gangs, it is clear that such incidents do occur. Despite this, Hallsworth (2011) has denounced the concept of 'weapon dogs', claiming that it is a term evoked through 'colourful inflated rhetoric'. However as Presdee notes (2000: 142), 'it is the users of weapons themselves who define what a weapon is, through the very act of violence'. Evidence of use of aggressive dogs as weapons does exist, although it is worth noting that given the cultural context of this use, it is almost certain that the issue is hugely underreported.

Cultural, media and marketing influences

In the western world, the phenomenon of status dogs, bull breeds and pitbulls is now largely situated within the cultural domain of urban and street life. This represents a significant change over the past few decades. The dogs are now symbolic of urban street culture and ghetto glamour, and for many have become the fashion insignia of hip hop and gangsta lifestyles, illustrative of underworld violence and illegal thrills. In the street world, they represent a form of cultural authority for the 'hood'. For others, they provide a mechanism by which their fantasy world of gangsters can now be made hyper-real. This is a relatively new image for these dogs in western society, and this shift in the way that they are perceived is one that has been sensed by the public but poorly articulated in the press (see Chapter Three). It is perhaps best summarised by the transition of the pitbull in popular culture from lovable family pet Petey in the Our Gang film series (see plate section) to dog-fighting champion Chato in the comic series Homies.

The Homies comic series, created by David Gonzales, appeared in the magazine *Lowrider* and depicts a series of Latino characters. The figurine merchandising is hugely successful across the US. The characters represent stereotypical images of barrio gang members, one of which is Mr Pit, the dog-fighting hero. A number of dog-fighting figures are available for collection. The media imagery and the subsequent merchandising situate the pitbull at the heart of the barrio, surrounded by homies, hip hop and gang life. As Allen (2007) observes, this completes the transition of the public cognition of the pitbull from family pet to black or Latino gangster accessory.

Hip hop

For many young men seeking to establish their male identity and their place in society in the absence of traditional working-class communities, the influence of music, film and media is paramount. Beatrice Campbell in *Goliath* (1993: 323) notes that young men were 'soaked in globally transmitted images and ideologies of butch and brutal solutions to life's difficulties'. Film, music and media offer instant opportunities to reframe and reconstitute unfocused, fragile masculinities in a contemporary way. By adopting the style, slang and attributes as presented by 'anti-heroes', hip hop 'gangstas' and rap stars, young men can at once affiliate with a contemporary urban context that speaks for and to them. This is a context widely understood by young people and needing little further interpretation or translation. It designates the young person as being contemporary and 'street', while reaffirming generational distance. This is not restricted to metropolitan areas. Winlow (2001: 67), writing of the north east of England, notes 'the effects of gangster films, for example, upon things such as speech codes, verbal style and vocabulary, and obviously criminal goals, practices and expectations were palpable'.

Central to this new influence of global media is rap and hip hop music. Sanders (2005) in his interviews of young black men in Lambeth notes how his interviewees felt a 'connection between their lives and the lyrics and meanings in the rap/hip-hop music which they believed expressed the reality of their lives' (2005: 139). Disenfranchised young people believe this music speaks to them/for them, articulating the reality and challenges of life on the street. Hip hop and rap provides a basis for a homology of cultural identity. It is adopted as the cultural motif for 'the street', for the ghetto boys and barrio chulos in the US. Hip hop artists, either musical or graphic, are quick to point out they are only illustrating and reflecting life as they see it, and experience it, on the street. Within this frame, aggressive dogs, pitbulls, violence, guns, girls, drugs and 'gangstas' all play their recognised part.

Hip hop itself is not viewed simply as music, but as culture. In this hip hop world of 'gangstas' and 'playas', status dogs are valorised and identified as an integral part of the 'hood', part of the habitus. In a constant dynamic of changing loyalties and constant watchfulness, they offer loyalty and are adopted as cultural insignia like trainers or designer brands.

Music and visual media help to situate this phenomenon in its cultural context, providing a rich source of aural and visual imagery. The relationship between urban street style and hip hop music is widely acknowledged. As such, music and media play a part in the explanation of the phenomenon of status dogs. The pitbull in particular is the breed of choice for many who associate with gang culture. The dog itself is now part of gangland habitus and as such finds representation in cultural modes that represent that lifestyle, including graphics, music, film and rap. Dogs are often represented in videos alongside celebrity musicians.

The hip hop artist DMX is particularly associated with pitbulls and status dogs feature in several of his music videos including 'Dogs for life', 'Where my dogs at', 'Ruff ryders' anthem' and 'Where da hood at'. Many of his tracks, and indeed his own record label, Bloodline, contain references to fighting dogs, such as the greatest hits album The Definition of X: The Pick of the Litter.[26] The album Grand Champ[27] is a paean to dog fighting[28] and raising bloodlines via breeding. His album, Year of the Dog ... Again[29] celebrates the links between dogs, guns and violence and suggests anthropomorphism. One track graphically illustrates the cultural links between hip hop and status dogs, typifying the widely held sentiment that the dog is now part of the habitus of the gang: 'It's all good, the dog is the hood' ('Where da hood at', Grand Champ album).

Status dogs feature in music videos of more mainstream artists, for example, Aaliyah in 'Back in one piece' (featuring DMX), and Eve in the track (featuring DMX) called 'Dog match', which valorises a dog fight.

DMX (real name, Earl Simmons) has previously been arrested for drug possession and reckless driving. In 2002, he pleaded guilty to 13 counts of animal cruelty for keeping pitbulls in unhygienic cages in his garage. He later starred in a public service announcement against animal abuse. In 2007, a further 12 pitbulls were removed from his home.

A new Cuban-American music artist, Armando Christian Perez, has adopted the stage name 'Pitbull' and achieved considerable success. Again, this indicates that the brand values of the pitbull are so strong and globally recognised that music artists are willing to use them to promote their stage image. This type of association does not exist with any other breed.

The image 'problem' of the pitbull

Many see this recent but highly visible cultural association between pitbulls, bull breeds and urban street gangs in the US as the cause of the pitbull's 'image problem' (Allen, 2007; Delise, 2007). It is also possible that the transition of the pitbull from family-friendly pet to a negatively viewed social pariah reflects the transition from the pitbull's association with a largely ethnically white Americana tradition to one with the black and Latino ghettos. But regardless of racial stereotypes, the pitbull still has a negative image in the US and is heavily associated with gang violence and dog fighting.

In the US, animal lovers, animal welfare organisations, rescue shelters and lovers of bull breeds who are interested in the traditional history and welfare of the stock are united in their attempts to try to recast the image of the pitbull and other bull breeds. Commercial TV in the US has also spotted a cultural niche and picked up on attempts to recast the negative image of the pitbull by making it central to a series called *Pit boss.*[30] This docu–soap TV series follows members' efforts in an organisation that was set up to rescue, train and rehabilitate pitbulls. Animal Planet has also recently aired the second season of a TV series entitled *Pitbulls and parolees.* The programmes show convicted felons working with pitbulls under the direction of a renowned pitbull trainer and dog rescue centre owner, Tia Maria Torres. They demonstrate how both felons and dogs can forge positive relationships and the stated aims include saving pitbulls from abusive situations and attempting to recast the image of both felon and pitbull.[31]

The image of the pitbull is routinely and universally marketed with the brand characteristics of aggression, exuberance, strength and loyalty. Such reputational attributes fit with the habitus of the gang and appeal to those in its social field, but the same characteristics appeal equally to those seeking to recast the image of the dog. Indeed the pitbull is so bound by its reputational characteristics that even those seeking to recast the image of the dog utilise and promote the same reputational characteristics. Thus the photographs, graphics, terminology, descriptors and imagery used by those who might be termed 'pro–dog–welfare owners' actually differs very little from those who have a more utilitarian relationship with their dog. It can be difficult to tell these groups of owners apart in terms of marketing audience. Products and merchandising to both groups routinely emphasise the canine attributes that are the very source of its appeal as a status dog. All the marketing products in relation to pitbulls, for example, emphasise size, strength, musculature and gameness. Even magazines such as *AtomicDogg*, aimed at responsible owners of bull breeds, present pitbulls in an almost fetishistic way (see plate section).

If the image of pitbulls and bull breeds is to be recast in the public consciousness, it is unlikely that such imagery will assist. It appears that bull breeds, specifically pitbulls, are trapped with an unshifting reputational brand image that has universal recognition and forms the marketing basis of all pitbull products, regardless of market sector. This brand image reinforces the image of the dog as urban and aggressive – the canine 'other'. Positive representation of the breed may help shift the stigma surrounding pitbulls by demonstrating the impact of positive and responsible breeding and ownership, but as long as the dogs are subject to such strong and uncontested brand values, any attempt to recast their image as positive will be problematic.

Pitbull products

The commodification of dogs suggests that the dog is viewed as a utilitarian commodity rather than a sentient companion. The dog itself becomes a product to be marketed. Pitbulls are either sold from kennels or acquired from independent (often amateur) sources via websites.

An extensive range of merchandising is also available for owners of status dogs. The UK is only just becoming a marketplace for this type of merchandise, but merchandising for bull breeds and pitbulls is prolific in the US. Items are both high and low in value, and can be unique customised products or mass-produced items. Most items rely heavily on the image, characteristics and attributes of the pitbull. The merchandising and accessories retain a number of noticeable features:

- Aggressive imagery. This reinforces the physicality of the dog and its aggressive potential. Images are often of pitbulls with bared teeth, snarling or straining on harnesses, poised to pounce or in a state of arousal. Such images convey the concept of 'gameness' to the buyer. Aggressive imagery is the most evident and by far the most widely used by commercial marketers for merchandising and for websites. Some images of pitbulls in harnesses come seductively close to fetish wear, suggesting animal requiring considerable 'control'. As merchandising targets the owners, not the dogs, its appeal to imagery is evident. Images are now heavily styled as 'American gothick' or gritty urban style, with depictions of camouflage or barbed wire, for example. Graphics and illustrations include visual representations of iron, steel and metal to emphasise musculature. Some graphics, fonts styles and iconography veer towards Nazi or fascist imagery. Imagery backdrops are often presented as elemental weather – lighting, storms or fire – to suggest the elemental nature of the dog. To appeal to urban dog fighters, backdrops and imagery often depict an urban wasteland and inner city, to convey the concept of survival in a post-holocaust world. This suggests the durability, resilience and toughness of the dog.
- Iconic Americana. Images of pitbulls suggest the iconic nature of the dog: its strength, its loyalty, its tenacity and its frontier spirit. Pitbulls and bull breeds are frequently draped in American flags,

including the confederate flag, or surrounded by trophies. Flags and banners are often associated with appeal to traditional 'dogmen' in the southern states, who valorise the dogs and the 'noble sport' and tradition of dog fighting

- Domesticated imagery. This includes images of pitbulls at play or as family pets. Such images seek to normalise the portrayal of the dog and to reverse or counter-balance the images portrayed by the above. These images are now heavily promoted not only by some retail organisations, but by bull breed hobbyist magazines such as *AtomicDogg*.

Merchandised products include the following:

- Dogwear accessories. These include leather and metal harnesses, often studded with metal spikes to emphasise the aggressive attributes of the dog. This fashion wear conveys the message that the dog should not be approached. In 2007, one dogwear accessory company called Dirrty Bones produced a controversial array of muzzles, refashioned as urban dog grills. The company marketed the collection as hip hop dog accessories. Three urban styles were produced to represent the dog in the urban/gang environment: the camouflage style, the bandana style and the hip hop bling style. Grills come plated with 18k gold and Swarovski rhinestones.[32] Collars are often heavily spiked, or studded with 'dragon claws', 'sharks teeth' or skull and crossbones.
- Dog health and muscle supplements. These are marketed with the intention of building big bones and big heads, promoting muscle growth, stamina, performance and endurance. Products are labelled Muscle Up, Formula MASS and Bully Max.
- Dog treats.
- Dog training equipment. Merchandise includes weighted collars, with pockets for stones. This item will build neck musculature. Other items include harnesses, anti-barking and biting muzzles and bite-protection sleeves.
- Owners' fashion merchandise. Owners can purchase from a wide range of fashion wear, including peaked caps featuring pitbulls, tee-shirts and sweat shirts, often depicting pitbulls lunging with teeth bared, set against urban or survivalist backdrops. Other items includes sports kit, sports bags and so on.
- Stickers, buttons, pins and banners. Car bumper stickers and schoolbook stickers are available, along with a wide array of badges. Many give warnings such as 'Don't mess with my Pits' or 'You had better start praying'. Children's collectibles include hood hounds, a

collection of 24 different dogs all associated with the 'hood'. These can be used alongside the Homies collection.

- Supplementaries (books, statues, photos, magazines). Monthly magazines such as *AtomicDogg* are used to market these products. The items also promote numerous shows, such as The Super Bully Show, The Bully Bash, The Official Dirty South Board. These are family fun shows where responsible owners enter their dogs into weight-pulling competitions and treadmill races or present their dogs for prizes in categories such as biggest head, widest chest, most compact dog and bully freak. These shows attract hundreds of people and take place every week across the US. They often feature headline rap and hip hop acts and a range of food and merchandise. One of the shows promotional websites[33] had almost 800,000 posts, demonstrating a wide audience. These sites and shows are legal, professionally run and largely attended by responsible owners and breeders. They may also be used to promote healthy dogs, healthy breeding and responsible ownership. However, they are always marketed in a way that promotes the very reputational brand attributes that so often create a negative public image of pitbulls.

Dog-fighting internet sites

In addition to legal shows, magazines and professional contact sites, there exists a world of illegal videos showing organised dog fights and chain rolling. Here viewers can become wholly immersed in the world of dogs and dog fighting, with accompanying specialist manuals, journals and 'sporting' magazines providing validation of dog fighting while commodifying and consolidating niche marketing. Dog-fight videos are often available to view on the internet, and DVDs are available for purchase.

Two video games recently available in the UK include dog fighting. In one, gamers select a wide range of weapons, including firearms, to be fight opponents. A pitbull is one of the choices in this weapons cache. This world enables gamers to participate in virtual acts otherwise deemed cruel and dehumanising by average citizens, and helps to normalise such acts. It allows participants to express and enact hidden desires and force the animals into even more distasteful gladiatorial or endurance challenges.

Recently, controversy erupted over a new Android app entitled KG Dogfighting (previously called Dog Wars) released by Kage Games LLC.[34] This online application provides instructions on conditioning a dog for a virtual dog fight. Once selected as an electronic game character, the dog can be provided with steroids, drugs and tyre-drag training before engaging in a fight. The makers of the game say they are confident that users will be able to distinguish between this virtual world and reality and claim that the game is a satire on dog fighting despite the fact that it is available to users as young as 13.

Pitbull imagery in the UK

The UK marketplace is different from that in the US in terms of merchandise for bull breeds, pitbulls and status dogs. However, all merchandise from any country is now available via the internet. The internet and other new technologies also mean that cultural references, such as hip hop, can be more easily shared. Hip hop has global resonance and young men in social housing estates in the UK will often feel this music and culture now speaks for them as much as it does for a barrio homie in Chicago as one of the focus-group interviewees in this study illustrates:

> 'Do you know DMX, he's got loads of pitbulls, and he fights them too.' (Male aged 16, London)

The cultural positioning of pitbulls in urban grime and hip hop music is reinforced by the habitus of the gang and the street. This is further reinforced by the global nature of the internet, which makes merchandise reinforcing the reputational branding of pitbulls available to young people in the UK. The status dog and notably the pitbull are now irreversibly situated in urban street culture. The status dog then is thus situated against a cultural backdrop that can be easily identified and referenced by young people, thus widening its appeal. Even national UK celebrities are keen to be seen acquiring a status dog to the dismay of this interviewee:[35]

> 'But then I watched in dismay an ad for a football computer game – with Wayne Rooney with a cane corso italiano, originally a fighting dog – quite difficult in temperament. He stood squaring up to a football team. We're working hard to address this and [...] they then go and do all this publicity with Wayne Rooney and a status dog.' (Police officer, West Midlands)

In the UK, the status dog, notably the pitbull, has quickly become an accepted and recognisable part of the urban community or the deprived estate. As such, it has entered the cultural landscape of the UK as it has in the US. Pitbulls are increasingly evident in amateur online videos produced by local gangs as well as in professional music videos, for example, 'Round here da estate',[36] 'Phenomenon – straight cockney' (Reppin Romford),[37] and in a TV advert for The E4 bunker[38] which shows two SBTs in Burberry outfits pulling on chains followed by hoodies.

In the UK, the pitbull and its association with dog fighting, aggression and 'the underclass' has even worked its way into politics and high culture. In a cartoon alongside a column in *The Times*, satirical cartoonist Gerald Scarfe lampooned UK Shadow Chancellor Ed Balls as a pitbull with an owner who seems ill prepared to handle a potentially aggressive animal.[39]

Opera, too, has recently played testament to the increased visibility of the pitbull in the UK. In January 2011, in a new production of Bizet's Carmen produced at the Grand in Leeds, director Daniel Kramer transposed the action to an urban project in Seville, Ohio with Escamillo owning a prize pitbull. The finale bull–fighting scene is depicted as a dog fight using a pitbull on a chain. When this author asked Kramer why he used this image, and whether he thought it was appropriate, he replied that he wanted to modernise the setting and make it contemporary but still to retain aspects of masculine brutality. As such, dog fighting was clearly a suitable transposition and was considered to be a well-understood element of the social context. Kramer considered the pitbull to be a metaphor for male aggression and one that is now a recognisable element of urban life in the UK as well as in the US. Speaking on the phone from his home in Hackney, Kramer added that as he looked out of his window into his neighbour's flat, he could see several pitbulls "milling around in [his] neighbour's kitchen".

Conclusion

There are several different motivations for owning a status dog. These motivations build on the characteristics and attributes of the dog's widely recognised reputational qualities. These reflect strong reputational brand values often used by marketers to publicise and sell merchandise featuring the dogs. The motivational typology proposed in this chapter identifies the different reasons for owners acquiring aggressive breeds and suggests that this reflects a motivational spectrum of different social fields and different functional uses of dogs.

Key among motivations is the need to build status through the acquisition of street capital. Status dogs allow for status advancement, commanding and demanding respect among social peers. In the social field of the gang, this quest for respect and street capital is greatly heightened. Aggressive dogs are valorised as part of 'ghetto family' or the habitus of the 'hood'. It is clear that dogs perform a range of utilities and functions within gang culture such as socialising and dog fighting. This is recognised in the US, where profiling dog fighters is now central to gang intervention activity and federal authority policing operations.

The UK situation is still emerging, although it is clear that status dogs are, on occasion, bred or trained to be aggressive. In the pursuit of criminal activity, this aggression may be directed towards individuals. The evidence presented indicates that dogs can and are used as weapons, including in the high-profile murders of Seyi Ogunyemi and Kodjo Yenga in the UK. It is only the extent of this practice that remains to be further identified.

The next chapter explores the methodological challenges of researching status dogs and sets out the methods used in this research study to seek evidence of this phenomenon.

Notes

[1] The Staffordshire bull terrier has long been known to be sociable and tolerant with children and often went by the nickname, the nanny dog.

[2] This raid on 15 August 2006 involved Ricardo Byfield and wife Lisa Harvey, known as pitbull 'royalty'. They were each jailed for commercial breeding of dangerous dogs and sentenced to six months in jail under the DDA 1991. They ran a 'stud' farm from their one-bed maisonette. When the police raided the premises, they found 21 illegal pitbulls, two dogues de Bordeaux, a rottweiler and an SBT. The house had treadmills, kennels and cages. One dog, covered in scars from fights, was estimated as being worth between £5,000 and £6,000 as a 'grand champion'. The couple also had links with a notorious dog-fighting ring in Ireland.

[3] 'Woman bred illegal fighting dogs in home', *Express and Star*, 22 October 2009, www.expressandstar.com/2009/10/22/woman-bred-illegal-fighting-dogs-in-home, accessed 13 March 2010.

[4] Jamie Doward, 'The "family pet" bred to be trained as a vicious fighter', *The Observer*, 5 August 2007.

[5] 'HSUS Englewood "Walk for Peace" honors son killed defending his dogs from fighting', 28 June 2008, www.hsus.org/press_and_publications, accessed on 25 June 2009 (no longer available).

[6] 'Football star battles dog-fighting scandal' by Ewen MacAskill, *The Guardian*, Saturday 25 August 2007, www.guardian.co.uk/world/2007/aug/25/us

[7] HSUS, cited in Gibson (2005).

[8] Gloria Campisi, 'Humane Society responds to huge jump in animal fighting', *Philadelphia Daily News*, 18 January 2011.

[9] Hanna Gibson, Dog-Fighting Database: Criminal profile of the Urban dog-fighter, ALHC.

[10] Regional Animal-fighting Investigations Division (RAID) pilot programme, Los Angeles Police Department and Los Angeles City Attorney's Office, 2004.

[11] Bill Morris, Liverpool City Safe, my research interview 2010.

[12] If an owner deliberately sets a dog on someone the owner can be arrested for assault and the dog seized for evidence as the weapon. Alternatively, or if deliberate intent is unclear or un-evidenced, the police may use section 3 ('Dog dangerously out of control') of the DDA 1991.

[13] Briggs, I. (2009) Paper presented at RSPCA Status Dogs Summit, April.

[14] 'Mayor backs anti-knife crime operation', www.london.gov.uk/media/press_releases_mayoral/mayor-backs-anti-knife-crime-operation, 2 June 2010, accessed 1 September 2011. The report notes that since May 2008 Operation Blunt 2 has resulted in more than 18,000 arrests. It adds that more than 9,500 knives have been seized and more than 500,000 targets searched, and that the number of incidents involving serious violence has dropped by 22%.

[15] Adam Fresco, 'Judge jails gang who stabbed star pupil, Kodjo Yenga', *The Times*, 10 May 2008.

[16] Elizabeth Pears, 'Dangerous dog trial judge: "Aggressive dogs make you feel bigger than you are"', *Wandsworth Guardian*, 1 April 2010.

[17] Interview with MPS police officer at Ealing Police Station, 21 December 2010.

[18] Michael Stringer, 'I fought off dogs, then owner set them on me', *South London Press*, 16 August 2010.

[19] Peter Dominiczak, 'Students savaged by gang's dogs', *Evening Standard*, 28 October 2010.

[20] 'Dog owner who gloated about fatal mauling on Facebook is jailed', *Mail Online*, 21 January 2011, http://www.dailymail.co.uk/news/article-1349284/Facebook-Dog-owner-John-Palmer-gloated-fatal-mauling-jailed.html, accessed 21 January 2011.

[21] Leanna Maclarty, 'Man jailed over horrific dog attack', *The Press and Journal*, 28 February 2011.

[22] Hannah Al-Taraboulsy, 'Stretford nan left for dead after being mauled by dog', *Warrington Guardian*, 30 September 2008.

[23] http://westminster.londoninformer.co.uk/2011/04/pimlico-thug-jailed-over-pitbu.html, Accessed 20/04/12

[24] Luke Traynor, 'Liverpool woman trained dog to attack police', *Liverpool Echo*, 25 May 2010, http://www.liverpoolecho.co.uk/liverpool-news/local-news/2010/05/25/liverpool-woman-trained-dog-to-attack-police-100252-26513195/, Accessed 25/04/12

[25] Elizabeth Pears, 'Man attacked by dog near Tottenham Hale retail park for phone', *Haringey Independent*, 2 March 2011, http://www.haringeyindependent.co.uk/news/topstories/8883768.Man_attacked_by_dog_for_mobile_phone/

[26] Released 12 June 2007 on Ruff Ryders, Def Jam label.

[27] Released 2003 and debuted at #1 on the US Billboard 200.

[28] A 'grand champion' is a dog that has won at least five pit-fight matches.

[29] Released 31 July 2006 on Ruff Ryders, Sony Urban, Columbia.

[30] Broadcast by Animal Planet, Discovery Channel, 2010-11.

[31] http://store.discovery.com/pit-bulls-parolees-seasons-1-2-dvd/detail.php?p=302544

[32] 'Pitbull urban wear by Dirrty Bones', Interview with Dirrty Bones' owner, 7 August 2007, *Format Magazine*, http://ifitshipitshere.wordpress.com/2007/08/14/pit-bull-urban-wear-by-dirrty-bones-2, accessed 1 July 2010.

[33] www.americanbullyworld.com

[34] Leslie Horn, 'Controversial dogfighting app rebranded "KG Dogfighting" back in the Android market', *PC Mag*, 30 April 2011, http://www.pcmag.com/article2/0,2817,2384707,00.asp

[35] The picture of Wayne Rooney with a status dog is used to promote the new electronic computer game FIFA 11 devised by EA Sports. The picture

shows Rooney restraining the dog. The dog appears in promotional stills and also in the video promotion for the game.

[36] 'Round here da estate', M16 Productions 2005, features status dogs. YouTube video posted by tegaffer with 1,210,926 views, accessed 20 December 2010.

[37] Phenomenon – 'Straight cockney' (Reppin Romford) Neath Films Ltd, 2006.

[38] E4 advert, 'The E4 bunker', January 2008. Posted on YouTube by traddie, accessed 22 January 2008.

[39] Ann Treneman, 'Dangerous dog Ed Balls on fearsome form that scares the Tories', *The Times*, 23 January 2011.

FIVE

Presenting the evidence

This chapter presents the evidence generated from the research study (see Chapter One for a detailed account of the methodological challenges of undertaking research into status dogs). The findings from the literature review are documented throughout the book and the critical discourse analysis of the media has been addressed in Chapter Two. The chapter begins by setting out the secondary data sourced from a wide variety of agencies, which indicates how these organisations have identified and recorded the appearance of the phenomenon of status dogs. This desk research indicates the emergence of the phenomenon and illustrates that aggressive bull breeds play a prominent role. The second half of the chapter sets out the findings from the primary research, evidencing more clearly the existence of the status dog phenomenon and confirming the typology. There follows a brief comparative analysis of this primary research with research by Maher and Pierpoint (2011), before concluding by asking the question, do owners of status dogs exhibit a propensity for criminality, violent or aggressive behaviour?

Agency data

Data was sourced from a variety of agencies:

- animal welfare agencies, including the RSPCA
- the Dogs Trust
- Metropolitan Police Service
- hospitals
- local authorities
- regional government.

RSPCA

The RSPCA has been at the forefront of raising awareness of status dogs. The phenomenon was mentioned in a briefing paper (RSPCA, 2007a) and a position paper (RSPCA, 2008); two conferences on status dogs followed in 2009 and 2010. The position paper acknowledges the issue as one of antisocial behaviour (ASB), where dogs are used to intimidate/fight other dogs, but they also refer to links with crime and gang culture. The RSPCA was alerted to the issue through increased calls and complaints by the public. B1 in Appendix B indicates an increase in the number of complaints to the RSPCA concerning status and dangerous dogs from 2006 to 2009. The society reported a 12-fold increase in complaints between 2004 and 2008.

The report of proceedings from the status dogs summit in 2009 noted that 'status dogs used in ASB are now beginning to be used in organised dog-fights' (RSPCA, 2009). B2 in Appendix B illustrates increasing reports of youths 'chain rolling' dogs. The RSPCA data, while incomplete, indicate regional variations in data. Organised dog fights are often completely clandestine and require in-depth investigations by the RSPCA Special Operations Unit to track and penetrate such groups over time, often involving transnational cooperation with other police forces. Moreover, they are seldom reported directly by the public, so the data only indicate the existence of the problem and not the extent of dog fighting. Notwithstanding this caveat, B3 in Appendix B shows reported dog fights at a peak in 2007. In 2008, 66% of reported animal fights related to youths chain-rolling dogs in the street.

The practice of chain rolling, however, is more likely to be reported by the public. A peak in the data in 2007 may well correspond to the widely publicised death of five-year-old Ellie Lawrenson by an illegally owned pitbull, which was followed by a pitbull amnesty in Northern Ireland and Merseyside that same year.

Not all owners engaged in organised or street dog fighting refer their dogs to a veterinary surgeon when injured (see Chapter Six). This fact further inhibits the collection of accurate statistical data. What can be stated, however, is that dog fighting takes place across the UK. In one London RSPCA animal hospital staff treated 22 dogs for dog-fighting injuries in one month (RSPCA 2010a).

These data are supplemented by the comments from Dr David Grant at the RSPCA Harmsworth Memorial Animal Hospital in north London. Speaking in 2009 for the RSPCA status dog appeal, Dr Grant commented:

> 'My staff are treating more dogs than ever for fight wounds and injuries sustained as a result of them being kept as status symbols by young people who think having a dog makes them look tough. We are seeing ... on average, three to five wounds every day. Even for a single fight it is a lot of work [to repair and dress wounds].'[1]

RSPCA data are often difficult to compare as definitions and time periods vary. While data quality is compromised in places, the society remains clear that the 'figures tie in with the increasing trend amongst teenagers and young males using stereotypically macho-type dogs as weapons of intimidation in urban areas of England and Wales'.[2]

The data may be further compromised by the underreporting of incidents. For example, the RSPCA claims that many people do not report attacks by status dogs through fear of retaliation:

> 'More and more attacks are taking place with these status dogs, and often people don't even report attacks to police because they are too scared. What's frightening is the victim goes and gets a dog himself and the problem grows. It's a vicious circle.'[3]

In its analysis of animal welfare data from 2005-09, the RSPCA (2010a: 10) reports an 'upsurge in breeding and ownership of so-called status dogs ... including mastiffs, SBTs and Rottweilers'. The report notes that the market for such breeds is now much reduced, as it has been 'flooded with puppies'. This development has led to an increase in the number of dogs being abandoned or neglected as their value falls (see also Chapter Seven). Staffordshire bull terriers (SBTs) and SBT cross-breeds constitute a large proportion of abandoned or neglected dogs. The report notes that in 2009, 615 SBTs or SBT cross-breeds were taken in by the 13 RSPCA regional animal homes. Animal rescue shelters have reported increased numbers of such animals being registered and one rehoming centre reported that 75% of its registered dogs were bull breeds (RSPCA, 2010a). The RSPCA also notes an increase in numbers of stray and abandoned dogs.

The Dogs Trust

The Dogs Trust is the UK's largest dog welfare charity and cares for over 16,000 dogs a year through a network of 17 rehoming centres. In its Stray Dog Survey 2010, the trust reveals that the UK's stray and abandoned dog numbers have reached an 11-year high. The trust also reported that across 311 local authorities a total of 17,834 status dogs were reported as having been handled between 1 April 2009 and 31 March 2010. While noting that some authorities did not respond and others did not provide figures for status dogs, this figure still accounts for 18% of all strays reported in the UK. The implications of stray and abandoned dogs are considered in Chapter Seven.

Metropolitan Police Service

Prior to the creation of the Metropolitan Police Service (MPS) Status Dogs Unit (SDU) in March 2009, the police addressed the issue of dangerous dogs via its Central Operations in conjunction with the Dog Section. The incidence of dangerous dog offences was regularly monitored. In the period 2001–06, only 69 persons were recorded on the MPS Crime Reporting and Information System (CRIS) as having been investigated for offences under the Dangerous Dogs Act (DDA) 1991 (MPS, 2007).

By 2006, the MPS was beginning to record a change in the pattern of offences relating to dangerous dogs in London. The number of dogs seized by MPS officers under the DDA 1991 had risen from 33 in 2005 to 147 in 2006 and by July 2007, local Safer Neighbourhood teams across London had listed dog-fighting behaviour as a priority on 73 occasions (MPS, 2007). The MPS, however, decided against adopting a dangerous dogs amnesty at this time.

By January 2009, the situation in London is reported as having changed significantly, with police data indicating a growing problem: 'Pitbull-type dogs have become a weapon of choice for a number of people involved in gang-related crime, drug dealing and anti-social behaviour' (MPS, 2009). From April 2006 to March 2008, 654 dogs were seized followed by a further 494 in the months April to November 2008. Also reported between 1 April 2008 and 1 December 2008 were 1342 spontaneous dangerous dog calls which were responded to by general-purpose dog units and 404 pre-planned operations. The MPS reported increasingly competing demands on its dog legislation officers (DLOs), arising from the increase in cases. Kennelling requirements and costs were increasing and by January 2009, 270 dogs were in kennels subject of court proceedings. Dogs were now kennelled for 182 days on average, making them increasingly volatile and aggressive. To address the increasing workload of its officers, and to encourage a more proactive approach to tackling the problem, the MPS decided to establish its dedicated Status Dogs Unit.

Table B4 in Appendix B illustrates the number of dogs coming into the MPS SDU by each London borough in the financial year 2010/11.[4] A total of 1,072 dogs came into the SDU, the largest number coming from the London Borough of Lewisham. Data must be interpreted with caution, as the boroughs presenting the highest number of dogs often also have active DLOs and police/local authority partnership activity underway. These more established local mechanisms are reflected in the data. It should also be noted that boroughs with a DLO or those designated as priority boroughs by the SDU are also the boroughs with the highest number of reported issues with status dogs. Spring and summer months appear to present higher number of inbound dogs. There are higher numbers of inbound dogs in spring and summer, and high figures may also reflect seizures of several dogs in a single raid.

In the calendar year 2010, the total number of dogs coming in to the MPS SDU was 1,107. Lewisham was again the borough with the highest count (87 dogs), followed by Tower Hamlets with 79 and Southwark with 63. In 2010, five boroughs (Haringey, Lewisham, Southwark, Tower Hamlets and Wandsworth) accounted for 30% of all inbound dogs to the MPS SDU.

The MPS SDU reports a steady increase of approximately 300 seizures per financial year since 2005/06.[5] The figures for 2010/11 indicate a slight decrease on the financial year 2009/10 of approximately 6%.

B4 in Appendix B records the dogs coming into the MPS SDU in 2010. The statistics appear to indicate slight seasonality with higher figures over the warmer summer months.

B5 in Appendix B indicates the breed or type of dog seized by the London MPS SDU under section 3 of the DDA 1991.[6] Of the 229 dogs seized, the pitbull is the breed/type most often seized (69), followed by the SBT or SBT cross-breed (59).

Hospital data

NHS data on animal attacks and injuries provides another source of information. However, this type of data seldom provided the level of detail useful to furthering the discussion, as the breed of dog involved in attacks is seldom recorded. Dog attacks and bites can therefore relate to minor bites from poodles as well as more serious bites.

Research carried out via requests under the Freedom of Information Act 2000 for records retained by hospitals and NHS trusts proved disappointing. The study attempted to locate data over a three-year period from August 2009 to October 2011, by gender, age and ethnicity, relating to the number of people admitted with:

- dog bites; and
- severe dog bites (dog attack).

Of 20 hospitals contacted in the FOI study, only 11 responded and only six of these provided data. Others held data, but only in personal records where costs prohibited access. Those responding but unable to provide data did not hold data in a way that would provide findings;

for example, they grouped bites with stings or recorded the nature of the injury rather than the cause. None returning data were able to give details on severe dog bites (dog attack). Some were able to provide admissions data and accident and emergency (A&E) data (although some double-counting has to be assumed). National coding in A&E departments precludes the collation of useful data.

With such poor data returns, only slight broad generalisations can be drawn:

- the Royal Liverpool and Broadgreen University Hospitals reported a steady increase in patients with dog bites from seven in 1999 to 41 in 2009;
- Whipps Cross Hospital, London reported increased patient admissions arising from dog bites from four in July 2008 to 15 in September 2010;
- patient admissions had declined slightly in University Hospitals, Birmingham. Male patients admitted for dog bites were aged 16-30 years, while female patients admitted for dog bites were aged 36-55 years;
- Alder Hey Children's Hospital, Liverpool reported an increase in admissions of patents treated for dog bites from 58 in 2008 to 79 in 2010. There was also an increase in females being admitted for dog bites.

Beyond noting increased hospital admissions, as opposed to those presenting at A&E, no conclusions can be derived from this data.

A further complication of assessing statistics from the NHS is that some data refer to A&E admissions, while others refer to general ward admissions. Furthermore many dog-bite injuries are not reported.

The Hospital Episode Statistics (HES) website proves a useful source for data on A&E admissions.[7] In the financial years from 2003/04 to 2007/08, A&E data reported a year-on-year increase in numbers of people attending hospital for dog bites/strikes. These increases ranged from 18% to 38%, and by 2008/09 had levelled off. An HES report on dog bites and strikes[8] for the period 1997/98 to 2007/08 reports an increase in the number of treated cases attributed to being bitten or struck by a dog. This is shown as a significant rise in numbers in all age groups, except under-10s. Interestingly, males between the ages of 10 and 40 are significantly more likely to account as a statistical entry as a 'finished consultant episode' (that is, patient was seen by a consultant) arising from dog bites/strikes than females in the same age groups. In the age ranges 45–65 and over 70 it is females who are more likely to be bitten.

NHS figures obtained by *The Guardian*[9] revealed that nearly 3,800 people in England required hospital treatment in 2007 following a dog attack. The figures represented a 40% rise over a five-year period. Of these, 2,510 involved adults and 1,277 involved under-18s. The majority of A&E admissions relating to dog attacks were in the north west of England. In 2006/07, dog attacks accounted for 426 adult admissions and 241 child admissions (under-18s) in the north-west region. Liberal Democrat health spokesman, Norman Lamb MP, who obtained the figures through parliamentary questions, commented that the rise was 'enormously disturbing'.

Statistics released by the Lancashire Teaching Hospitals to the *Lancashire Evening Post*[10] show an increase in the number of those requiring hospital treatment for dog bites from 24 in 2002/03 to 74 in 2008/09. Citing the consultant plastic surgeon at the Lancashire Teaching Hospitals NHS Foundation Trust, the paper reports that these bites can require skin grafts and reconstructive plastic surgery.[11] While such data on their own must be treated with caution, it is noteworthy that local practitioners and police in Preston (one of the hospitals included) had reported an increase in dog fighting and status dogs in the area.[12]

Other articles revealed 500 people requiring hospital treatment in the period 2001/02 to 2007/08 at Bradford Royal Infirmary A&E.[13]

In Wales, data obtained from South Wales Police via an FOI request by the Assembly Member for Cynon Valley revealed that cases of hospitalisation resulting from dog attacks had risen by 60% from 1999/2000 to 2010.

Data for Merseyside reported through *Hansard*[14] indicate that the total number of 'finished admissions' as a result of being bitten or struck by a dog have stayed more or less the same between 2006/07 (287 cases) and 2008/09 (275 cases). A&E admissions (outpatients) are likely to be considerably higher. In response to an FOI request from the BBC,[15] Whiston Hospital on Merseyside reported that cases of dog bites had risen from 60 in 2000 to 175 in 2009. Much of the rise was among children aged under 10 and adults aged 40–45. Status dogs such as pitbulls and rottweilers were reported as being responsible for the majority of attacks.

Clearly not all the cases presenting at hospital or illustrated in the data above involve status dogs or aggressive bull breeds. The data do, however, indicate a rise in the number of attacks and injuries from dogs. It remains to be proven what lies behind this increase in attacks evident in hospitals across the country. It is most likely that it relates in some way to an increase in the prevalence of bull breeds and status dogs.

Local authority data

In response to increased complaints from borough residents some local authorities began to review local provision for addressing dangerous and status dogs via local action plans, scrutiny reports and partnership responses. These are considered in Chapter Eight. Few local authorities collate their own data on the issue of dangerous dogs, or if they do, it is very recent. In response to increased complaints from residents, some local authorities have begun to review local provision for addressing dangerous and status dogs via local action plans, scrutiny reports and partnership initiatives. These are considered in more detail in Chapter Eight.

Merseyside City Council

Following the death of Ellie Lawrenson from a pitbull attack in Liverpool in 2007, Merseyside police initiated a citywide operation to encourage residents to hand in illegal dogs. Termed 'an amnesty' by the local press, the operation resulted in hundreds of dogs being handed to the police and the city council. Police data for this operation were not retained, but in an interview in the *Liverpool Echo*, the Assistant Chief Constable reported that during the one week hand-in 654 calls were received from the public and 97 pitbull-type dogs were handed in and euthanised.[16] The tragic death prompted proactive police raids in Liverpool, which uncovered the problem of multiple dogs living at one address, often a small terraced house, and in one case stored in a lock-up unit.[17] The raids resulted in the following seizures:

- 3 January 2007: six pitbulls at a house in St Helens;
- 5 January 2007: seven adult pitbulls and one puppy in Croxteth, Liverpool;
- 6 January 2007: 14 pitbulls seized from a lock-up unit in Liverpool.

London Borough of Lambeth

In 2009, Seyi Ogunyemi was brutally murdered in the London Borough of Lambeth in an incident involving status dogs (see Introduction). The incident gained much public attention: the RSPCA reported that the borough had the highest level of dog fighting in London,[18] and the local press (*Streatham Guardian*) made an FOI request to the borough that revealed there were three dangerous dog attacks a day in Lambeth.[19] As a result the issue became a high priority for the local authority, which initiated a profiling analysis of dogs in the borough.[20]

This profile provides a useful in-depth view of crime data relating to dangerous dogs in one borough. The key findings are as follows:

- Fifty-eight dangerous dog offences were carried out in Lambeth in 2008.
- By 2009, Lambeth was the highest-ranking MPS borough for volume of dangerous dog offences.
- In 2008, most of the stray dog arrivals at Battersea Dogs & Cats Home (BDCH) came from Lambeth (340). Of these, 54% were public strays, an increase of 26% from 2007. The majority of dogs received by BDCH were SBTs (58%) and a further 13% were other bull breeds.
- In an analysis of 40 dangerous dog offences from January to August 2009, 70% of victims were found to be male with 34% of these aged under 18 years. Approximately 50% of victims were ethnically white (north European) and the remainder ethnically black. One in five of the victims had injuries considered to be moderate or serious.
- Of the 45 suspects involved, 26 were male. The main ethnicities were reported as black (19) and white (north European) (14). Forty-two per cent of suspects were said to be under 30 years of age.

Even after taking into account limitations regarding the accuracy of primary data entry, this does illustrate a useful localised profile of one London borough. The data should be read in conjunction with Table 5.2 which documents the prevalence of status dogs and dog fighting in Lambeth. Read together, the data are suggestive of a high number of status and dangerous dogs in Lambeth owned by young men in deprived areas of the borough.

Summary of evidence from the secondary data

As the phenomenon of status dogs is a recent one, evidence is only just being formally collated. Terminology is still being tested/shared and often remains subjective. The creation of specialist units such as the MPS SDU significantly improves the collation of statistical evidence, and its availability and quality. Prior to this, no specific data were collected on status dogs. In order to carry out any research on the topic of status dogs and formulate a picture of what effect it has had on different agencies, data need to be sourced and retrieved from numerous sources. The variable quality of the data available also has to be taken into account at the analysis stage. Other useful data remain unobtainable without in-depth and costly analysis.

Difficulties in sourcing and collating data do not, however, inhibit forming a broad picture of events and their impact – in short, it is clear that all agencies involved agree that there has been an increase in the number of status dogs, dangerous dogs and dog attacks and that inner city boroughs and young men are most often involved.

It is also clear that bull breeds are recognised as a key element in the proliferation of status dogs and dog attacks. Other issues such as an increase in the number of strays are linked to dog fighting and chain rolling, as injured dogs are often abandoned. The question is, does this amount to sufficient evidence to claim that a problem exists.

What we can say is that:

- The RSPCA reports a 12-fold increase in complaints about young men with aggressive dogs or status dogs between 2004 and 2008. There has been an increase in the number of public complaints and reported concerns about status dogs.
- There have been increased reports of dog fighting.
- Incidents are likely to be underreported.
- The number of status dogs seized by the MPS rose from 33 in 2005 to 1,107 in 2010, an increase of approximately 300 seizures per financial year.
- Pitbulls and SBTs feature highly in seizures.
- Hospital Episode Statistics indicate a year-on-year increase in the number of patients presenting with dog bites/strikes, with young males comprising a significant proportion of victims.

The Lambeth profile provides a useful insight into the data now required in order to provide sociologists with the opportunity to undertake further analysis. Strict guidelines are required to capture full profiling data, for example, on victims' and offenders' age, gender and ethnicity and so on. Incidents should be crime mapped and analysed alongside other relevant data, for example on the location of incidents (social housing, parks, areas of multiple deprivation), to establish hidden correlations and patterns, and improved understanding of the range and type of incidents.

To answer the question posed above, I do think the data indicates some dramatic changes, some of which are concerning and some alarming. However it remains at this stage only a partial picture of the phenomenon and further work is required to complete this picture. I shall now report findings from my primary research.

Primary data

Findings from participant observations in parks

During my own research, I observed aggressive or PBT dogs in 19 of the 40 field sites visited (see Table 5.1). This included six out of the 10 destination case-study sites; no such dogs were observed in the remaining four sites during my one-hour research visit. Aggressive/PBT dogs were observed by other park users interviewed in 34 of the 40 (85%) of the field sites. This included positive sightings by these random park users in all 11 designated case study sites. While such field observations have a necessary methodological caveat and do not claim to be scientific, they do nonetheless illustrate that aside from the data presented in reports, it was possible to witness aggressive/PBT dogs in a range of London parks on almost any given day throughout the summer of 2010. It further indicates the high degree of visibility of such animals in these open spaces and a high degree of recognition among general members of the public. and are a common sight in locations throughout London.

A range of factors could account for the absence of such dogs in the remaining four case-study field sites, including local authority action following the negative media reports, weather, time of day, season and location in the park.

Findings from qualitative interviews with practitioners and professionals

As may be expected with professionals working with dogs in a range of roles, all 37 (100%) of respondents were aware of the issue of aggressive/status dogs and all acknowledged the issue had presented itself to them professionally in the course of their daily work. As one interviewee said, "Yes there are a lot of status dogs around, lots of Staffies and we have seized pitbulls around the estate" (police officer, Southwark).

There was a high degree of consensus among practitioners that the issue was real and that it involved young people using certain breeds that they believed would give them status: "There's no doubt a lot of young men are using big, tough-looking dogs, aggressive dogs, to intimidate other people" (police officer, Greenwich).

Table 5.1: Visual observation of pitbull-type (PBT) dogs in London parks in 2010

Name of park	PBT dog observed during field visit	Month visited	Media reports of aggressive/ PBT dogs in that park	Aggressive/ PBT dogs seen using the park by other dog-walkers
Ruskin Park		June		Yes
Norwood Park	Yes	August		Yes
Streatham Common	Yes	August	Yes	Yes
Tooting Common		May	Yes	Yes
Max Roach Park		May		Yes
Northbrook Park	Yes	August	Yes	Yes
Southall Park	Yes	August	Yes	Yes
Brockwell Park		July		Yes
Dulwich Park		June	Yes	Yes
Crystal Palace Park	Yes	June	Yes	Yes
Ladywell Park	Yes	July		Yes
Hillyfields Park	Yes	September		Yes
Mountsfield Park		August		Yes
Blythe Hill Park		November		
Peckham Rye Common		July		Yes
Knights Hill Playing Field		August	Yes	Yes
Clapham Common		July		Yes
Burgess Park	Yes	August		Yes
Southwark Park		December		Yes
Waverley Park		July		
Kennington Park	Yes	June		Yes
Myatts Field	Yes	June		Yes
Vauxhall Park		May		Yes
Ealing Common		August		
Acton Park		August		Yes
Finsbury Park	Yes	December	Yes	Yes
Victoria Park	Yes	July		Yes
Battersea Park		April	Yes	Yes
Lammas Park		August		
Brentford Park		August		
Forster Memorial Park	Yes	August		Yes
Downham Rec Ground	Yes	August		Yes
Larkhall Park	Yes	June	Yes	Yes
Walpole Park		August		Yes
Pitshanger Park	Yes	August		Yes
Gunnersbury Park		August		Yes
London Fields	Yes	June	Yes	Yes
Plumstead Common	Yes	July	Yes	Yes
Hackney Downs	Yes	July	Yes	Yes

The breeds identified by respondents included bull breeds, notably pitbull and STB cross-breeds, mastiffs and other large dogs noted for their size or aggression, such as akitas, rottweilers and presa canarios. Dogs proscribed under the DDA 1991 were also identified as falling within this category.

> 'We had a bad incident in Brockwell Park [Lambeth]. This gentleman was walking his dog and there was a Staffie with another gentleman. The dogs began fighting, he was trying to keep this dog off his own dog. The Staffie bit his arm really badly, but he didn't want to press any charges.' (Park ranger, Lambeth)

All respondents were able to give numerous examples of this kind.

Findings from qualitative interviews with a range of respondents, including local residents, local police officers, local professionals and gang-affiliated young people in Lambeth

Of the 27 respondents questioned about status dogs and dog fighting in Lambeth, 100% (27) were aware of status dogs in the borough; had witnessed status dogs in the borough; were aware of dog fighting taking place in the borough; were aware of status dogs linked to gangs in the borough; and were aware of dog fighting specifically linked to gangs in the borough. Table 5.2 indicates the findings from these interviews. Of those interviewed, 40% had witnessed dog fighting among gangs, mostly chain-rolling fights but also organised dog fights. All believed that status dogs were used by young men to gain respect and several mentioned aggressive dogs being used for personal protection or protect drug deals. Three respondents believed that dog fighting was now in decline in the borough.

Having conducted these interviews and developed a typology of motivations/functions for owning status dogs, the findings were then tested in the field by undertaking qualitative interviews with the owners/handlers of aggressive breeds.

Findings of qualitative interviews with owners/handlers

A total 42 dogs were owned among the 33 respondents. Most of these dogs were SBTs (16), followed by pitbulls (nine) and pitbull or SBT cross-breeds (nine). B6 in Appendix B indicates the research findings.

Table 5.2: Public perception and awareness of status dogs and dog fighting in Lambeth

Interviewee	Aware of status dogs in general	Witnessed status dogs	Aware of dog fighting	Witnessed dog fighting	Aware of status dogs linked to gangs	Aware of dog fighting linked to gangs	Witnessed dog fighting among gangs	Comment
Resident & professional 1	Yes	Yes	Yes		Yes	Yes		
Resident 2, resident 3	Yes	Yes	Yes	Yes, Yes	Yes	Yes	Yes, Yes	Both have seen chain rolling and heard more organised dog fights
Resident 4	Yes	Yes	Yes	Yes	Yes	Yes	Yes	Chain rolling been seen often
Resident 5	Yes	Yes	Yes	Yes	Yes	Yes	Yes	
Professional 2	Yes	Yes	Yes		Yes	Yes		
Professional 3	Yes	Yes	Yes		Yes	Yes		
Professional 4	Yes	Yes	Yes		Yes	Yes		
Professional 5	Yes	Yes	Yes		Yes	Yes		Notes evidence of drug dealers using dogs too
Professional 6	Yes	Yes	Yes		Yes	Yes		
Police 1	Yes	Yes	Yes		Yes	Yes		Notes Pit bulls have been shot in the borough
Police 2	Yes	Yes	Yes		Yes	Yes		Seen Pit bull type dogs on raids of offenders homes
Police 3	Yes	Yes	Yes		Yes	Yes		Dog fighting exists but it appears to be in decline
Police 4	Yes	Yes	Yes		Yes	Yes		Dog fighting exists but it appears to be in decline
Police 5, police 6	Yes	Yes	Yes	Yes, Yes	Yes	Yes	Yes	Have both seen chain rolling
Police 7	Yes	Yes	Yes		Yes	Yes		
Gang-affiliated YP1	Yes	Yes	Yes		Yes	Yes		
Gang-affiliated YP2	Yes	Yes	Yes	Yes	Yes	Yes	Yes	Dog fighting exists but it appears to be in decline
Gang-affiliated YP3	Yes	Yes	Yes	Yes	Yes	Yes	Yes	
Gang-affiliated YP4	Yes	Yes	Yes	Yes	Yes	Yes	Yes	
Gang-affiliated YP	Yes	Yes	Yes	Yes	Yes	Yes	Yes	Family member attacked by gang dogs
Gang-affiliated YP	Yes	Yes	Yes	Yes	Yes	Yes	Yes	
Gang-affiliated YP	Yes	Yes	Yes	Yes	Yes	Yes	Yes	
Gang-affiliated YP	Yes	Yes	Yes		Yes	Yes		
Gang-affiliated YP	Yes	Yes	Yes		Yes	Yes		

The coding analysis used to categorise each respondent is set out in Chapter One.

Of the 33 owner/handler respondents successfully completing interviews, only two kept their dogs solely as pets or companions. No other latent reason could be identified for their owning a dog.

Of the respondents analysed, 18 respondents were identified as having dogs to convey status (54%); seven for protection[21] (21%); one for status/protection (3%); one for breeding (3%); two for breeding/status (6%); one for dog fighting (3%); and two for breeding/dog fighting (6%).

A total of 21 respondents (64%) were associated with status functions, four (12%) with breeding functions, and three (9%) with dog-fighting functions.

The majority of respondents using dogs for protection were female (five out of seven) and all of these respondents were aged between 28 and 60 years of age.

One woman felt embarrassed by how members of the public viewed her:

> 'When I walk him [an SBT] I see people clearing out of the way 'cos they think he's vicious. He pulls on his lead and his eyes go bloodshot so they bulge and he looks worse than he is. You see everybody clearing the pavement and I go, "Oh sorry," it's embarrassing.' (Mature female, Norwood Park, Lambeth)

In contrast, only five of the 21 total respondents using dogs for a status function were female and all of these were aged under 18 years. The breeds used for protection were overwhelmingly SBTs. Two respondents owned a rottweiler and an American bulldog, respectively. The men who used dogs for protection were considerably older than average, aged between 35 and 40 years. These findings concur with findings from interviews with practitioners and professional staff, in other words that women tend to acquire such dogs for protection.

The breeds used for status were see below predominantly pitbulls, SBTs or pitbull and SBT crosses:

> 'I got 'em 'cos I like 'em dogs. They are powerful. This one, Killer, will go for anything. He doesn't like other dogs. Other people don't like 'em dogs. They get out of the way. This dog will take you out. He is really powerful. Muscular. When he gets angry, he's scary, man. Them's tough them dogs.' (Male, Harmsworth Memorial Animal Hospital, with pitbull–Staffie cross)

Other breeds such as the bull mastiff and American bulldog were used, along with two crosses, both of which involved bull breeds. Those seeking to use aggressive breeds to acquire status were mostly men aged 16-30 years. Women in this category were aged 12-17 years. This finding concurs with the findings from interviews with practitioners and professional staff, namely that bull breeds and mastiffs are most commonly used by those seeking status, and that young people aged 12-30 years are most likely to use dogs to convey status. It was common to hear such assurances as, "He's got a bit of pitbull in him, but he's harmless."

The observation by the interviewer that some people seem to try to make their dogs look even bigger and more menacing drew the following response:

> 'Yeah, that's what we are doing with him. We feed him meat, mince and things like that. We boil it down so it dries out, no seasoning 'cos it can make 'em sick. He'll eventually bulk up. This is the fur he will grow into when he gets bigger.' (Young females, Northbrook Park, Lewisham, with a pitbull described as a Staffie cross)

The breeds identified as being used for breeding and/or dog fighting were either pitbulls or SBTs. (The five pitbulls in this category were all owned by one person.) Those involved were all male aged 17-29. This finding concurs with the findings from interviews with practitioners and professional staff.

> 'I just got an 11-week-old Staffie pup, its good colouring. I'm goin' to use him as stud for breeding. I had four other Stafffies all rescued from Battersea Cats and Dogs Home. They were expensive to keep. You feed 'em red meat if you want 'em bigger.' (Male, Lewisham)

> 'I'm looking to breed her if I can find a match. Have been offered opportunities. I could get up to £2,000 for a purebred akita pup.' (Male, Lambeth, with pitbull/akita cross)

Dog fighting was positively identified with one respondent and strongly suspected with two others:

'He eats a lot, cost £40 a week. He eats meat and tripe to build him up and make him stronger. He will bulk out much more. They get a lot of muscle on them – it makes them look more fierce. He's had a lot of fights with other dogs. Nothing organised though – just fights with other boys. Mostly with Staffies. They tend to fight their own, you see, he doesn't bother other dogs.' (Male, Lewisham)

The breeds involved here were pitbulls, akitas and SBTs. Respondents were male aged 25-30 years. This concurs with the findings from interviews with practitioners and professional staff.

Many of the respondents were aware of the controversy regarding status dogs. Those categorised as using the dog as a pet/companion or for protection – personal or domestic – were keen to distance themselves from this debate and criticised those who would seek to use their animals in this way.

Of those categorised as using their dogs to acquire status, a small number stressed the positive attributes of their dogs and clearly cared for them. Their dogs were well groomed and healthy.

'He's such a beautiful dog, lovely coloured coat and very healthy, I just love him. He's very passive.' (Male, with Staffie cross)

Others, however, clearly could barely handle or control their dogs and had little or no identifiable relationship with the animal:

'I've got a rottweiler/Staffie cross who's eight years old and since he's been neutered, instead of getting quieter, he's got wilder. He's an absolute nutter. I can't bring him to hospital, they have to sedate him out here. He's lost the plot. He's so aggressive to people and dogs, and I can't take him to the park. I only exercise him in my garden.' (Female, Harmsworth Memorial Animal Hospital)

One respondent demonstrated the lengths to which some are prepared to go to acquire a status dog when he revealed he had illegally imported his akita:

'I got her from Turkey. You can get 'em from there, they are much cheaper. You can do it all legal and they'll give you all the papers 'n' stuff. You don't have to put 'em in quarantine when you bring 'em back. You can pick up papers in Turkey to avoid all that.' (Male, Harmsworth Memorial Animal Hospital)

Some owners were aware of the stigma attached to certain breeds:

'He's four years old, had him since a puppy. Has to go to vet for an injection. He goes through a lot of food and he's expensive to keep but he's a good guard dog. He has a bit of pit in him, but I probably shouldn't say that and I keep that quiet, you know.' (Female, on tube train, with pitbull–Staffie cross)

Findings from the focus group

To consider further the issue of dog fighting and how it relates to the typology, I conducted a focus group (August 2010) of four Asian boys aged 16 to 17 years. All four owned aggressive dogs, including an American bulldog, a bull mastiff, an akita and several different types of pitbull. One boy (17 years) was both a breeder and a dog fighter. The others owned aggressive dogs but did not purposefully fight them. The boys displayed both impressive knowledge and surprising gullibility and ignorance about their dogs. They were very knowledgeable about dog fighting, but also clearly believed several urban myths.

For these boys, it was clear that protection also meant the potential to attack people:

Interviewer: 'Why do people have pits, Staffies and rotties?'

A: 'They're good guard dogs.'

B: 'They are vicious and aggressive. It's for when you get into rows with people, most people tend to use their dogs.'

Interviewer: 'To protect themselves or to set upon someone else?'

B: 'Both of these things. It's the same thing, both of them.'

There was a shared belief that it was both possible and easy to alter dog's physical characteristics:

'You can get all that stuff done to dogs, cut off the tail, you can expand the jaw, do all that kind of stuff, but it's not healthy for the dog.'

'Some people inject their dog with steroids. They put it in their head and their skulls split. Then the dogs go mad and will only obey the trainer.'

'People do genetics and try to breed pitbulls with lions 'n' stuff. They do all this breeding in different countries, it makes them really vicious.'

The 17-year-old boy bred red-nosed pitbulls with his uncle. Out of a litter of 16, 13 survived. Female dogs were sold for £600 and males for £400. Five dogs with rare colouring were sold for £650 each. A total of £7,250 was realised from this litter. This respondent had breeding books and downloaded information from the internet.

Another boy had an akita that was soon to be mated and bred, with an estimated value of £2,000 per puppy:

'That's what a lot of people do though, if you ain't using your dog for guarding or protection, it's basically just for money.'

The boys were aware of people feeding raw meat to their dogs in order to make them bigger. Although some of the dogs owned were illegal, the boys displayed both a limited and keen understanding of the law:

'When I go out I put muzzles on 'em, so that's allowed innit?'

'Well you don't really say they are pitbulls, you say they are bulldogs or cross-breeds.'

The respondents realised the need to bond with the dogs, while they are still puppies, and those who failed to do so often failed to control them. Dogs were sometimes given away when they got older and were considered to be "too much hassle". One boy gave one of his pitbulls to a friend to look after. The friend then entered in a dog fight in Bradford and the dog died: "I thought it was going to a good home...."

All the boys had attended organised professional dog fights in large warehouses in downtown Bradford as spectators. Two had attended dog fights on farms outside Bradford. They were aware of dog-fighting videos on the internet and knew of Michael Vick, one of the most famous professional players of American football in the US. They were also aware of Asian men fighting their dogs in Bradford's Lister Park at night. The dog's size was thought to be crucial to its value as a potential fighting dog. The boys suggested that a prize blue- or red-nose pitbull ready for fighting could be sold to a fighter for up to £10,000. Such sales were said to happen on big farms outside Bradford. In the Bradford warehouse matches attended by the boys, five matches were typically viewed in one evening, with over 150 people attending, including women. Mixed matches between different breeds often took place, for example, an akita versus a rottweiler. None of the boys said he had enjoyed the experience.

Various myths about dogs went unquestioned, with one respondent commenting: "All American pitbulls have jaw locks. You can't get 'em off." Resolutions included throwing water on the dogs, and poking their eyes. Kicking was considered pointless.

In terms of status dogs, several different narratives were evident:

> 'Whenever there is a beef and fights and stuff, if it's the worst case then people will bring their dogs.'

> 'It's just, like, to get the owner bigger and more respect or something.'

> 'It's a fashion in a way ... but you also get respect.'

In terms of cultural influences, all the boys had heard of rap and hip hop stars renowned for owning pitbulls, such as DMX and Snoop Dog:

> 'Most rappers are involved, like Giggs, he did a video with six or seven of his dogs in the video, he's from Southwark.'

It was evident that the respondents looked after their dogs and they also had clear views about how dogs interacted with humans:

> 'Always buy a dog as a puppy to build up trust, 'cos later you don't know what they are thinking and they can "switch out" on you, as in attack you.'

> 'I got jumped once by a gang of boys who tried to rob me and my dog jumped up and bit him on the balls.'

Table 5.3: Type and number of previous convictions of those with dogs seized under Operation Navarra, Lambeth, July 2009

	Address 1 / Occupant 1	Occupant 2	Address 2	Address 3	Address 4	Address 5	Address 6	Address 7	Address 8
Ethnicity					African Carribbean				
Conviction									
ABH			2						
Assault						1			
Assaulting police		1							
Attempted robbery				1					
Breach of Order		2				1	3		2
Breach of Bail Order		1	5			1			1
Common assault		1				1			
Criminal damage			2						
Driving without insurance		1							
Failure to comply with order		1							
Fraud									4
Handling stolen goods									
Making a false statement					1		1		
Justice								1	
Possession of cannabis	2	2				2	4		
Possession of Class A drugs			2				1		
Possession with intent to supply							2		
Obstructing police			1						
Robbery				1					
Shoplifting			6	1					2
Theft from person									
Threat to kill									1

Police identity codes are based on perceived ethnic identity. These are listed in the following ways:

IC1   White person

IC2   Mediterranean/Hispanic person

IC3   African/Afro-Caribbean person

IC4   Pakistani, Indian, Nepalese, Maldavian, Sri Lankan, Bangladeshi, or other (South) Asian person

IC5   Chinese, Japanese or South-East Asian person

IC6   Arabic, Egyptian, Tunisian, Algerian or Maghreb person

IC9   Roma, Romany, or Gypsy person

IC0   Origin unknown

Table 5.4: Type and number of previous convictions of those with dogs seized under Operation Colverin, London Borough of Greenwich, April 2010

Conviction	Address 1 Occupant 1	Address 1 Occupant 2	Address 2	Address 3	Address 4	Address 5	Address 6	Address 7	Address 8	Address 9
Ethnicity	White	White	White	African or African-Caribbean	White	White	African or African-Caribbean	African or African-Caribbean	White	White
ABH							1	4	1	
Assault				1					1	
Assaulting police				1				1		
Attempted murder				1				1		
Attempted robbery										
Breach of Order								2		10
Breach of Bail Order										
Common assault				1		1	2	2	2	
Criminal damage						1	1	3		
Driving without insurance	1			1				9	1	
Failure to comply with order										
Fraud								3	2	
Handling stolen goods	1						1	3		
Making a false statement										
Perverting the course of justice										
Possession of cannabis					1		1	1	4	
Possession of Class A drugs				1			2	1		
Possession with intent to supply							2	2	1	
Obstructing police										
Offensive weapon							1	2	2	
Robbery		1		1	1	1	1	1		
Shoplifting		1						1		
Theft from person	1						1	2		
Threat to kill										

Different breeds were grouped according to function:

> 'Some people like rottweilers, they keep 'em 'cos they are guard dogs. Anyone in the UK will have them as guard dogs.'

> 'Pitbulls are mostly fighting dogs. People buy 'em and fight 'em. That what it's all about.'

> 'Dobermans are running dogs, you can't outrun them.'

> 'Staffies are just pets.'

The respondents had all witnessed aggressive dogs attacking other dogs or other animals such as cats: "We saw a pitbull rip off a cats head." They were protective and caring of their own animals but realised that other owners often mistreated their dogs. They were hugely knowledgeable about different breeds and their capabilities and talked for over 90 minutes about breeds and their functions, characteristics and abilities, in ways that were similar to boys discussing the functions and capabilities of sports cars.

Links to criminality

Much of the debate surrounding aggressive dogs, dangerous dogs and bull breeds has been about their potential connectivity to criminality. However, between 2001 and 2006, only 69 cases recorded on the MPS CRIS involved people being investigated for offences under the DDA 1991. Of these, only 11 recorded the dog as being used as a weapon in the commission of other offences (MPS, 2007). Prior to 2011, CRIS did not 'flag' the role of dogs in the commission of a crime. This fact further compromises data quality and suggests serious underrecording of such incidents.

I thus undertook further research to determine what evidence exists to suggest that those owning dangerous dogs as defined by section 1 of the (DDA 1991) are likely to have a criminal offending history. This research study involved identifying police forces that had recently undertaken targeted operations to seize such S.1 dogs and negotiating the offender profiles of the dogs' owners. Forces approached included the Metropolitan Police Service (Lambeth, Greenwich, Ealing, Merseyside Police Service and West Midlands Police Service. The results of this study are are discussed in the following section and summarised in Tables 5.3 to 5.5.

Metropolitan Police Service, Lambeth – Operation Navarra

In July 2009, the MPS SDU undertook Operation Navarra to raid 12 homes, using 60 officers to target known gang members and seize 20 dangerous dogs. Sergeant McParland, acknowledging an increase in young men using dogs as weapons, described it as an operation "targeting gang members using dogs in violence and crime". Table 5.3 illustrates the type and number of previous convictions of those who had their dogs seized. The nine arrestees had 62 previous convictions between them, the most common being for drugs offences and for breach of an order.

Operation Colverin, Greenwich

Operation Colverin was a joint operation between the MPS SDU and Greenwich police, undertaken in 2010 in response to local residents' concerns and to intelligence from partnerships with social housing managers and the RSPCA. It involved 35 officers using 15 search warrants over two days, during which time police arrested nine people, including seven for owning pitbulls. Fifteen dogs were seized in total. One owner had elaborate training equipment on his premises, including cattle prods. The arrestees had a total of 91 convictions between them, with one individual responsible for 37 offences. Five of the nine arrestees had previous convictions for drugs, six for robbery, five for common assault and one for attempted murder (Table 5.4).

Metropolitan Police Service, Ealing

Following the involvement of the MDP gang in two serious incidents (see Chapter Four), the Ealing police gang unit worked closely with the MPS SDU and targeted strategic and operation activity towards gangs. Ealing police worked closely with MPS SDU between March 2009 and April 2010 to tackle gang activity in the borough, with the following results:[22]

- the seizure of 66 status dogs linked directly to gangs and violence;
- the identification of gang members from film footage of them fighting dogs;
- the seizure of a pitbull from a suspect arrested for serious assault;
- the recovery of a quarter of a kilo of heroine as a result of linking gang members to dogs;
- the seizure of three pitbulls from a driver arrested for possession of drugs with intent to supply;

Table 5.5: Type and number of previous convictions of those with dogs seized in Merseyside, April–September 2011

	1	2	3	4	5	6	7	8	9	10	11	12	13	14	15	16	17	18	19	20	21	22	23	24	25
Ethnicity (W = White; A/AC = African/African Caribbean)	W	W	W	W	W	W	W	W	W	W	W	A/AC	W	W	W	W	W	W	W	W	W	W	W	W	W
Conviction																									
ABH	–										–							–							
Assault	–	–		–		–			–							–		–			–	–	–		
Assaulting police					–													–							
Attempted robbery						–																			
Breach of Order	–					–				–															
Breach of Bail Order																					–	–	–		
Common assault	–	–						–		–												–			–
Criminal damage				–	–			–	–	–						–									
Driving without insurance	–	–		–										–		–			–		–		–		–
Failure to comply with order		–		–	–							–					–		–			–			
Fraud							–																		
Handling stolen goods																–									
Making a false statement																									
Perverting the course of justice																									
Possession of cannabis	–	–	–		–					–		–							–	–		–			–
Possession of Class A drugs	–	–	–		–							–							–			–			–
Possession with intent to supply	–										–											–			
Obstructing police	–						–																		
Offensive weapon												–								–					
Robbery																	–		–	–					
Shoplifting	–				–		–		–		–					–			–				–	–	–
Theft from person																								–	
Threat to kill																							–		

- the seizure of two pitbulls while executing a drugs warrant and two pitbulls while making arrests for other offences;
- the arrest of gang members for animal cruelty.

Merseyside Police Service

Merseyside police reviewed the cases of 25 individuals who had their dogs seized under section 1 of the DDA 1991 from April 2011 to September 2011 (see Table 5.5). Of these, 23 had a total of 87 previous convictions between them. Eleven individuals (44%) had convictions for driving without insurance and 11 (44%) had convictions for shoplifting. Ten individuals (40%) had convictions for drugs and over one third (35%) had convictions for assault.

The propensity of the owners of seized dogs to have a criminal profile led Merseyside Police Service to consider whether this criminal activity extended to other family members and domestic household occupants:

> 'In the past we dealt with only that owner alone. Now we consider any criminality links at all in the house. That is important. Owner may be OK but son may be a gun crime nominal and he is the one who walks it – or it is really his, more likely. It is very common.' (Police officer, Merseyside)

Police officers working on issues of dangerous dogs report that they are increasingly undertaking joint police operations in relation to drugs, firearms and gangs:

> 'We have all our teams, from different forces. Basically they're looking at drugs, organised crime and criminality, gun crime and we are tying in to them now all the time, and it's becoming more and more regular that if you are on earlies, you are going to be on a raid with someone. In there with your shield and fire extinguisher trying to drive that dog back from the door so others can get in, hopefully, to get some evidence.' (Police officer, Merseyside)

The dog unit is working alongside the regional gun crime team and the Serious Organised Crime Agency to check owners' links to major crime groups or other criminal activities. Operations for dog seizures are increasingly subject to complex planning arrangements.

West Midlands Police Service

Research analysis was conducted on the number of prohibited dogs seized by West Midlands police in 2010 whose owners had previous convictions for drugs, violence, weapons and assault.[23] During 2010, officers seized 147 prohibited dogs, of which 21 were stray and no owner located. A total 47 of the 126 dogs whose owners were known were owned by individuals with no previous convictions for the aforementioned offences.

Of the 126 known owners, 79 had previous convictions in the categories listed. Twenty-four of these individuals were under 25 years of age; 38 were aged between 25 and 34; and the remaining 15 were over 35 years of age. In terms of ethnicity, 44 of the 79 individuals were white, 26 were black and 9 were Asian. Sixty-one individuals were male and 18 were female. The offending history profile of those 79 individuals with convictions indicates that the majority (70%) had at least one conviction for drugs offences (55); 53% (42) had at least one conviction for assault; 49% (39) had at least one conviction for violence; and 11% (nine) had at least one conviction for weapons offences. In terms of multiple offending, 63% (50) had more than one conviction. Of the 79 individuals, 25% (20) had at least one conviction for drugs, violence, weapons or assault; 35% (28) had at least two convictions; 24% (19) had at least three convictions; and 3% (three) had four or more convictions.

Links to drugs

One of the main reasons for gangs using dangerous, illegal or aggressive dogs is the protection of entrepreneurial businesses relating to illegal drugs. This takes a number of different forms.

First, dogs may be offered as personal protection for street dealers and 'shotters' as they transport drugs and money from stash to the street and vice versa: "Yeah bruv, a dog will keep you from getting any hassle, a big 'un, a mastiff" (gang 'younger', London).

Second, dogs may be used to guard the stash or drugs 'fortress':

> 'You have your dog there as well, a key-purse safe to make sure that if anything goes wrong you can rely on the dog, maybe 'cause you can't have the gun. It's basically another way of having a weapon without having a weapon.' (Gang 'elder', London, cited in Harding, 2012)

If the 'serving' of drugs is undertaken from the same house as the stash, the dog is not necessarily considered 'good for business'. Many visiting clients will not care for dogs and it is not wise to make them feel uncomfortable. Others may use the dog to sit on the money stash so that only the dog's owner can entice the dog to move aside. Dogs may also be left unguarded on the premises:

> 'It's also used as a minder for the premises. You do get flats with furniture in them and a stash of drugs is left there. The dog then guards it and never actually leaves the premises. It just shits and pisses through the floorboards. The dog's life revolves around staying in the flat and protecting whatever is stashed there. The dealer won't live there – 'cos the dealer will want as few links as possible to him and his work. He'll have a warehouse, a lock-up or flat and the dog is there purely to protect his money or drugs or weapons.' (Police officer, West Midlands)

Third, gang members may train bull breeds to act as roaming guards to protect drug cultivation or large-scale hydroponics. In a raid on an address in Croydon suspected of being a cannabis factory, police found eight pitbulls and eight other dogs being bred as fighting dogs.[24]

> 'Guarding hydroponics we've had before – guarding a big shed of plants in Bellvale area of Liverpool and two pitbulls roaming this brilliantly constructed shed, all mesh. This is at the back of a normal house. So yes, here we are struggling to get the pitbull issue away from the criminal issue.' (Police officer, Merseyside)

Police and gang members confirmed in interviews that the presence of bull breeds in drug houses is effective for two reasons:

- to slow up any police entry; and
- to prevent other dealers or gang members from raiding their stash.

GLA report

In November 2009, the London Deputy Mayor, Kit Malthouse, hosted a working breakfast for agencies on weapon dogs in London to highlight the issue and discuss potential responses. Later that month, the Greater London Authority (GLA) produced a report entitled *Weapon dogs –*

the situation in London (GLA, 2009). The report notes that London was experiencing 'a serious rise in the number of dangerous and status dogs. These are increasingly being used in crime and as weapons for intimidation – "weapon" dogs' (p 3). The report states: 'Causing fear or intimidation by having a powerful-looking dog is one of the reasons for the increase in "weapon dogs" among young people' (p 4). It should be noted that the term 'weapon dog' is used throughout the report to denote a dog used for the purposes of intimidation.

In January 2011, the GLA agreed a motion for immediate action to deal with the problem and pledged support for a review of legislation and tougher penalties for owners.

Gang injunctions

In 2011, the UK government introduced gang injunctions via the Policing and Crime Act 2009 as a tool to deal with serious gang violence. Their use enables local authorities and the police to impose civil prohibition orders on individuals to tackle gang violence. These prohibitions, which are similar to antisocial behaviour orders, act as an injunction that can result in imprisonment if breached. Prohibitions may include preventing gang members being in charge of an animal in a public place, if it has been proven that the gang member has engaged in, encouraged or assisted gang-related violence.

Summary of findings from primary data

The research undertaken for this study confirms the typology of five main categories of motivation for owning aggressive or illegal dogs:

* pet/family companion
* protection – personal or domestic
* status – fashion
* status – entrepreneurial by breeding or dog fighting (professional circuit)
* status – image and identity, sometimes by chain rolling.

Other findings are as follows:

* Status dogs are commonly visible across numerous London parks, and were witnessed by the researcher in 48% of parks visited and reported by the public in 85% of parks visited.

- Mature women are those most likely to use aggressive breeds for protection. Men who own dogs for this reason are also likely to be mature (aged 35–40 years).
- Young men aged 16–30 years are most likely to use dogs to convey status. Females involved in this category were aged 12 to 17 years. Bull breeds and mastiffs were the most common breeds for this function.
- Those using aggressive breeds for entrepreneurial purposes of breeding were all male aged between 17 and 29 years.
- Some dogs used to convey status were well presented, groomed and well cared for with very proud owners.
- Many dogs had been 'gifted' or acquired from friends and others purchased from the internet. Those who had dogs as pets/companion and for protection had a better sense of the dog's history and background. Of those using dogs to acquire status, only those who had owned the dog since it was a pup had this knowledge. Several of those with status dogs were unclear, unable or unwilling to give an account of the dog's background.
- Dogs categorised as pets/companions or for protection had good temperaments and were better socialised than dogs used for other reasons. Dogs used to convey status often had difficult temperaments and could not be touched (with the exception of those who were well groomed).
- Some respondents were eager to discuss breeding and fighting early in the conversation. Others were quick to identify the function of the dog as providing them with a sense of status. These respondents valued and praised the attributes of the dog in ways that would elevate status.
- Owner/handlers who were having a dog for status and also dog fighting were reticent to give any details.
- Those categorised as using dogs to acquire status often hid the true breed at the start of the interview, only to later reveal it was in fact really a proscribed dog, adding quickly, "I shouldn't really admit to that."
- Some dogs are 'traded up', like mobile phones.
- Dog fighting was not commonly reported but clearly took place. Different levels of dog fighting were distinguishable from the interviews.

Comparative analysis with other primary research

Comparative analysis with other research into this topic is limited, as few other studies exist. One recent contribution is that undertaken by Maher and Pierpoint (2011). In this study, 25 youths were interviewed across a range of unspecified urban locations in south Wales. The study used detached youth workers to access 'hard-to-reach dog owners', although both animal owners and non-animal owners participated in the research. Three focus groups were undertaken and five individual interviews. In addition, seven practitioners were interviewed. Over half the 25 youth respondents identified themselves as gang-affiliated.[25] An unspecified number of the youths were dog owners and 19 dogs, mainly STBs, were owned by the youths. The youths claimed that friends owned a further 73 dogs (of which the majority were bull mastiffs, SBTs or American bulldogs, although this was not verified by the authors and the dogs were not viewed). The number of friends referred to was also unspecified.

The authors' report detailed the activities of nine youths (36%) who were involved in animal abuse, including cruel training techniques, abandonment, neglect, withholding medical treatment, poor breeding practices, lack of exercise or socialisation, drowning the runt of a litter, kicking stabbing or beating dogs and chopping off dogs' tails. Dog fighting, chain rolling and other animal abuse were also identified.

Maher and Pierpoint talk of 'active' abuse – intentional and direct harm, such as docking tails, stabbing and beating. Passive abuse is identified as 'behaviours which result in abuse, but is not intended or direct' (pp 412-13), such as drowning puppies, harsh discipline/training, neglect or withholding medical care. Here, they claim abusers may recognise the behaviour as cruel. Dogs, they claim, were more likely to be victims of 'passive abuse' than other animals, which were more likely to suffer 'active abuse'. No figures are given to support this conclusion. The distinctions, however, are unconvincing and the categories are human-centric, that is, derived from the perspective of the abuser and whether or not they believe their behaviour is abusive. The supporting quotation to this conclusion illustrates a runt of a litter being drowned for its lack of monetary value. The authors fail to identify the financial imperative behind many of the abusive actions and fail to identify this line of argument as central to any discussion regarding status dogs. 'Passive', as a descriptor, also implies a lack of agency on behalf of the abuser, which is not the case.

A more practical categorisation might instead relate to forms of abuse having a direct physical impact on the animal, for example, stabbing, beating or docking, or actions having an indirect physical impact on the animal, such as poor socialising. This categorisation, which favours the animal perspective, reveals the majority of the abuse to be 'active', using the authors' terminology.

Maher and Pierpoint also note that dogs may be shared among group/ gang members. This important finding is, however, misrecognised by Maher and Pierpoint. This was also an important finding from my research study, which identified that dogs are 'shared' or 'pooled' for various reasons:

- insufficient domestic space;
- lack of proper socialising, meaning that the dog is unsuitable to stay in a family home;
- lack of empathy towards the dog, leading some families to view it as a 'yard dog' and not a family pet. This view is common among Asian families, but may also signify that the dog is being used for other purposes, for example, to enhance status or for dog fighting (see Chapter Six). In addition, the dog may be illegal and thus moving it from house to house is an attempt to conceal its true ownership;
- financial cost sharing, for example, 'gang dogs', where several members club together to purchase the animal.

In addition, dogs may be owned by one family, but fought by someone else, so that it can recover from its wounds at one home before returning to another.

The key issue arising from these potential scenarios is that any dog moved frequently across a variety of owners, experiencing varied environments and varied and erratic discipline, will be badly socialised and and ill tempered. Eventually such dogs will be almost impossible to keep domestically inside the family home due to its poor socialisation. Such dogs are then often abandoned or neglected when group/gang members cannot agree whose responsibility it is to care for the dog or finance any treatment required. This lack of socialisation further elevates the potential risk of holding, owning or managing that dog – especially in a public place. Once abandoned, such dogs pose a risk to the public or to the welfare agencies and authorities charged with taking it in.

Maher and Pierpoint also state the 'reason that most youths gave for dog ownership was for companionship and/or socialising with friends' (p 414). Two issues arise here. The research fails to identify whether or not the youths were gang-affiliated and the nature of the socialising and companionship is unclear. What is also interesting is that 11 out of 25 respondents (44%) did not mention this as their main reason for owning a dog. Maher and Pierpoint only briefly allude to the fact such dogs may play a part in building social capital (see Chapter Four of this book). This function, whereby dogs are 'seen by youths as companions and as playing a role in socialising' (p 414), is seen by the authors as an 'intrinsic function' of the ownership (Beverland et al, 2008), as opposed to an 'extrinsic' function, such as behaviour that earns rewards and acknowledgment from others. This is misrecognised by Maher and Pierpoint. Where the latent (or primary) function of the dog is to acquire status this is, by Beverland et al's, definition, an 'extrinsic' function. Socialising with the dog provides an opportunity for the owner/handler to elevate his status among his peer group or gang. Thus rewards are both sought and gained. Such is the power and authority conveyed by the aggressive breed that in any socialising event the dog will be the centre of attention. Socialising therefore is purely on the terms of the owner/handler of the dog. It becomes his opportunity to lead and dictate the action, for example, where the group goes and how to get there. Socialising will most likely still occur if the dog is absent. The presence of the dog permits the individual to gain/acquire further advantage and reward through socialising. This fact is not well articulated by respondents in their study and is not addressed by Maher and Pierpoint.

Maher and Pierpoint acknowledge that youth in gangs will offer protection to the dog and that mutual trust and loyalty exists as a 'unique bond' between dog and owner (p 414). Moreover, they identify dogs being used as weapons; 11 out of 25 (44%) youth respondents acknowledged using their dogs as weapons in this way. In addition, six respondents (24%) used their dogs in chain rolling or dog fighting. Entertainment was identified as the main reason for this, although it is unlikely the authors explored transactional relationships here or considered that this activity may be used to settle arguments/debts. In a small-scale study such as theirs, it is arguable that these figures are really quite high. Notwithstanding the small sample, the percentages involved are relatively high, and it could be argued that the relevance of these figures is underplayed

Significantly, the figures indicate that in south Wales in 2010/11, youths who were both gang-affiliated and non-gang-affiliated were using dogs to acquire status in their peer groups, and engaging in a wide range of animal abuse and in organised dog fighting and chain rolling. A significant percentage (44%) were using dogs as weapons.

My own research study did not specifically enquire whether dogs were used a weapons, although this information was sometimes volunteered by respondents. It is thus not possible to compare these findings with those of Maher and Pierpoint.

Is status dog ownership linked to deviant behaviours?

Clearly, it would be wrong to claim that all owners of status dogs are inclined towards, or participate in, criminal behaviours. However, the survey evidence indicates that status dogs are favoured by some criminals. Having considered motivations for ownership, it is evidently possible that status dogs, notably aggressive bull breeds, can be attractive to criminal elements. For some, this raises the question, do owners of status dogs exhibit a propensity for criminality, violent or aggressive behaviour? Such research remains outstanding in the UK, although a number of recent studies have been conducted in the US.

For example, Barnes and colleagues (2006) examined the association between ownership of high-risk ('vicious') dogs and the presence of deviant behaviours in the owners as indicated by court convictions. In this study, dogs were classified as 'vicious' by breed (bull breeds) or by action (having bitten or attacked a person or animal). Analysis showed that owners of high-risk (vicious) dogs had significantly more criminal convictions than owners of licensed low-risk dogs, 'Findings suggest that ownership of a high-risk (vicious) dog can be a significant marker for general deviance and should be an element considered when assessing risk for child endangerment' (Barnes et al, 2006: 1616).[26] The results found that owners of high-risk dogs had 'significantly more criminal convictions and traffic citations in all categories except crimes involving children' (p 1626), and that ownership of a high-risk dog 'is a much stronger predictor of criminal convictions, specifically aggressive convictions, than gender and licensed status combined' (pp 1629-30).

Elsewhere, Arluke and colleagues (1999) examined links between animal abuse and subsequent violence against humans. They found that rather than animal abuse necessarily leading to violence against humans, it is one of many antisocial and deviant behaviours adopted by perpetrators, including both personal and property crimes.[27]

The results of the Barnes et al study was supported by research undertaken by Ragatz et al (2009) in their study of whether owners of 'vicious' dogs differed from non-owners in terms of antisocial behaviours and personality.[28] The findings revealed that type of dog ownership made a 'significant difference in criminal behaviour' (Ragatz et al, 2009: 699). According to findings, owners of vicious dogs were significantly more likely to admit to violent criminal behaviour when compared with owners of large or small dogs, or the control group.

They were also more likely to engage in a wider variety of criminal behaviour, including violent, property, drug and status crime, compared with others. When compared with the control group, owners of high-risk vicious dogs scored significantly higher on impulsive sensation seeking. Examining psychopathic traits, 'the owners of high-risk dogs endorsed significantly more characteristics of primary psychopathy (including, carelessness, selfishness and manipulative tendencies) than small dog owners' (Ragatz et al, 2009: 703). No significance difference in secondary psychopathy traits (impulsiveness or self-defeating behaviours) was noted. The authors concluded that the 'research indicates psychopathy is predictive of a greater propensity to commit multiple criminal acts' (p 699). Again the authors find that ownership of 'high-risk vicious' dogs 'may be a simple marker of broader social deviance' (p 703).

Other research has considered links between animal abuse and cruelty and interpersonal violence among humans. Flynn (2011), in a review of the research on connections between animal abuse and interhuman violence, provides a useful summary of recent findings. Findings suggest that :

- Animal cruelty is a symptom of psychological conduct disorder and may also lead to an inhibition or distortion or empathy (Flynn, 2000).
- Animal abuse can be a marker for family violence and is also linked to a variety of interpersonal violence, including bullying, juvenile delinquency, adult violent crimes and other nonviolent crimes (Flynn, 2000).
- Animal abuse can be a more reliable marker of family violence than the reverse (DeGue and DiLillo, 2009).
- Among schoolchildren who abused animals, almost all reported greater exposure to domestic violence (Baldry, 2003).
- Early exposure to animal abuse and committing cruelty alone may be indicative of other forms of antisocial behaviour (Henry, 2004).
- Violent criminals were nearly three times more likely than non-violent criminals to have committed childhood animal cruelty (Merz-Perez et al, 2001).

The US research is limited but informative, and it is notable that there is no comparable UK research. In this absence of this, we must rely on the personal accounts of professionals and practitioners and their interactions with owners, gang-affiliated or otherwise. Such accounts, unless recorded via interview, can lean towards anecdote. Nevertheless, it is possible to collate observations and form a picture of character types.

From around 2007, staff at the Harmsworth Memorial Animal Hospital in north London began to notice an increasing number of diffident young men presenting dogs that had clearly been involved in fighting and displayed multiple injuries

> 'Re the injuries to the dog the owners lie and claim the dog fell down the stairs or was "run over". They also delay seeking treatment – sometimes leaving it four days or up to two weeks later.' (Director, RSPCA Harmsworth Memorial Animal Hospital)

Those presenting with injured dogs are largely young men from inner-city social housing estates. They often have poor social skills, are unable to read, write or sign forms and are often unable to articulate the injuries or how they occurred. They frequently deny the dog is theirs, or use a girlfriend's name when booking in the injured animal for treatment so they cannot be traced or challenged.

> 'Many of these characters who come in are really damaged people. They are abusive of staff. They won't pay the bill upon completion of treatment. They get abusive when the bill is presented to them. They kick off in the waiting room. They often come in late at night. We even had one guy in the waiting room who went berserk in the waiting room. Our other clients locked themselves in the toilet out of fear.' (Director, RSPCA Harmsworth Memorial Animal Hospital)

As a result of threats to staff and other clients, the hospital has increased security over the past five years by installing double-lock doors with an air-lock for receiving animals, desk security screens, CCTV and a security guard.

Staff report that the owners frequently display no empathy for the injured dog, no insight into their role in causing the injuries, or realisation of animal cruelty:

> 'Two weeks ago I had a pitbull-type dog who had lost an eye. I stitched it up. The man was abusive and quite nasty. He walked out without paying his bill. Later the police called me up to say the dog had been taken home and had

attacked him and his girlfriend and had locked its jaws on his girlfriend in their flat in north London. When the police arrived the dog was shot dead along with two others. The woman's arm was hanging off and she needed 10 hours of emergency surgery to save her arm.' (Director, RSPCA Harmsworth Memorial Animal Hospital)

More than one third (36%) of those interviewed by Maher and Pierpoint (2011) acknowledged that their friends and associates abused animals, although youths clearly differentiated between activities they considered cruel (dog fighting and baiting) and not cruel (chain rolling, hitting a dog during training). Although not reviewed by Maher and Pierpoint, neutralisation techniques (see Chapter Six) are also evident among their respondents.

Conclusion

This chapter set out to capture for the first time evidence of the phenomenon of status dogs by obtaining the views of practitioners, professionals and young people who own status dogs such dogs.

It is clear that the issue of status dogs is a real one: certain aggressive and bull breeds of dog are widely used to convey status, mostly by young men aged 16–30. Bull breeds and mastiffs are most commonly used for this purpose. Status dogs can be well groomed or badly socialised, depending on their owners/handlers. These dogs are also used for protection (mostly by mature females) and for entrepreneurial purposes such as breeding and dog fighting (by men). The dog's history is often of little concern to those using the animal as a status dog. Dogs may be gifted and shared among peers, and traded up and discarded or abandoned if they no longer perform their function. Dogs used for protection are usually better socialised than those used for other purposes.

There is evidence of dog fighting and the use of dogs as weapons: pitbulls and pitbull cross-breeds are favoured for this. Fighting, often for money or entertainment, is evident but not commonly reported, although different levels of dog fighting are distinguishable. Breeding, often random breeding, is a further entrepreneurial function for some breeds.

The next chapter looks in some detail at what is involved in a dog fight before examining how dog fighting, as an activity, operates at three distinct levels.

Notes

[1] RSPCA status dog appeal, www.youtube.com, accessed 1 November 2009. (no longer available).

[2] www.rspca.org/archivednews, accessed 31 October 2009 (no longer available).

[3] RSPCA Dangerous Dog Unit leader, Chief Inspector Jan Eachus, quoted in *Streatham Guardian*, 'Three dangerous dog attacks a day in Lambeth', 2 April 2009.

[4] Source: MPS SDU (private correspondence with author).

[5] 'Dangerous dogs seizure and disposal 2008-2010', MPS Publication Scheme, www.met.police.uk/foi.

[6] Source: MPS SDU (private correspondence with author).

[7] Admissions for dog bite/strike 2001/02 to 2008/09 by age group and NHS Trust, Hospital Episode Statistics – Accident and Emergency, www.hesonline. nhs.uk.

[8] 'HES on ...dog bites and strikes', Hospital Episode Statistics Report, 2008, www.hesonline.nhs.uk, accessed 29 August 2011.

[9] James Meikle, 'Rise in A&E cases after dog attacks', *The Guardian*, 28 February 2008, www.guardian.co.uk/society/2008/feb/28/health, accessed 3 November 2009.

[10] 'More than 80 people hurt by "danger dogs"', *Lancashire Evening Post*, 3 February 2010 and 'Danger dogs attacks"are on the rise"' – 2 December 2009.

[11] Aasma Day, 'Dangerous dogs blamed for rise in animal attacks', *Lancashire Evening Post*, 25 July 2008.

[12] 'Shame of city dog fights', *Lancashire Evening Post*, 5 July 2009.

[13] Anika Bourley, '500 left needing treatment after dog attacks', *Bradford Telegraph and Argus*, 31 August 2009.

[14] *Hansard* written answers, Dangerous Dogs: Merseyside, 9 December 2009, column 471W, question raised by Dr Pugh, response by Ann Keen, www. publications.parliament.uk.

[15] BBC News, 'Hundreds treated after dog bites', 31 March 2010, http://news. bbc.co.uk/1/hi/england/merseyside/8597356.stm, accessed 25 April 2012.

[16] *Liverpool Echo*, 'Devil dog amnesty cost taxpayer £160K', 18 June 2007.

[17] *Liverpool Echo*, '14 Pitbulls seized in police raid', 8 January 2008.

[18] *South London Press*, 'Shame of dog-fight borough', 2 June 2009.

[19] Matt Watts, 'Three dangerous dog attacks a day in Lambeth', *Ealing Times*, 2 April 2009.

[20] Safer Lambeth Partnership, 'Lambeth dogs profile', Executive report, September 2009.

[21] Karen Delise notes that 'it is estimated that 40% of the people who obtain dogs, do so with protection in mind' (2002: 6).

[22] Safer Ealing Partnership, 'Dangerous dogs', 11 December 2009; MPA, 'Update on dangerous dogs', 16 September 2010.

[23] The offences were categorised as follows: drugs – possession or supplying of drugs; violence – public disorder, robbery, threats of violence; weapons – possession of any weapon and/or firearm; assault – any offence against the person.

[24] MPS website, 'Croydon police 18 dogs seized by SNT', http://cms.met. police.uk/met, accessed 31 July 2011.

[25] Maher and Pierpoint use the Eurogang definition; see Klein and Maxson (2006).

[26] The study sample consisted of 355 owners of either licensed or cited dogs that represented high- or low-risk breeds.

[27] A study group of 153 convicted animal abusers were compared with a control group of a similar number of non-abusers. When matched for age, gender, area and socioeconomic earnings, the authors found animal abusers were 3.2 times more likely to have a criminal record and 5.3 times more likely to be the perpetrator of a violent crime.

[28] A total of 869 college students completed online questionnaires regarding ownership, criminal behaviours and personality.

SIX

Off the chain: the issue of dog fighting

The past few years has seen an upsurge in the popularity of illegal dog fighting in the UK, as reported by the RSPCA,[1] and also in the US as reported by the Humane Society of the United States (HSUS).[2] It is possible that the increase in both organised dog fighting and 'chain rolling' (impromptu dog fights where dogs are kept on the leash) mirrors the increase in the number, popularity and availability of 'status dogs', although this theory is as yet unproven.

In recent years, dog fighting has been subject of considerable media coverage, but little, if any, academic research. There is scant UK research into what UK dog fighting actually involves, how and when it occurs, who is involved and the nature of their involvement. The evidence base in the UK is also limited, although the data that do exist suggest an increase in dog-fighting activity. Similar trends of increased numbers of dangerous dogs and of dog fighting are reported in the US, Denmark, the Netherlands and Finland.[3] However, any link between dog fighting and UK urban street gangs remains largely unresearched.

This chapter reviews why people get involved in dog fighting, the different levels of illegal dog fighting, and how it links to status dogs, breeding and training. It examines a US typology of dog fighting and considers if this model fits the current UK situation. It also considers the findings from recent UK research before considering whether the evidence supports the suggestion of an increase in, or resurgence of, this activity.

Why do people fight dogs?

One reason given by sociologists for dog fighting is that it represents a way for the dog fighters 'to validate their masculine identities while remaining only on the periphery of actual violence' (Evans et al, 1998: 210). Operating as a 'sport', dog fighting provides an arena of social competition and for 'doing' masculinity by emphasising aggression and violence. Evans and colleagues note that those engaged in the 'sport' of dog fighting refer to their groups as 'fraternities'. From interviews conducted with 31 dogmen, they find that elements of the sport 'represent symbolic attempts at attaining and maintaining honour and status' (Evans et al, 1998: 209) in what is a predominantly white working-class activity in the southern states of the US. In this subcultural world, dogs are viewed as reflections of their owners: 'mean and tough guys have the kind of dogs that [demonstrate] they are men' (Evans et al, 1998: 214). Evans and colleagues (1988) found their respondents hoped that the actions of their dogs would have enduring symbolic value, that is, where the actions of his dogs come to 'display attributes of his own character unseen in other areas of his life' (Evans et al, 1998: 216). This finding, while pertinent for ethnically white, rural, professional dogmen, undoubtedly also resonates with the views expressed by urban and often black or Latino young men in US public housing projects and young men in UK social housing estates.

Solomon (2008), in a study of professional dogmen, argues they struggle to gain respect in a violent subculture (both dogs and men have to fight regularly). As a result, he believes that 'dog fighting as a sub-culture and practice adopts a street orientation' (2008: 70) (see Chapter Four for further discussion on gangs). It is therefore credible that the re-emergence of dog fighting in the US is strongly linked to the emergence of 'street culture', as both retain similar social field values; for example, the pitbull is part of the habitus, the imperative is to compete and fight for respect; and the dog is a symbolic representation of the self.

The University of Chicago and the HSUS interviewed 165 dog fighters in 2008 to examine why young men and boys become involved in dog fighting. Findings include the following:

- the appeal of dog fighting comes from a desire to appear 'tough';
- the image of certain dogs supported the perception of toughness;
- dog fighting was used to work out street conflicts among gang members;
- dog fighting was a means to earn money;
- dog fighting was a reflection of young people's obsession with competition;
- dog fighting was seen as 'exciting' (University of Chicago Survey Lab (2008).

Cultural criminology may also offer some insightful perspectives with regard to dog fighting. Drawing from sociology and criminology, it offers a theoretical approach that places criminality within a cultural context, determining crime as a cultural product. It focuses on situated meanings of crime, rules and transgressions, with particular reference to identity, style, youth culture and the media. While offering an interpretative perspective for understanding youth criminality (Hayward, 2004), it has also been criticised for overly focusing on 'minor' illicit transgressions (Ferrell et al, 2008) and romanticising and embracing marginalised groups (Hall and Winlow, 2007).

Cultural criminologists argue that there are those who seek 'delight in being deviant' (Katz, 1988: 312). Some refer to the 'deviant leisure' pursuits of the oppressed and disposed (Rojek, 1995), while others note a 'quest for excitement [that] is directly related to the breaking of boundaries, of confronting parameters and playing at the margins of social life' (Presdee, 2000: 7).

Some individuals involved in dog fighting relish their role at society's margins, transgressing social boundaries and social norms while seeking to stimulate emotions 'through the pursuit of danger, pleasure and excitement' (Ferrell and Hamm, 1998).

Bahktin (1984) argues that some individuals seek to create 'a second life', away from official monitoring and rationality where people can indulge in activities such as crime (or dog fighting), opening them up to wholly new illicit experiences. This concept certainly fits with Michael Vick, the former Atlanta Falcons quarterback and National Football League (NFL) sport star and multimillionaire convicted of attending dog fights and breeding dogs for fights. Presdee (2000: 8) argues that this 'second festive life [is] expressed through carnival acts'. Dog fighting, either as chain rolling or organised, professional-circuit events, can offer a performance of violence and carnival that, albeit risky and unconstrained, offers 'unscripted drama'.

Dog fighting in the UK and the US can be viewed as largely a transgressive act – one that crashes traditional social norms and boundaries. It is both oppositional and (as with the ownership of aggressive status dogs) also attractive.

Even for spectators of dog fights there exists the possibility of a quick escape from the mundane. This is especially the case with chain rolling, where dog fighting provides an injection of adrenaline in a day that was otherwise exactly the same as yesterday. Gambling takes places spontaneously at such bouts, offering 'heightened pleasures through heightened risks' (Ferrell, Hayward and Young, 2008: 72). This was confirmed by one dog fighter interviewed for the current study:

> 'Gambling, yeah, that's the reason people do [fight] 'em. You can gamble with anyone really but the main man, he's the one who holds the bets. It depends on whose dog it is. If it's your dog and you know your dog is gonna win it, then you put your money on it – maybe about £500. If it wins,

you get the money back and the winnings and the organiser gets his cut.' (Professional UK dog fighter)

Analysing dog fighting from the perspective of cultural criminology offers up two further explanations. First, dog fighting, as a performed event with acts of excess and excitement, can be described as a form of carnival. Dog fighting, or similar events such as joy riding, may therefore be one form of carnival pleasure that is not mass marketed or available through mass entertainment. It perhaps offers something to young people that is not mass produced, but oppositional: a semi-spontaneous opportunity to 'play outside the rules' and seek instant gratification and illicit excitement. It also offers proximity to danger, accident and death. This perhaps highlights the difference between chain rolling and organised dog fighting: the former is more spontaneous, while in the latter, professional 'dogmen' seek to create a 'sport' governed by rules and procedures.

Second, if dog fighting can be considered a carnival event, such events often have an underlying resistance to a hegemonic position. In other words, it suggests not only that those involved in dog fighting enjoy it as a sport, but also that it embodies their view of life, and a life lived through opposition; of 'sticking it to the man', of revelling in acting outside the law, morals and conventions, an observation echoed by Robert Soloman (2008). Subscribers to this view of life are more likely to be those involved in organised, professional-circuit dog fighting rather than youths who 'chain roll' their dogs in local parks or on social housing estates. It is, however, also likely that attempts to challenge or change the behaviour of those who have constructed their 'carnivalesque' life as a 'different way of being' will not be easily dissuaded by reasonable argument that their actions are cruel or inhumane. This insight may prove useful for local authorities and agencies working with young men engaged in this activity.

A darker analysis might suggest that those engaged in dog fighting are taking symbolic revenge on that emblem of family-oriented life, the dog. By forcing dogs to engage in barbaric acts of gladiatorial combat, they somehow undermine the animals' place in society and in family life. For them, the dog does not form part of inclusiveness and contentment, but is used to operate in an excluded world where it is forced to fight for its own survival. This implied narrative has echoes with the lives of many socially excluded young men who feel they too must fight for survival. Dogs may therefore represent an anthropomorphised version of themselves – or perhaps who they would like to be – puffed up, muscular, angry, aggressive, ready to fight to win or survive, using street skill and brute force in a pit not of their own making. This metaphor for life may be unspoken, but for some, pertinent. This narrative is also reflected in the public's perception of status dogs as the embodiment of increasingly visible subterranean values.

Dog fighting foregrounds the brutality of the fight, the skill in opposition, the tenacity of not giving in, of being 'game'. This is the opposite of the nurturing domesticity embodied in the comforting commercial imagery of animals as family pets. For some participants, dog fighting suggests the 'pet in the underworld', a world upside down. A fighting pet embodies anti-establishment social mores – the antithesis of domesticity and conventional values. A pet that will fight for its master will bring honour and then social advancement: a passport to something better (Solomon, 2008).

For young men who chain roll dogs, there may indeed be few opportunities for 'carnival' expression, although drugs, joy-riding, video-gaming are often cited as possibilities (Presdee, 2000; Ferrell, Hayward and Young, 2008). Owning a status dog to set on another dog offers opportunities for staging a spectacle and retaining a position of powerful influence over spectators convened at your convenience. Status is therefore not simply gained or acquired by owning a status dog – it can now be conjured up and orchestrated through an event devised by the owner, who takes centre stage as producer and ringmaster.

In this cultural context, fighting dogs offers a variety of outcomes that have considerable appeal to some young men:

- proximity to danger – death, law, guns drugs, gambling, risk, money, secrecy;
- heightened excitement – gambling, secrecy, hidden venues and last-minute arrangements, the secret society of friends and the exclusive invite-only nature of events;
- oppositional status;
- the clannish nature of a secret society offering bonding social capital;
- an opportunity to build into a 'sport', allowing for upward mobility by skill and dedication and the possibility of reaching the elevated status of dogman. This may be a passport to social status among an elite band of 'brothers' or social circle;
- the vicarious enjoyment of seeing dogs amplified, built up and engaging in combat;
- lure of competition, preparation and so on, which brings purpose and focus to lives;

- identity, either group or individual – the opportunity to construct an identity of opposition, brotherhood and shared understanding of the hard hand that life has dealt.

Dog fight DVDs/videos

A noticeable feature of contemporary dog fighting in the UK, the US and other countries is its interface with modern multimedia technology, which offers opportunities for video filming and then broadcasting imagery. This has created a whole new category of dog-fight spectator or video voyeur. Broadcast as entertainment, these images permit young people to engage in 'leisure-time violence' (Hall and Winlow, 2006). For cultural criminologists, dog-fight DVDs and their ubiquitous social transmission on mobile phones effectively normalise brutal and violent images as entertainment or 'sport', permitting local youth to commission their own personalised audiences (Ferrell et al, 2008).

Images of street chain-rolling fights or organised dog fights, often from outside the UK, are transmitted via personal technologies and often become available on DVD. The spectacle is commodified and packaged for illicit audiences. As cultural criminologist Mike Presdee noted, 'Viewers/voyeurs then act as validation and help to re-commodify the event by viewing it and passing it on as a commercial treat to be enjoyed or discussed' (Presdee, 2000: 54). As images are uploaded, either for mass consumption, or by critics by way of condemnation, they re-enforce commodification.

Others seek only to view dog fights on the internet, 'participating without attending, pleasure without guilt' (Presdee, 2000: 30). However, the addictive nature of the voyeur is such that it encourages a taste for ever-darker images of more violent fights. What participants first view with horror soon becomes normalised and so begins the quest for video clips more explicit and more gruesome than the last – a sort of dog pornography, which no doubt retains its own fans and enthusiasts.

Before examining the links between status dogs and dog fighting or gangs, it is important to have an understanding of what the dog fight entails, who is involved and the different levels of involvement. In considering these aspects, I draw on recent UK evidence.

How dog fighting works

Although dog fighting was a common activity in the UK until 1835 when it was made illegal,[4] it is to the US we need to look for current dog-fighting literature. The US also has a long history of illegal dog

Table 6.1: Dog-fighting vocabulary

Term	Meaning
Ace	A pit dog of exceptional quality ability and skill, with more wins than a grand champion
Blood stopper	A powder for the checking and stopping of minor bleeding
Bloom	Dogs in top condition are considered to be in full bloom
Campaign	A fighting dog's career
Champion	A dog with three winning fights to its name
Conditioner	A person responsible for conditioning the dog and shaping the pit for the contest
Convention	A large dog-fighting event, often with music and food available
Cur out	To quit from a lack of gameness
Dogmen	Professional trainers and handlers
Drag fight	A fight where the dogs spend long intervals out of hold
Drain	A means of providing a discharge of fluids from wounds
Fanged	When a fang penetrates a dog's lip and gets stuck
Grand champion	An undefeated dog with five wins
Gameness	Assessment of quality of tenacity, mood and willingness to engage in a fight
A 'game test'	To set the dog up for competition and make sure the dog is ready to be put in the pit for money
The keep	A period of up to six weeks training prior to a dog fight
Non-prospect	A dog who fails to live up to training expectations
Off the chain (OTC)	Allowing the dog off the chain to engage in its fight
On fire	On good fighting form
Pit/box	A pit or ring 8-20 feet square, with 2-3 feet wire mesh around it
Pit weight	A dog's conditioned weight or match weight
Prospect	A young aggressive dog identified as a potential fighter
Purse	Money/takings agreed as the winnings
Rape stand	A stake to which bitches are tethered to allow dogs to mate
Register of merit	Registered document proving champion dog's ability
Roll/rollin'	A dog's first fight; or permitting a dog to briefly fight another possibly to initiate and school the dog in fighting
To unfang	Allow a handler to remove a dog's lip impaled on its teeth
Sanctioned match	A match where dogs have been weighed in and agreed as ready to fight
Scratch lines	Starting lines
Show	A dog fight
Turn	A recognised fault during a fight when a pit dog turns its head and shoulders away from its opponent. However different rules can give this ruling a different meaning

Sources: Silverman, J. 'How dogfighting works' (www.howstuffworks.com/search. php?terms=dog+fighting); R. O'Meara, 'Dog fighting in Britain – the shocking truth', *K9 Magazine*, 31 August 2007

fighting, which remained popular until the 1930s when it began to demise. Animal fighting was outlawed by several US states by the Federal Animal Welfare Act 1976. Nonetheless, during the 1980s, fighting dogs, in particular the pitbull breed, saw a huge upswing in popularity in the US (Jessup, 1995). Writing in 1984, Dr Carl Semencic notes that, 'today in spite of strict laws that prohibit dog fighting in the United States, the sport seems to be growing in popularity at an incredible rate', (Semencic, 1984: 37) and remains a 'half-billion dollar industry' (Ortiz, 2010: 15). This development was paralleled by a considerable proliferation of urban street gangs (Maxson, 1998: 1-11). Unfortunately, no centralised databases of illegal dog fighting exist in the US, so available data is both weak and locally based. Currently, dog fighting remains particularly popular among people from Russia, Eastern Europe and Central Asia, including Pakistan and Afghanistan.

Rules for dog fighting were 'codified' in the US in 1920 by reputed dogman[5] Al Brown. They are widely known and adhered to by dogmen worldwide and are widely referenced by Semencic. The 15 rules advise on refereeing, including 'unfanging' dogs which are locked together, and prohibitions of poison or hypodermics. Modern or 'Cajun' rules allow for slight alterations to Al Brown's rules; here, dogs are allowed to have 'time out' in the corner and carpeting may be provided to allow dogs a better purchase. As with street or gang subculture, dog fighting has its own vocabulary (see Table 6.1), widely used to codify aspects of the 'game' and to imbue quasi-respect and authority (Semencic, 1984: 39-47).

Most organised dog fighting occurs in a 'pit', squared off on all sides, which can be constructed and dismantled at short notice. Fights average an hour in duration but can last from three to seven hours. The dogs are 'forced' to fight by owners and can be whipped, beaten or stabbed to ensure they are 'on fire'. Dogs may fight up to 10 times in a three-week period, depending on its injuries, which may be extensive. Owners of a match-winning dog (the champion), develop all-important bragging rights, allowing status elevation within the dog-fighting fraternity and opportunities to secure higher value fights for future engagements. Pitbulls are the favoured dog for the pit.

> 'People have taken that instinct of a pitbull to bond to a human, to really love its owner and they totally manipulated it, so that they're using it to engage in a fight with another dog. The underworld combined these elements, realising they could train the dog to become a vicious fighting

creation.' (Sergeant Steve Brownstein, Chicago Police Department, interviewed in *Off the chain*)[6]

Those who are neither professional, organised dog fighters nor chain-rolling youths are often termed 'hobbyists'. They may organise dog fights at the weekend with friends alongside gambling and drinking. Some establish dog-fighting pits in lock-ups, garages or even bedrooms. Doors may be sawn in two to provide for videoing of the match and to allow spectators to peer over the top half.

Dog fighting is largely, but not exclusively, a male-dominated activity. Participants may range from bored young people chain rolling their dogs in the local park to organised groups with connections to criminal activity.

In the US, there is increasing evidence that dog fighting is closely linked with gang activity (Degenhart, 2005; Gibson 2005; Randour and Hardiman, 2007). Recent gang prevention strategies in Chicago have begun to investigate the link between animal fighting and gang activity. This was prompted by high levels of dog-fighting arrests; for example, from 2001 to 2004, the Chicago Police Department arrested 332 people for dog fighting, of whom 91% were male and 59% were members of criminal gangs (Degenhardt, 2005).

The HSUS has developed a typology of the different levels of dog fighting. Its research indicates three distinct levels, ranging from impromptu street-level fighting, to dog fighting by enthusiasts or 'hobbyists' to organised and professionally staged dog fights (see Table 6.2).

Table 6.2: Three levels of dog fighting

Level	Activity
1: 'Off the chain' fights	• One-on-one impromptu street fights • Arranged by teens (some of whom are gang-affiliated) • Little/no money involved • No dog-fight rules employed
2: 'Hobbyists'	• Fights in abandoned buildings or garages • Often gang-affiliated • Gambling involved • Trunking – placing dogs in car boots (trunks)
3: Professional	• Sophisticated dog rings • Carried out in a pit • Spectators, handlers, referee • Hundreds of thousands of pounds wagered

Source: Hardiman (2009); Ortiz (2010)

Research by Francesa Ortiz (2010) at the South Texas College of Law and Kelly Daley (2010) at University of Chicago (and HSUS) has begun to flesh out each distinct level, considering participants' roles and activities and the benefits acquired from dog fighting. Although similar research has yet to be undertaken in the UK, professionals in the RSPCA and the Metropolitan and West Midlands Police Services believe that a similar typology applies to the UK (Evans, 2010).

The next section examines what evidence exists in the UK for dog fighting and whether it supports the adoption of the HSUS typology. As published research data are limited, media reports of arrests and convictions and press reports regarding public complaints are a useful source of data. Such sources may present methodological limitations when establishing an evidence base, but they provide a useful starting point.

Level 1: 'off the chain' rolling

The RSPCA reports that two thirds of all dog-fighting reports received relate to youths using their dogs as weapons in streets and parks. These reports (as shown in Appendix B, B3) have risen from 37% of all calls in 2007 to 66% of all calls in 2009.[7] Table B2 in Appendix B illustrates a range of statistics provided by the RSPCA from 2006-08. A total of 634 incidents involving dangerous dogs are recorded,[8] of which 293 incidents (46%) relate to impromptu fights with dogs. While these data can only ever be illustrative rather than wholly reliable, they indicate a high proportion of incidents involving young people and chain rolling or impromptu fights. Such findings are supported by practitioners, for example, park wardens and rangers[9] and local veterinarians,[10] witnessing an increase in dogs presenting with fight injuries.[11]

The widespread popularity and prevalence of aggressive-looking or vicious dogs has become an issue of public concern (Rawstorne, 2009). In many cases, the sheer volume of status dogs in a neighbourhood may increase the level of impromptu chain-rolling incidents. Anecdotally, status dogs and potential fighting dogs are much more visible on the streets and in parks (see Table 5.1). However, such incidents are not the sole preserve of gang-affiliated youth and may appeal in general to bored teenagers.

The issue of fighting dogs has also currently attracted increased media attention. A BBC Three documentary, *My weapon is a dog* (2009)[12] considered the issue of dog fighting. The investigative journalist and radio broadcaster, Rickie-Haywood-Williams, noted,

'I've noticed a new must-have accessory – dogs – the bigger, fiercer and scarier the better. Sometimes it feels like every park or street corner will have a group of guys, hanging around with the same types of dog, Staffies, bull mastifs, bull terriers. It's not just Croydon or even a London thing, it's happening all over the UK and is leading to some pretty nasty incidents.'

Despite this, incidents involving youths and dogs are relatively rarely reported. Many people may be unaware that 'rolling' is illegal and if the event appears impromptu (or passed off as accidental), even those aware of its legal status may not consider it worth reporting. Such incidents are often largely obscured from public view or concluded in a few minutes. Prosecutions are thus even less likely, although a 19-year-old Liverpool man was given an antisocial behaviour order (ASBO) in May 2009 for allowing dogs to fight each other in the street.[13]

In the US, Kelly Daley of HSUS identified a graduation from street-level to mid-level fights (Daley, 2010). In the UK, lack of research precludes support of this supposition. Undoubtedly, some young people come to view dog fighting as 'sport', overcoming their initial reticence at the gruesome spectacle by mythologising the events as 'gaming' or 'sporting' fixtures. They may then be keen to train their dogs and match them against others for financial gain.

Level 2: dog fighting enthusiasts or 'hobbyists'

The second level of the typology relates to those taking a more active part in quasi-organised matches. Such people are often referred to as enthusiasts or hobbyists. Matches may be hastily convened on a regular basis in domestic homes or converted garages, with onsite gambling.

In September 2009, a Lincolnshire mother of three was among several people convicted of dog fighting using a purpose-built pit in the garage of her home. Undercover reporters established links to organised crime in Northern Ireland as well as to 'kingpins' in the dog-fighting underworld in England. Offenders were arrested with the help of RSPCA officers working across eight counties. Thirty-five fighting dogs were seized, of which most were battle scarred.[14]

In March 2010, a man was banned from keeping dogs for life following a conviction for dog fighting at Accrington Magistrates' Court.[15] In July 2010, a dog fighter was convicted in Caerphilly Magistrates' Court following identification in several illegal magazines that contained reports of dog fights.[16]

Other examples of hobbyist dog fights may only come to light after a person has been arrested for an unrelated offence and the offender's mobile phone holds gruesome footage of a recently organised fight.

Level 3: professional fights (professional circuit) and dog-fighting rings

Dog fighting 'rings' are not uncommon in the US and Ireland.[17] It is clear that professional fights at this level also occur in the in the UK, although it is not possible to estimate numbers of fights or those involved.

In one synchronised raid in England involving 50 police officers from three forces, 14 pitbulls, training equipment and videos of dog fights were seized.[18] An undercover investigation for the BBC's Panorama programme in 2007 gained access to one of the biggest and most notorious gangs, the Farmers Boys in Northern Ireland, who were smuggling fighting dogs from Eire (where pitbull ownership is legal) and trading extensively in the UK. Their 'legendary' dog fights took place in a so-called 'party house', where losing dogs were ceremoniously drowned in the infamous 'Tandregee bath'.[19] During its 17-month award-winning investigation, the BBC uncovered 15 illegal dog-fighting gangs in Northern Ireland, and it became clear that dog-fight professionals would travel across Europe to attend a match or source breeding stock.

In the UK, dog fights or 'shows' may involve an estimated 10-50 people, with larger events relatively uncommon. One interviewee for the current research study claimed:

> 'There'll be 30 to 40 people there. You take your mates with you and once you get to know the organiser he will let you know when it's on.' (Professional UK dog fighter)

In September 2007, a Birmingham Magistrates' Court convicted 26 men for hosting dogfights in a converted kitchen showroom. It cost the RSPCA over £100,000 to bring the prosecution. In 1990, 29 men were arrested in Fife, Scotland for dog fighting in the biggest UK event in modern times.[20] Such events, however, do not appear to be on the same scale as those in the US, where a large match may also host barbecues and attract as many as 200 people including families. The respondents interviewed for this research study (see Chapter Five) indicated that they had attended organised dog fights in Leeds and Bradford in the past two years and with between 50 and 150 people in attendance.

The dog-fighting world is mostly secretive and exclusive but also professionally organised,[21] with publications such as *The Sporting Dog Journal* reporting matches and charting the rise of champions. The internet provides easy opportunities to make or establish contacts alongside adverts for upcoming matches. The existence of dog-fighting rings suggests that well-organised groups work together, publicising matches in a clandestine manner, as this interviewee reported:

> 'The fights are interesting. You'll get a week's notice of it, "Go to such 'n such a place." There will be loads of cars there in a circle. The dogs will be in a pit in the middle. To try to get the dogs going, they edge the dogs together then toss them onto each other. Once they are snapping they let them off the chain and they lock on. I got bit trying to separate two dogs.' (Professional UK dog fighter)

Authorities are often the last to find out that they have taken place. Meetings are pre-arranged at a secret location only revealed by phone text 30 minutes before the match begins. Criminal connections are characteristic of those involved in dog fighting, both in the UK and the US. At this level, the underground world of dog fighting, and any involvement in it, is strongly linked to organised crime, urban gang culture and criminal activity (Gibson, 2005; Ortiz, 2010). This is notably the case in the US and is becoming increasingly evident in the UK (Harding, 2010).

The type of dog used varies:

> 'It's usually pits against pits. A good dog, a big pit, will weigh eight stone. They match 'em for weight. There is the referee who takes the money and sets it up. Once you go there, like in a car park or a secluded place, you see how it works. The set up a fight-pit with barriers. It's quite nasty to see, actually. If it's not your dog, it's better.' (Professional dog UK fighter)

The number of matches also varies:

> 'It depends how many dogs are there, usually about eight dogs so there are about six matches. The dog fights twice in one evening. They try not to go for the kill, it's a bit messy. If the dog is healthy it will fight, 'cos you can't put up a dog that ain't healthy. When you get a good healthy dog,

that's when you get high bets – the money is up. It's about five minutes for most matches – so no really long matches. The dog will get damaged though, it will.' (Professional UK dog fighter).

While acknowledging the limitations of data from the RSPCA, the media, the courts and the police, it appears that there is indeed evidence of dog-fighting activity in the UK. A full fit with the HSUS typology may be emerging, but is at yet inconclusive. To advance the hypothesis that UK dog fighting does indeed fit the HSUS typology, it is important to consider the evidence in conjunction with evidence from additional sources including veterinary and welfare agencies, local authority managers of public space and criminological gang research.

Breeding fighting dogs

There is a great deal of money to be made by unscrupulous dealers in breeding fighting dogs. Profit comes from high turnover rather than the quality of the breeding. A breeding pitbull could produce up to 12 puppies valued at £300-£500 each, although market saturation has recently lowered some market values. High turnover comes from unscrupulous breeders who sell puppies that may die only a few days later. To maximise turnover, some breeders will use a 'rape post' staked into the ground, where unwilling bitches are tethered for mating. Unwanted dogs will be sold off to local families who are often conned into believing they are buying a Staffordshire bull terrier but actually are getting a pitbull cross.

The type of dog used for fighting may also be influenced by changes in demand or minor shifts in fashion as this interviewee indicated:

'I saw a half-wolf/half-husky from Ireland the other day, very big aggressive dog. But the dogs at the moment are Turkish dogs – Anatolian shepherd dogs,[22] about three feet high. They are used to attack bears in Turkey. They are vicious and they don't like anyone.' (Professional UK dog fighter)

Other attributes or gender may also be important:

'Girl dogs can be a bit clingy so boy dogs are the best in the ring. However, my mate has got a girl dog and she's quite tasty in the ring. The dogs are all different characters – noisy ones, quiet ones. But the quiet ones are the more aggressive ones.' (Professional UK dog fighter)

The internet has almost certainly increased opportunities to access both breeders and dog-fighting enthusiasts, operating as an open market for trading in all dogs. However, websites relating to so-called status dogs are frequently referred to as 'gaming sites' to attract potential gamers and to hide from the scrutiny of the authorities.

'You have to say it's a long-legged Staff if you are going to sell 'em on the internet, 'cos then people will know it's a pit.' (Professional UK dog fighter)

Both men and women breed dogs for fighting. In October 2009, a Wolverhampton woman was given a six-month suspended jail sentence for breeding fighting pitbulls and selling them for £200–£300 each while claiming unemployment benefit.

Two different groups of breeders exist: professionals, who largely breed fighting dogs with gameness, and street fighters, who largely breed dogs for size and ability to intimidate, rather than fighting tenacity (Ortiz, 2010: 23). As a result, professionals and hobbyists have often accused street fighters and gangs of ruining the pitbull breed through indiscriminate breeding.

Dogs with 'champion blood' are highly valued as breeding stock and their pups command more money. Fighting dogs develop fighting histories or CVs, documenting shows and wins. To maximise breeding stock, breeders must obtain the fighting history of the dog and may bid for stud rights. To do so, and to ensure verification, breeders – even respectable kennel breeders – must establish and maintain contact with those in the world of dog fighting. Thus co-dependent/interdependent relationships are established between unsuitable owners and breeders, with each group reinforcing the other's networks of contacts in the underworld of fighting dogs.

So-called breeders without such contacts may use false or embellished histories, stoop to stealing dogs from unsuspecting owners or take dogs away under threat of violence. Others import/export dogs using false documents. Where such breeders are discovered with aggressive or illegal dogs, prosecution may follow, with dogs taken into care and/or destroyed. In 2007, police found 26 dogs in a one-bedroom council house in Northolt, London. The attendant documentation showed some were grand champions, having won several fights.[23]

Training (the 'keep')

Training a dog to fight may take place at any of the three levels specified earlier. However, the more serious, professional or highly staked the fight, and the more dedicated the owner, the more serious, rigorous and organised is the training programme. The less formal training regimes generally appropriate for chain rolling are described in the next section.

Dogs in the keep may be placed on treadmills or leashed to a rotating wheel, chasing live bait, to build up stamina and muscles. One man in Blackburn[24] converted his terraced house into a training centre for fighting dogs in this way. Live bait may be used to coax the dog to bite and provide practice in pouncing, ripping and killing. Small dogs, cats and rabbits are often used as bait animals, sometimes tethered to a bait stick and at other times set free to face the fighting dog. Their snouts may be bound with duct tape to prevent them from injuring the fighting dog and thus lowering its overall value. Bait animals may be caught wild, stolen or acquired under false pretences by direct approaches to animal shelters or from unsuspecting families offering pets 'free to a good home' in local newspapers.

Many dogs trained to fight grow up in an environment of violence and aggression. The dogs remain brutalised and conditioned to violence, subjected to doping and performance enhancements. Dogs may be encouraged to leap up and hang from old tyres on chains in order strengthen their jaws. Some trainers may give the dogs steroids to develop muscles. Training may take place in swimming pools, often for hours at an end. Dogs are frequently beaten and antagonised to ensure enhanced aggressiveness, responsiveness and violence. Dogs may be doped with their jaws held open by metal retainers in order to file their teeth to sharp points to inflict maximum damage and. Ears may be cut off in a 'fight cut' to encourage dogs to go straight for the neck rather than biting off the ears.

So-called 'professional' breeders take pride in the 'professional' training regime and treatment of their dogs, often feeding them only on red meat and exercising them on mills (see Table 6.3) The living and training environment of those dogs operating at the lower end of the scale, perhaps purchased via the internet by a would-be enthusiast, may be cramped and unhygienic, with overcrowding common.[25] A police raid on a one-bedroom flat in Bethnal Green, London (March 2009) uncovered 14 dogs including six pitbulls.[26] Such raids often reveal a host of items favoured by breeders and trainers, including 'breaking sticks', match report logs, fight histories and weighing scales. Other types of training mechanism are listed in Table 6.3.

Table 6.3: Training mechanisms for dog fights

Type	How it works/purpose
Chain and axle	A device used to chain a dog up in proximity to other dogs while providing limited 'freedom'
Jenny mill	A chain and pulley mechanism to train dogs
Slat mill	A free-spinning treadmill with slats, used for training
O rings	Circular neck rings used in training to reduce injuries to the neck or reduce head movement
Bull snap	A device for attaching a dog to chain
Breaking stick	A wedge-shaped stick used to separate fighting dogs
Turntable	A flat running board that revolves under the dog as it treads
Swim tank	A large tank in which chained dogs swim in order to build up muscles

Source: J. Silverman, 'How dogfighting works', www.howstuffworks.com; A. Turner, www.ukandspain.com/dangerous-dogs

While some people breed dogs for profit, others breed them for fighting, and many websites offering such dogs for sale boast of tough training regimes. Investment in breeding could be £2,000 to £3,000 over two years, and investment owners seek to recoup 10-fold by entering the dog into fights. A seasoned champion will fetch more in potential future breeding if it survives.

The body shape of dogs is often altered to make them into better fighting dogs. Physique may be enhanced by feeding on red meat or high-protein foods and supplements. This gives the dog more musculature as well as more weight in the ring. Sometimes dogs are starved before a fight to increase aggression and also to make the skin cling to the bone. This makes it harder for another dog to grab hold of the skin.

In order to keep the dog-fighting industry thriving, a regular supply of new dogs is required – both as potential fighters and live bait. Bait animals will be family pets stolen either opportunistically or to order. The BBC has reported[27] on pets being stolen in Northern Ireland to be used for 'blooding' dogs in illegal fights. Stolen pets can end up in a 'dog training camp', fed to dogs in training to fight.

'Street surgery'

Violent training regimes and multiple dog fights take their toll on animals in the form of torn flesh, scarring, severed arteries, gouged eyes, severed eyes and ears, and even severed limbs and disembowelling. A two-hour fight can lead to extensive injuries. Scarred dogs are often paraded by owners or prospective fighters as a signifier that the dog has been through many battles and survived. Sometimes 'false' scars are inflicted by knives to give the dog the appearance of a fighting pedigree.

As one professional dog fighter interviewed for the research admitted, "The dog does get some bad injuries, you know, the holes in their necks ... it's massive, nasty."

RSPCA vets in north London have reported dogs being stabbed, mauled or savaged in fights to the death. Dogs are often brought to the vet several days after a fight, some displaying maltreatment such as cigarette burns. Deaths occurring days later from loss of blood is common:

> 'I have seen two or three dogs entering the hospital as a result of fighting today. They are always Staffies and pitbull-type cross-dogs. The dogs suffer fighting, shooting, stabbing, scalding, beatings. Then there is a delay in getting medical attention for the animals. It is shocking to see the animals cruelly treated and left for 10 days with wounds before coming into treatment, and during this time they are likely to harm humans.' (Director, RSPCA Harmsworth Memorial Animal Hospital)[28]

As dog fighting is illegal in the UK and US, owners often attempt to treat injuries themselves rather than attending a veterinary surgery, despite the dogs having serious injuries. This might include rudimentary stitching of cuts and tears in flesh or injections of fluids or antibiotics in so-called 'street surgery'. Owners have no qualifications to perform such surgery and dogs often suffer further before dying. In the US, vets have found dogs that have had wounds stapled together and been given lethal injections of household fluids to kill them. The documentary *Off the chain,*[29] includes graphic accounts and images of botched attempts at patching up injured dogs.

It is not uncommon for dogs with severe injuries to be left to die as they not considered worthy of further investment.

> 'You've got to have somebody to stitch 'em up at the fight, or you dump 'em on a vet or at the RSPCA. If it's bad the dog will be killed after the fight. It depends upon how bad the injuries are, how bad the dog is really, and if the man doing the fight says it can be saved, then they will. If the

dog is a pup then you leave it on the doorstep of the vet. But you can't do it yourself: you have to pay someone to do this for you.' (Professional UK dog fighter)

In 2009 in south London, a dog injured in a dog fight was thrown off a tower block to its death.[30] Injured dogs have also been reportedly wired to mains and electrocuted.

Trunking

A relatively recent practice favoured by east-coast US gangs is 'trunking'. This involves placing two aggressive fighting dogs in a car boot (trunk), closing the lid and driving off. The driver will then play loud music to drown out the sounds while driving round the block. Bets are placed on which dog will survive or come out top. Amateur dog fighters often use this technique to avoid attracting the attention of the police and to circumvent possible surveillance of dog-fight sites. Large sports utility vehicles with spacious boots (trunks) are preferred.[31]

Trunking takes place at the hobbyist level in the typology described earlier, and can be used by dog breeders as a training method. Such activities can build a dog's reputation and enhance the owner's bragging rights.

Similar practices have been identified in the UK, as this interviewee described:

> 'We've had back-of-a-van fighting, similar to trunking, in the borough, just last year. This was adults rather than gangs.' (Police officer, Ealing)

Dog fighting links to gangs

The phenomenon of dog fighting (and status dogs) is increasingly associated with gangs, both in the US and the UK (Harding, 2012). It is recognised that the social pariah status afforded by some breeds of aggressive dog, such as the pitbull, has resonance and meaning with gangs (Gibson, 2005; Ortiz, 2010). In her analysis of dog-fighting laws in the US, Ortiz notes that gangs 'gravitated towards fighting dogs – pitbulls in particular – because they not only served as protection ("four-legged guns"), but also provided status' (Ortiz, 2010: 23). It is possible that bull breeds provide all aspects of the functional requirements presented in Table 4.2 in one: breeding opportunities, fighting opportunities, status and protection.

Police officers in Chicago have noted how the ferocity of dog-fighting appeals to gangs: "There is a marriage between dog-fighting and gangs. Dog-fighting is violent and that is what gangs like."[32]

For gang-affiliated young men the venues used for urban dog fights are familiar territory: abandoned buildings, suburban streets or specially adapted houses or yards. For those organising a match and ensuring the attendance of those prepared to bet on a fight, criminal contacts are a prerequisite. If an illegal dog fight (or 'game') is taking place, guns and drugs are probably close by. In the US, Ortiz (2010) cites a survey of dog fighters in the Chicago area undertaken by the University of Chicago and HSUS that indicates that gang members 'use street-fighting not only as a way to appear tough and gain street credibility, but also as a way to earn money, fight boredom, and work out street or gang conflicts' (Ortiz, 2010: 60).

In the UK, such research has yet to be undertaken and similar correlations lie beyond current evidence. Anecdotally, however, many police officers and local authority representatives would offer the view that criminal activity lies very close to dog-fighting activity.

Does the HSUS typology fit the current UK situation?

The HSUS typology (see Table 6.2) presents clearly defined and grouped activities that escalate in seriousness, cruelty and professionalism. They provide a useful template against which to assess dog-fighting activity. It is now worth considering if this typology fits the contemporary UK scene.

Reported incidents

Accurately establishing facts regarding UK dog-fighting activity remains problematic because of limited evidence from statistical sources. The RSPCA, as principal source of data, indicates a steady rise in public reports of dog fighting over several years, with a high of 358 incidents in 2007, followed by a slight decline. This decline may relate to increased media coverage and intensive intelligence-led policing operations pushing the activity back underground. Relating the RSPCA data directly to the typology is problematic, as these data are incomplete. As the typology has not yet been formally adopted in the UK, data collection methods do not match. Police service data that relate to incidents and convictions do not permit interpretation of activity levels that may facilitate matching against the typology.

Moreover, unless witnessed by the general public, many dog-fighting incidents go unreported or unrecorded. Given such clear limitations of the evidence base, it is difficult to establish the full dimensions and prevalence of this activity in the UK.

The limitations of the RSPCA data are also evident in the context of their regional scope, that is, they do not allow for regional analysis, although other sources suggest regional variations in how the phenomenon is experienced across the UK. Some regions have recorded significantly higher dog-fighting figures than neighbouring regions. The RSPCA claims that 'dog-fighting has rocketed to a "phenomenal" level in the West Midlands',[33] where cases have risen by more than 1,000% in three years. While level 1 dog fighting largely relates to reports of urban youth, levels 2 and 3 make take place in either urban or rural locations. While the first typology of dog fighting described earlier largely relates to urban areas, the second and third typologies may take place in either urban or rural locations, but again, the limitations of the data preclude any robust analysis of locational variations.

Legislation

Legislation has recently been developed to protect dogs and prosecute those involved in organising or attending fights. Section 8 of the Animal Welfare Act 2006[34] makes it an offence to train or cause an animal to fight (or attempt to do so), receive money for admission, and publicise or attend a dog fight. Although the legislation is comprehensive in its coverage of dog-fighting activities, the public remains largely unaware of the Act. As public reporting of dog fighting largely relates to the chain-rolling incidents of the first typology, there are few successful convictions under the legislation. In 2008, the RSPCA succeeded in bringing 16 convictions, rising to 31 in 2009.[35] Again, existing data do not allow us to match against typology. The legislation is largely aimed at dog fights in the second and third typologies, as impromtu fights are unlikely to involve publicity, formal attendance or paying observers.

Any participating dog is likely to be injured in a fight. Those incurring severe injuries may be considered unworthy of further investment and left to die. Others may be drowned or electrocuted.[36]

The relevance of the typology for the UK is located in activities associated with dog fighting, namely breeding and training. Here an increased fashion for aggressive or status dogs has led to a burgeoning market in irresponsible back-street breeding of both status dogs and fighting dogs. While dog fighting may be difficult to locate or unlikely to be witnessed by outsiders, the training required to prepare a dog for fighting offers up further evidence of incidents in both the first and second typologies.

Any statements about the illegal activity of dog fighting in the UK must be made with reference to data limitations. The data are not presently robust or expansive. However, it does appear that street-level dog fighting (chain rolling) has been increasing for several years. In some urban areas, it may even have peaked due to a crackdown from statutory authorities.

Table 5.2 in Chapter Five sets out residents' and professionals' perceptions and awareness of status dogs and dog fighting in Lambeth. All respondents were aware of dog fighting taking place in Lambeth and all linked dog fighting to gang activity. Eleven respondents had witnessed dog fighting by gang-affiliated youths in Lambeth.

Respondents commented that street fighting was the most common form of dog fighting in Lambeth, a view supported by police and RSPCA, although fights in the other categories were also known to occur. Three respondents felt that visible dog fighting in Lambeth was declining, possibly due to recent enforcement activity by police and authorities, suggesting it had gone underground. A higher number of residents and gang-affiliated young people in Lambeth had witnessed dog fighting, often among known gangs with activities based on local estates where gangs operated or claimed territory.

These interviews were followed up by seven qualitative interviews with police personnel with a specific remit to address dangerous and status dogs across the Metropolitan Police Service (MPS), the West Midlands Police Service and Merseyside Police Service (shown in Chapter Five).

Table B2 in Appendix B illustrates that the most common type of dog fighting in the UK is chain rolling by young men, often, but not exclusively, gang-affiliated. Organised dog fighting also exists. Going by the evidence of equipment found in the homes of breeders, organised dog fighting is more common than suggested by the number of recent convictions. Not all incidents occur in metropolitan areas; for example, the table includes convictions in Wales and Lincoln.

Of particular interest are reports from West Midlands and West Yorkshire police services of dog-fighting activity within the Asian community. In some cases, this is known to take the form of organised dog fights. Following the conviction in 2007 of 26 Asian men for dog fighting in Alum Rock, Birmingham, BBC Radio 4 journalist Amardeep Bassey[37] investigated dog fighting within the Asian community in the West Midlands. He found wide acceptance of dog fighting, indicating a different cultural perspective, often linked to traditional rural homelands in Pakistan and Afghanistan where dog fighting is a long-established and legally endorsed cultural tradition.

Interviewed by Bassey, Chief Inspector Ian Briggs of the RSPCA's Special Operations Unit commented that "dog fighting is up 400 per cent in the past three years in the UK. Out of all the work we do, 98 per cent of the dog-fighting work we do in our unit is to do with Asian gangs."[38]

Inspector Briggs believed his team was only 'scratching the surface', as information about one fight uncovers yet another. One Pakistani man interviewed says he attended a recent fight in Birmingham where over £50,000 in cash changed hands. Mr Bassey says "there is evidence that the popularity of dog fighting in the Asian community is being influenced by what is happening" in Pakistan and Afghanistan. DVDs and videos of dog fights in both countries are available for purchase in Birmingham within 24 hours of the fight finishing. A Birmingham youth worker reported local UK Asians travelling to Pakistan and Afghanistan to spectate at dog fights. Other UK residents pay Pakistani or Afghani locals to keep their dogs for them and fly over regularly to watch them participate in fights. There are concerns among some practitioners and police that this central Asian cultural tradition is leading to an increase in the acceptability of dog fighting among some Asians in the UK, or if not acceptability, then indifference to the fact that it remains an illegal activity in the UK.

The interviews with police staff indicate that dog fighting in the UK is known to take place, but with some interesting regional/local variations.

UK regional variations of dog fighting

The level and type of dog fighting in the UK varies from region to region. According to one interviewee in the current study, professional dog fights are relatively uncommon in Merseyside:

> 'Yes, we know it goes on, but they hide it really well, it's not a usual occurrence to be honest. Dog fighting is kept very, very underground. Professional dogmen do not parade their dogs in public like the boys with pitbulls in parks who are chain rolling.' (Police officer, Merseyside)

Such a lack of visibility may simply mean that dog fighting is more professional and thus better hidden from view. In Merseyside, police have seized dogs from professional and hobbyist dog fighters who have been training multiple dogs on treadmills. One trainer, known to the police for previous criminal activity linked to gangs, firearms and drugs, boasted to the police of 'sleeve training' and 'attack training' with dogs that he then supplied to local people.

Proactive policing, dog wardens, high-level publicity and media interest – including a BBC documentary that reported on the prevalence of pitbulls and dog fighting – are offered by the police as reasons for the apparent decline in the number of reported cases of dog fighting in Merseyside. Police claim that members of the public are now reluctant to walk their pitbulls but will still walk American bulldogs and mastiffs in local parks.

While officers in London's MPS Status Dogs Unit had not witnessed an escalation in the severity of dog fights from chain rolling to more organised activity, they recognised that there was a fine line between the two, particularly in the activities of gangs such as MDP in Ealing. Officers are able to assess the dogs injuries and judge the level of their involvement in fighting:

> 'When dogs come in you can see injuries on the dogs. If they've got injuries on the front then it's going from a "chain fight", from a roll. If they've got injuries all over, it's from a traditional fight or a full-on meeting in the park.' (MPS SDU officer)

There was recognition of the involvement of young Asian men of Pakistani backgrounds in dog fighting in Tower Hamlets in east London and Hounslow in west London. In Ealing, west London, officers also noted that chain rolling was the most prevalent form of dog fighting, with low-level gambling and recording of fights on video common:

> 'Chain fighting will take place on an open space or courtyard, not in cultivated parks in the borough. Yes there is chain rolling – both within the gang and between the gangs.' (Police officer, Ealing)

Despite the observations of police in different regions and research findings from qualitative interviews in Lambeth, it remains difficult to quantify the scale of the problem in the UK. As shown in Tables B2 and B3 in Appendix, reports of dog fighting rose, then declined, but remain low in overall terms. Successful convictions are even lower. It will therefore be difficult to quantify the overall extent of dog fighting in the UK until the data is more robust. That said, it seems evident that dog fighting at all three levels of the HSUS typology takes place in the UK and that formal adoption of the typology should be considered by all UK agencies. Doing so will allow greater coordination of data and improve opportunities for monitoring the growth of trends and current activity.

How dog fighting behaviour is rationalised

For an activity that appears to most of us to be excessively cruel, it can be hard to understand the motives of people who become involved in dog fighting. Rationalisation for participants is easier to understand when viewed as a process of circumstance and applied techniques. An understanding of participants' circumstances and the neutralisation techniques they use as justification for their activities makes it easier to understand their rationale for becoming involved. The circumstances of multiple deprivation dictate that large aggressive dogs form part of participants' habitus, and the social fields dictate that it is a requirement to fight for scarce resources of street capital. Dogs thus become a functional vehicle by which people fight for status and success. The final rationalising behaviour is through the application of techniques of neutralisation (Sykes and Matza, 1957). 'Neutralisation techniques' are ways of justifying actions with the intention of diluting the societal norm or rendering it meaningless. Through such justifications, the offender ultimately weakens his ties to societal norms and thus makes the act of deviance possible. Sykes and Matza suggest five ways in which offenders try to justify their actions before committing a deviant act:

- denial of the dog as victim;
- denial of responsibility – 'the dog loves to fight';
- denial of injury to the dog;
- appeal to a higher authority – 'it's a noble/valorised sport with a glorious history';
- condemnations of the condemners – their behaviour is seen as normal and misunderstood while humane workers are extremists and 'humaniacs' (see also Forsythe and Evans, 1998).

In an attempt to explain the sociology of dog fighting, Forsythe and Evans (1998) suggest that denial of responsibility and denial of victim are the least effective justification techniques. By employing excuses and justifications, conventional values can be neutralised, thus allowing people to drift into illegal activity if they believe they will profit from it.

While Forsythe and Evans were considering the perspectives of professional dogmen in the US, it is not known whether chain rollers and street fighters use the same neutralisation techniques. More research is required in this area, and to consider whether these techniques used in the US are relevant in the UK.

Conclusion

Dog fighting is a long-established cultural activity across the world. In the UK, it appears to be in resurgence or at least increasingly evident in a range of new forms. It remains poorly researched, with most existing research relating to the US. The available data are therefore neither comprehensive nor robust.

The current UK evidence suggests that involvement in dog-fighting matches the typology established by HSUS, though clearly the issue of traditional cultural perspectives within the Asian community needs further examination.

The extent of dog fighting in the UK and its regional variations also remain unquantified, and are areas that would greatly benefit from further research and the central collation of data. If public authorities are to address the issue, there is an urgent need to quantify the phenomenon and to develop a greater understanding of those involved at all levels. Collation of data should be the primary focus of a new strategy to address the issue of status dogs and illegal dog fighting.

The next chapter considers the implications and potential risks of an increase in status dogs for public spaces and asks how these breeds and their owners interact with the community.

Notes
[1] BBC News 'Hundreds involved in dog fights', 31 August 2007, www.news.bbc.co.uk/1/hi/uk/6972763.stm, accessed 7 November 2010.

[2] www.humanesociety.org

[3] Malthouse, K. (2009) 'Muzzles are not enough: dogs are weapons', *The Times*, 2 November.

[4] Humane Act 1835.

[5] 'Dogmen' are defined as ' individuals who participate in the underground subculture of dog fighting' by Robert Solomon (2008).

[6] *Off the Chain*, documentary by Bobby Brown (director) and David Roma, Richard Velazquez and Troy Garity (producers), Allumination Studios, ASIN: B0009UVCKS.

[7] RSPCA www.rspca.org/archivednews, accessed 31 October 2009.

[8] It should be noted that this set of statistics comes with the caveat that the data are incomplete. Neither West Yorkshire nor Greater Manchester reported. The data therefore only refer to five metropolitan areas.

[9] As widely reported by practitioners attending the MPA dogs forum meetings and MPA status dogs briefings held in 2010/11.

[10] RSPCA Status dog appeal, www.youtube.com, accessed 1 November 2009.

[11] RSPCA (2009) www.rspca.org/archivednews, accessed 31 October 2009.

[12] BBC Three, *My weapon is a dog*, broadcast on 21 May 2009, broadcaster Rickie Haywood-Williams, producer Elizabeth Byrne, director Derek Jones.

[13] *Liverpool Echo*, 'Asbo for Liverpool teen who encouraged dog fights', 18 May 2009, www.liverpoolecho.co.uk.

[14] *This is Lincolnshire*, 'Woman faces jail over dog fight', www.thisislincolnshire. co.uk/news, accessed on 25 September 2009.

[15] Simon Thacker, 'Dog fighting ringleader given a lifetime ban', *Accrington Observer*, 1 April 2010, http://menmedia.co.uk, accessed 17 September 2011.

[16] BBC News Wales, 'Dog fighting is a "massive problem"', 16 July 2010, accessed 16 June 2011.

[17] www.humanesociety.org/issues/dogfighting, accessed 17 January 2011.

[18] *The Sun*, 'Cops smash "dog fight ring"', www.thesun.co.uk, 10 April 2008.

[19] BBC News, www.news.bbc.co.uk/go/pr/fr/-/1/hi/programmes/panorama, 31 August 2007.

[20] Presentation by Inspector Ian Briggs (RSPCA, 2009).

[21] The most in-depth exploration of dog fighting in the US is by Robert F. Soloman (2008).

[22] Also known as akbash or karabash dogs.

[23] David Doyle, 'Fighting dog breeders caged', *This is Local London*, 27 May 2007.

[24] *Lancashire Telegraph*, 'Treadmill to train vicious dogs', 11 June 2007.

[25] Alex Hayes, 'Man bred fighting dogs in one-bedroomed Wembley flat', *Harrow Times*, 26 November 2008.

[26] *East London Advertiser*, 'Illegal dog-fighting fear as pet is savaged to death in street', 12 March 2009.

[27] BBC News, www.news.bbc.co.uk/go/pr/fr/-/1/hi/northern_ireland, 2 November 2005.

[28] Presentation to RSPCA (2009).

[29] See note 6.

[30] *South London Press*, 'Fight dog is hurled to its death ...', 13 March 2009.

[31] *Hidden in darkness: Trunking is dog fighting's ugly secret*, video accessed on YouTube, 12 May 2009.

[32] Agustina Guerrero, 'Police say dogfights becoming gang game, bouts increasing all over Chicago', *Chicago Tribune*, 20 July 2001, citing Sergeant Steve Brownstein from Chicago Police Department and reporting an increase in dog-fighting activity among gangs.

[33] Mike Bradley, 'Illegal dog-fighting has rocketed to a "phenomenal" level in the West Midlands, the RSPCA revealed today', *Birmingham Mail*, 19 March 2009.

[34] www.legislation.gov.uk

[35] RSPCA (2008) 'RSPCA seize horrific dog fighting footage from London man', www.rspca.org, Press release, accessed 15 August 2010.

[36] BBC News Liverpool, '"Fighting" bull terrier dog found dead in Runcorn canal', 2 November 2010.

[37] BBC Radio 4, *Inside the world of dog fighting*, broadcast on 30 July 2009, broadcaster Amardeep Bassey.

[38] See note 37.

Pete the pup and companions in the Our Gang comedy *School's Out*, 1930
Source: The Internet Archive, http://archive.org

Newspaper headlines regarding the murder of Seyi Ogumyemi, 2009/10
Source: author

This page and opposite (top): cover and inside images from *AtomicDogg* magazine illustrating how bull breeds are valorised

Source: author

Above: 'Hood hounds' collectible toys
Source: author

Metropolitan Police Service Status Dogs Unit seize animals under Operation Navarra, Lambeth, July 2009.
Source: PA Photos

Anti-dog-fighting posters by HSUS
Source: Reproduced with kind permission of The Humane Society of the United States, www.humanesociety.org

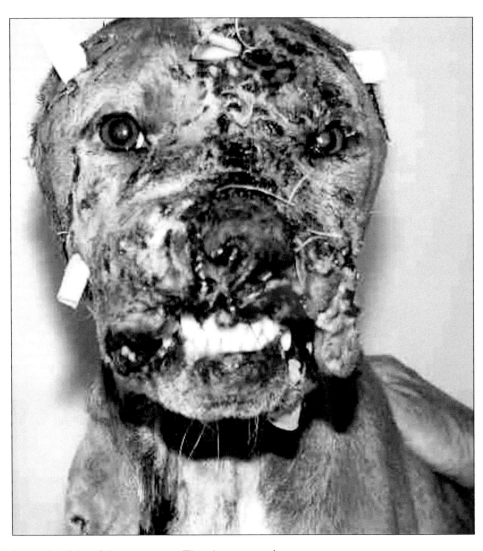

Example of dog-fighting injuries. This dog survived.
Source: www.pet-abuse.com/cases/4402/. Image reproduced with kind permission of
Tri-County Animal Rescue, www.tcar.us

A youth smoking a spliff with his pitbull terrier dogs at home in London, 2006
Source: PYMCA; photographer: Oliver Grove

Local boys with status dogs watch police activity following a double stabbing in East London in which one boy died, 2009
Source: Getty Images News; photographer: Peter Macdiarmid

Local boys with status dogs photographed on the Benchill Estate, Manchester, 2009
Source: News Team International

SEVEN

Implications of status dogs in public space

Having established the nature of the status dog phenomenon, we now turn to the impacts on communities and consider the implications for people who share public spaces with status dogs. Growing numbers of bull breeds and status dogs has led to their increased visibility in parks, high streets and housing estates. This, coupled with increasing media attention, has led to heightened public recognition and awareness of these breeds. An increase in public anxiety is often the result, and is reflected in changes in how people use public places; for example, an unwillingness to frequent areas such as local parks where such breeds are visible or by crossing the street when faced with a bull breed on a chain in the street.

Chapter Four examined the effects that status dogs can have on owners. In this chapter I shall focus on a third aspect: what are the implications for the community of such breeds? How and to what extent do these breeds and their owners interact with the public?

The implications for communities present in a variety of ways:

- dog attacks on adults
- dog attacks on children
- dog attacks on dogs
- dog attacks on working dogs
- damage to the environment: trees, playground equipment, etc
- intimidation of users of public space.

Dog attacks may be triggered by a number of factors, including hot weather, noise, being chained or cooped up for prolonged periods, pack instinct or change of home or owner. Failure to socialise or condition a dog early in life to the noise and interaction of children may lead the dog to consider children as a potential threat. Doctors in Bradford Royal Infirmary studied 1,621 victims of dog bites presenting at the A&E department and compared the number of bites with the lunar phase of each month. Their conclusions, published in the *British Medical Journal* (Bhattacharjee et al, 2000), noted that the full moon was associated with a significant increase in animal bites to humans. However, a later piece in the same journal (Dobson, 2003) rejected this conclusion, but noted that the risk of people being bitten increases at weekends and during summer months.

Controlling such dog attacks is complicated by the fact that the Dangerous Dogs Act (DDA) 1991 does not apply on private property. Uncertainty as to what is public and what is private – particularly in the context of housing estates – has led to further confusion among the authorities about how to control and act in such cases. It is likely this has further compromised data quality for some agencies.

Dog attacks on adults

Over the past five years, the UK press has reported many examples of attacks on members of the public by status dogs. These are too numerous to list, but many describe attacks where the victim has required hospital treatment and surgery. The average costs of an attack have not been evaluated, but where adults require time off work for hospital treatment, the costs can be high. Attack locations vary and include domestic homes, parks and other public areas (see Chapter Four for further data on such attacks).

However, in the UK, fatal dog attacks remain a relatively rare event. Dog expert, Karen Delise (2002), in her analysis of fatal dog attacks in the US, notes that 'it was not surprising to find that a substantial number of the "dangerous" breeds that caused fatalities were owned by young adult males' (2002: 26-8). Analysing fatal dog attacks in the US from 1965 to 2001 Delise records 431 fatalities. While 36 different breeds of dog were involved, 21% of all fatal attacks were by pitbulls, 16% by mixed-breed dogs and 13% by rottweilers. Single dog attacks accounted for 68% of incidents and 32% were multiple dog attacks. Three quarters of all fatal dog attacks occurred on the property of the owner (2002: 88-112).

Delise's analysis has identified several common factors in many fatal attacks (Delise, 2002: 21-54). These include:

- chained or restrained dogs;
- dogs obtained for protection, guarding, fighting or status
- multiple dogs and pack mentality
- irresponsible ownership/breeding
- newly acquired dogs
- dogs in families with newborns and negligent parents
- certain types of dog, namely pitbulls, mixed-breeds and rottweilers.

In the UK, fatal dog attacks on adults are even less frequent than those on young children. In November 2007, three rottweilers owned by Jason Bloor, aged 35, of Blackpool attacked a local woman and killed her pet poodle. Bloor was given a 12-month suspended sentence supervision order and had to pay compensation, but was not banned from owning dogs. He later purchased two German shepherd dogs that went on to kill his 21-year-old flatmate in May 2009. Bloor, who also owned three Jack Russells, could not be charged with failing to control the dogs, as the incident occurred on private property.[1]

More recently, on 23 December 2010, 52-year-old Barbara Williams was attacked and killed by a Belgian mastiff at her home in south London. The dog was shot dead by the police. Originally used by the Belgian army to pull carts and light artillery, these dogs are not banned under the DDA 1991.

Dog attacks on adult workers also continue to be problematic for some sections of the workforce. In December 2008, postman Keith Davies 'had his arm nearly ripped off' in an attack by two rottweilers. His union, the Communication Workers Union (CWU), called on police to take the issue of dangerous dogs more seriously.[2] The CWU has noted[3] that there are 6,000 dog attacks on postal workers every year (approximately 12 per day), although not all these are by status dogs. In some cases, postmen now carry peppermint spray or anti-dog hissing devices to deter dog attacks. The CWU website[4] hosts a series of case studies of recent dog attacks. In addition, the union has been central in lobbying the government for a change in legislation to plug the current legal loophole that prevents prosecutions in cases where the attack occurs on private property. CWU claims that thousands of postal workers and telecom workers are injured each year through dog attacks. Its campaign has successfully achieved legislative change in Scotland and Northern Ireland, but not in England, despite the Prime Minister David Cameron's apparent open support for such a move.[5] To progress their views, the CWU has established the Bite Back campaign.

Alongside postal workers, council workers and visiting health and charity workers are vulnerable to dog attacks. For example:

- A Lambeth council worker was injured in a dog attack by a SBT in November 2009.[6]
- A housing charity worker visiting a student was attacked by a pitbull in Sutton, south London in May 2009. The attack, which occurred at the owner's premises, left the charity worker requiring operations, skin grafts and 100 stitches.[7]

Dog attacks on children

A particularly distressing element of the proliferation of status dogs is that of dog attacks on young children. The size and weight of aggressive bull breeds far exceeds that of young children, and injuries inflicted in minutes can be horrific or fatal. When the attack is combined with the ability of some breeds, such as pitbulls, to hold and tear, the attacks on children can results in multiple life-changing injuries, requiring plastic surgery, skin grafts and amputations. Table 7.1 gives details of the most recent serious dog attacks on children in the UK, including six fatalities.

It is of interest that five of the six child fatalities listed occurred while young children were being supervised by their grandmothers and the dogs that attacked them were known to them. In the remaining incident, the parents were responsible for looking after an unknown dog. In these cases, a close relative often owned or housed aggressive dogs on the premises. For example, after the fatal attack on Zumer Ahmed, police found a Neapolitan mastiff and a dogo argentino. It is also possible that the grandmothers were unfamiliar with the behaviour of the dog in their care. Following Delise's identification of key factors involved in fatal incidents, there appears to be a confluence of multiple factors involved in the UK fatal incidents, including a new dog being poorly supervised by an adult with little or no relationship to the dog, poorly socialised animals in cramped or crowded conditions, the presence of a child or new arrival, issues of territory and lack of vigilance.

While these fatal attacks occurred in private property and domestic homes, it is not uncommon for dogs to attack randomly in streets or parks if they mistake children's noisy play for the noise and excitement of a dog fight. Several recent incidents have occurred seemingly at random, when the dog attacked 'out of the blue' with no provocation.

Dog attacks on dogs

The most common form of attack in public is a dog attack on another dog. These events occur daily and frequently go unreported. Parliamentary discussions regarding dangerous dog legislation refer to numerous attacks (as reported in *Hansard*), as do letters to local authority councillors or the local press. An examination of one local newspaper, the *Lewisham Mercury*,[8] reveals a typical array of headlines relating to such events:

Table 7.1: Recent dog attacks on children in the UK

Date	Fatal	Incident
05/06/12		Two-year-old boy mauled by SBT in Swindon
21/01/12		Six-year-old girls has ear ripped off by SBT in north-east London
23/04/11		Seven-year-old savaged by SBT in Cleethorpes
09/11/11		Two-year-old boy savaged by pet Alsatian cross in Gloucester
26/01/11		Seven-year-old boy attacked by pitbull in West Ham, London
25/12/10		Eleven-year-old boy attacked by Shar-Pei
01/09/10		Ten-year-old girl needs 150 stitches after attack by Japanese akita in Kilmarnock
20/08/10		Ten year old seriously injured in attack by two rottweilers in Dundee
21/08/10		Eight-year-old Sky Barker needs 175 stitches following attack by Japanese akita in W. Yorkshire
17/04/10	Fatal	18-month-old girl, Zumer Ahmed, killed by American bulldog in Crawley
22/03/10		Two-year-old girl loses jaw during attack by family bullmastiff in south London
11/08/09		Seven-year-old girl savaged by SBT in Bolton
26/02/10		Five-year-old boy 'scalped' by rottweiler attack in Essex
30/11 09	Fatal	Four-year-old Jean-Paul Massey killed by pitbull attack in Liverpool
04/11/09		Eight-year-old girl attacked by SBT in Leeds
16/10/09		Two year old mauled by two SBTs near Leeds
19/05/09		Five-year-old Andrew Osbourne attacked by dog that jumped into his garden
07/02/09	Fatal	Baby Jaden Mack snatched from baby basket and killed by bull terrier, south Wales
09/10/08		Baby attacked by bull terrier, Mitcham, London
09/06/08		Six year old attacked by SBT, Folkestone
02/06/08		Seven year old savaged by Japanese akita, Undercliffe, Yorks
29/05/08		Nine-year-old girl attacked at children's party, Castleford , Yorks
28/12/07	Fatal	One-year-old Archie-Lee Hirst, savaged to death by rottweiler, Wakefield, Yorks.
26/12/07		Seven-year-old boy attacked by Japanese akita, Cardiff
21/08/07		Six year old savaged by two rottweilers, Ballymoney, Co. Antrim
09/04/07		Two year old savaged by pet SBT, Blackburn
15/01/07		Nine year old savaged by three rottweilers, Newcastle-under-Lyme
01/01/07	Fatal	Five-year-old Ellie Lawrenson, mauled to death, St Helens, Merseyside
26/09/06		Two year old mauled by rottweiler, Bognor
23/09/06	Fatal	Five month old baby Cadey-Lee Deacon killed by two rottweilers, Leicester
12/08/06		11-year-old girl savaged by SBT, Liverpool
21/07/06		Five year old needs plastic surgery following dog attack, Liverpool
18/07/06		Seven year old scarred for life by dog attack, Runcorn
28/05/06		Nine year old savaged by pitbull terrier, Liverpool
12/01/05		Two year old mauled by Japanese akita, Llansteffan, Wales

Source: Turner, A. www.ukandspain.com/dangerous-dogs; various UK newspapers recording date of incident or date of report

- 'Vicious Staffie savaged my cat', 24 June 2009
- 'My poor pet was savaged and law has let me down', 17 February 2010
- 'Dog mauled in vicious attack', 20 April 2011
- 'Police shoot danger dog – suspected pitbull bites pet and owner', 24 August 2011.

Attack scenarios include dogs that are being walked with or without a leash suddenly attacking other animals; dogs leaping fences into private gardens to attack domestic pets; and stray dogs appearing to attack suddenly and at random. Such events usually happen quickly and often in front of the owners of the victimised pets. Occasionally there are reports of youths goading their dogs to attack other dogs.

Roll and Unshelm (1997) report that dog attacks on other dogs occurred between the same animals in 31% of cases. The aggressor dogs were mostly handled by men and 75% of incidents occurred in public places. Both aggressors and victims in such incidents are reported as being male and generally unneutered (Sherman et al, 1996).

Dog attacks on working dogs

Dog attacks on other dogs sometimes involve working dogs, notably guide dogs, as the victims. In one recent attack, a 19-year-old youth was given a three-month suspended jail term for having a dog out of control in a public place. He was also fined £1,700. His pitbull dog had made an unprovoked attack on a blind woman's guide dog, leaving them both unaided. This high-profile attack in October 2009 led to the then Cabinet minister David Blunkett, MP to describe the problem of attacks on guide dogs by aggressive breeds as 'a hidden calamity', long overdue for public airing.[9]

In a survey by Brooks and colleagues (2010) on dog attacks on guide dogs in the UK, researchers analysed 100 incidents of attack between November 2006 and April 2009, looking at the number, severity and impact of the attack, alongside characteristics of victim and aggressor. Of the attacks analysed, 61% were on dogs in harness working with an owner/handler. Of the dogs attacked, 62% were male. The majority of attacks (61%) occurred in public places between 9am and 3pm. Thirty-eight per cent of attacking dogs were bull breeds. Veterinary attention was required in 41% of attacks and there was additional injury to the handler or a member of the public in 19% of attacks. In 45% of incidents, the attack affected the working ability of the victim dog and two dogs had to be completely withdrawn from service. The most common attacking dog was a bull breed (38%) or a cross–breed (17%). Attacks occurred in public areas on 97% of occasions, mostly in town centres and shopping areas (26%) and public parks (23%). Victim dogs were proportionally labradors and golden retrievers and in 40% of incidents were behaving in a friendly manner towards the aggressor before the attack. Where injuries occurred to humans, bull breeds were responsible on 52% of occasions.

The study identifies several concerns, including that the aggressor's handler only apologised to the victim's handler in six of the incidents. In many attacks, the aggressor's handler left without assisting or indicating to the victim's handler that their dog required medical assistance. Guide dogs subject to attack can be severely traumatised and subsequently unable to perform their duties. There are approximately 4,500 working dogs in the UK supported by the Guide Dogs organisation. The cost of maintaining each one is approximately £50,000 throughout its lifetime. Non-availability of a working guide dog can severely affect the life of a user and an injured dog may have significant financial implications for both user and agency. Clearly, for many unsighted people such attacks are highly distressing, frightening and potentially dangerous.

Status dogs have also been recorded attacking police horses in the course of their duties.[10]

Damage to the environment

In addition to attacks on humans, aggressive dogs and bull breeds may also inflict damage to the public space environment. Aggressive and status dogs, and those in training to fight, need regular exercise. Professional dog fighters (dogmen) will rarely exercise their dogs in public. Those dogs that are seen being trained in parks and other public places tend to be used in street fighting or impromptu dog fights. This type of activity has been widely reported in the UK media over the past two years, with many reports citing the fear it generates among the general public (*Birmingham Mail*, 2009).[11]

Training dogs to fight in parks can cause damage to the environment itself. Owners and handlers may train their dogs to savage trees to build strength in the dogs' jaws/shoulders and to encourage them to jump and grip. There are reports of dogs savaging trees in parks and green spaces in Peckham, Battersea, Hampstead and Barnet in London and also in Liverpool and Manchester. One Islington councillor believes that more than 80% of trees in Laycock Street, Islington have suffered what appears to be dog damage.[12]

The Guardian (2009)[13] has reported numerous such incidents in London and Bristol, and 'widespread' incidents in Liverpool prompted the council to deploy non-toxic chemicals on tree trunks to reduce attacks. According to one report, there have been more than 20 dog attacks on trees in St George Park in Bristol, where terriers are hung from branches, and other dog attacks on young tree stems on the Blaise Castle estate.[14]

In Barnet, London, in 2009, a 22-year-old man was fined £60 after inciting his Staffordshire bull terrier (SBT) to bite tree branches in Oak Hill Park.[15] Barnet Council reports that damage by dog attack and dog 'training' on trees in Oak Hill Park has caused more than £10,000 worth of damage.[16] In Southwark, south London, Southwark Council reported the loss of 18 trees in a six-month period in 2010.[17]

Elsewhere, it was reported[18] that in Northern Ireland playground equipment had been used to train dogs, with play equipment ripped to shreds. Training may take place in other public spaces. In Lewisham, in October 2009, complaints were made about dogs being trained to fight in the grounds of the restored Georgian library.[19]

The London Tree Officers Association (LTOA) believes that dog attacks on trees in London are increasing, with one London borough estimating damage caused in excess of £1million (LTOA, 2010). In an LTOA survey in 2009 officers were unanimous that the problem of dog attacks on trees was increasing. Damage includes:

- bark stripping, which damages the living part of the tree just below the bark and can cut the connection between root and crown;
- branch chewing, which creates wounds on the tree leaving it open to decay and disease.

Damaged or dying trees diminish the character of the park or green space and may make it appear unsafe or unappealing. Dead trees may have to be removed at considerable expense. To prevent trees from being damaged and removed, dog attacks on trees are now often a neighbourhood policing priority. Local authorities can now take protective measures against such damage, such as employing wardens to patrol parks and installing fences, although barriers are expensive and often make the park less attractive.

Intimidation of users of public space

As well as being used for dog fighting (either organised or amateur) status dogs are often used to patrol and enforce territoriality. Young men or gang-affiliated young people may use aggressive bull breed dogs to intimidate rivals and push them off their own neighbourhood territory or 'endz'. Dogs may also be used to intimidate rival gang members on their own territory, or to secure contested territory, for example in a local park or sports ground. Dogs may also help to deter any perceived potential threats. In the UK, the RSPCA claims that this is now a common aspect of the use of status dogs in certain neighbourhoods and is affecting the use of public space. In gang-affected areas, the threat of a status dog is aligned with its potential use as a weapon.

While undertaking research in Brixton Market in south London in 2010, I witnessed the arrival of a well-known local gangster:

> Stripped to the waist the muscled young man held two large Pitbulls. The dogs looked incredibly fit and were bulging with muscles to match his own. They were both chained and harnessed. He held a tight grip on them as they strained forward. Without a word the busy marketplace quickly cleared a wide route for man and dogs. All eyes were upon him and his dogs. Several people moved away completely. Surrounded by attendant gang members, this was clearly a special outing to make a statement. As he moved past me I could see he had three Pitbulls tattooed across his back. (Field notes, Harding, 2012)

One aspect of intimidation is the association in the public mind of many of these breeds with owners/handlers who are irresponsible and undesirable. Again, media portrayals will have had an impact here, and owing to the strong cultural associations now being made with pitbulls and criminality, it will be difficult to shift this public perception. The intimidation factor is increased when people consider the possibility that the owner/handler of the aggressive breed may not understand the character of the dog or how to control it, as they are assumed to be irresponsible.

Another issue is that of chain rolling. Impromptu chain rolling may occur quickly in parks or open spaces and last only a few minutes, but such events are noisy and attract attention. They also alarm other dogs and other users of the public space.

Park users have often been among the first to raise issues of public safety with local authorities or through reports to park rangers or wardens. This has prompted some local authorities to take action against persistent offenders:

- In Battersea, London, a man who used his rottweiler to intimidate and harass other park users was given an ASBO. He was now banned from entering Clapham Common and Battersea Park for five years.[20]
- A 19-year-old Liverpool man was given an ASBO in May 2009 for allowing his dogs to fight each other in the street.[21]

Many recent attacks have taken place in public parks where excitable children are most at risk from dogs trained to attack and kill. In April 2009, a nine-year-old boy was knocked off his bike and attacked by a bull mastiff in Battersea.[22]

An intelligence briefing for the Greater London Authority Strategic Crime Analysis Team reports on survey findings of the public perceptions of safety in parks and open spaces with regard to dangerous dogs (GLA, 2011). The findings of the telephone survey[23] in 2010 indicated that:

- 43% of interviewees think that nuisance/dangerous dogs in their parks are a problem, with 12% indicating they are a big problem;[24]
- 39% of residents in higher social classes (AB groups) think nuisance dogs are a problem compared with 50% of those in lower social class (DE groups);
- 50% of residents of social rented housing and 41% of home owners think nuisance dogs are a big problem in their parks.

Impact

The use of aggressive dogs in public spaces can have a wider negative impact on local communities, particularly children and families. This might include:

- reduced or curtailed park visits through fear of attack;
- restrictions on freedom of movement within the park;
- a need for increased vigilance of children;
- fear of confrontation with an owner of an aggressive breed;
- inability to make use of recreation facilities destroyed by dogs (for example, swings);
- concern regarding visual damage to the environment;
- displacement (altering times of visits to parks/open spaces);
- a fear of entering a park or open space on one's own and preferring to do so only in company;
- altered routes through open spaces;
- a decline in the use of public spaces.

Strays

The proliferation of status dogs, a result of increased supply and demand, notably over-breeding, has affected the number and breed type of strays in the UK. Status dogs that become strays may present a threat to public safety, particularly if they are large or aggressive dogs. Status dogs may become too expensive or unruly for owners, who may then neglect or abandon them. The RSPCA estimates that there are 50,000 stray dogs in the UK.[25] Many of these are SBTs and pitbull-type dogs. In 2010, the RSPCA reported that SBTs and SBT crosses accounted for 22% of stray dog intake (up from 18% in the previous year) (RSPCA, 2010). Regional variations were evident and one centre reported 75% of dogs in its care as bull breeds. As a result, the RSPCA has tried to improve the image of SBTs and focus on rehoming them.

A similar increase in stray and abandoned bull breeds and SBTs has been noted by other animal welfare agencies. The Battersea Dogs and Cats Home in south London reported in 2001 that the number of SBTs and SBT crosses entering the shelter has increased by over 300% since 1996.[26] In August 2011, two thirds of the dogs housed were SBTs or SBT crosses. The majority of these were under two years old.

In 2010, the Dogs Trust, the UK's largest dog welfare charity, carried out a wide-ranging of survey of status dogs among partner agencies. It reported that 126,176 dogs were picked up by local authorities in the period 1 April 2010 to 3 March 2011 (GfK NOP, 2011). This is a 4% increase on the previous year and takes the number of stray dogs handled by councils in the UK to an 11-year high.[27] The survey found that a large number of dogs were also rejected by their owners, who refused to claim them once found and identified. It commented that 'this new trend is worrying as it appears some dog owners no longer view their pet as a valued family member or have not considered the true cost and responsibility involved with owning a dog'.[28]

The majority of dogs, stray or abandoned, are seized by local authorities (77%) and a further 16% are brought into shelters by the public, with 7% handled by the police, vets, RSPCA and include dogs seized under the DDA 1991. The majority of dogs (48%) are reunited with their owners and one quarter (25%) are passed on to welfare organisations or dog kennels. Approximately 6% of stray dogs are euthanised. Dogs that are microchipped are easier to return to owners. The Dogs Trust estimates that compulsory microchipping would save the government an estimated £20-£23 million a year.

The Dogs Trust survey also asked respondents to report the number of status dogs they handled and how many of those were euthanised because of aggression.[29] The survey reports a total of 11,099 status dogs as having been handled between 1 April 2010 and 31 March 2011, or 11% of the national total.[30] Some authorities did not respond to the survey and others did not provide figures for status dogs handled. Table 7.2 indicates the numbers of strays and status dogs handled by regional

Table 7.2: Numbers of stray dogs and status dogs handled by local authorities in each region from 01/04/10–31/03/11

TV region	Number of local authorities	Total number of strays	Change in number of strays (%)	Total number of status dogs handled	Number of status dogs destroyed due to aggression
Tyne Tees	13	11,119	↑32	1,208	27
Granada	28	19,119	↑13	1,333	124
Yorkshire	20	10,081	↓19	983	89
Central	55	20,995	level	2,569	119
HTV	23	12,529	↑10	868	44
Anglia	28	6,242	↓15	495	39
Carlton	53	14,547	↑1	1,641	97
Meridian	39	10,002	↑21	860	78
West Country	15	4,346	↑48	346	4
Border	6	1,523	↓11	269	9
Grampian	8	2,107	↑7	152	15
STV Central	18	3,399	↓7	375	15
Ulster	26	9,119	↑3	NA	NA
TOTAL	**332**	**128,128**		**11,099**	**660**

Source: GfK NOP (2011)

Notes: In order to maintain comparability with methods used in previous surveys, the national total is calculated separately from the regional totals. As a result, the individual region figures do not always equal the UK total. The key findings from this survey are based on actual numbers reported by each authority (for example, the number of strays); however, at some points reference is made to 'estimated' figures. The figures have been grossed up to make estimates for each TV region, based on the assumption that authorities responding are representative of authorities as a whole. Where figures are shown for Wales, West and Tyne Tees and Border TV regions, these are additional to and do not make up part of the overall UK totals.

It is also worth noting that the 26 authorities within Northern Ireland only provide data on the number of strays seized by the local authority, the number brought in or surrendered by the general public, the number reclaimed during the statutory local authority kennelling period, and the total number put to sleep. Where all other figures are reported these are based on the 306 responding authorities in Great Britain.

local authorities during this study period.[31] The highest number of status dogs handled was in the Central TV region (Midlands) followed by Carlton (London). This figure is reported as having decreased from the figure of 17,834 nationally reported the previous year, which accounted for 18% of all stray dogs in 2010.

The Dogs Trust believes that a combination of factors has led to the increase in numbers of strays and cites the recession alongside a high number of unwanted bull breeds. It also notes a trend for people disposing of dogs when they no longer want them. This finding concurs with previous discussions around the commodification of dogs, and changing public attitudes or societal views about the role of dogs and how they are now perceived, for example, as tradable and functional commodities.

These figures also indicate high numbers of status dogs loose in public spaces and a proportion of these are clearly so aggressive they are unsuitable for rehoming. This indicates a potential risk to the public arising from the increased number of status dogs. The figures also reveal the extent of status dog ownership nationally. It is not possible to determine which typology of owners is most responsible for strays. The implication is, however, that many families take on bull breeds (for one of the four motivational reasons discussed earlier in the book) then find they cannot afford its upkeep or manage its behaviour.

The Dogs Trust also retains data in relation to dogs handed in to its 17 rehoming centres in the UK (approximately half the dogs in its care). It monitors two groups:

- trend dogs – SBTs, SBT crosses, akitas, mastiffs and bull breeds;
- toy dogs – bought as fashion accessories.

In the past five years, the Trust has seen a 21% increase in trend dogs (status dogs) and a 39% increase in toy dogs handed into its rehoming centres. Of these 48% or 493 were under two years of age.

In 2010, the 17 rehoming centres had eight times as many dogs handed in than in 2005 because owners could not cope with the breed traits.

Behavioural problems among relinquished dogs has also notably increased. In 2010, the number of dogs handed into rehoming centres because owners could not cope with behavioural issues had nearly tripled since 2005.

These data indicate that owners are frequently unaware or ill prepared for the responsibilities of owning and managing a dog, and that people are unaware of the breed traits of the dogs they choose. This finding fits with the increased number of people acquiring dogs from the internet, on a whim or for fashion. It also supports the conclusion that some owners are not prepared for the challenges of owning or training bull breeds, or for the growing financial cost of keeping them, and thus choose to abandon them.

Conclusion

Increased breeding and ownership of status dogs and bull breeds has resulted in increased visibility and presence of such dogs in the UK's open, green and public spaces. This has resulted in large numbers of people expressing anxiety or even fear over the presence of such dogs and has led to changes in how people both view and use public spaces. There may be significant implications here for families with young children, but there are also implications for adults at work, for example, postal staff and those using guide dogs. One of the most common outcomes of the proliferation of status and aggressive dogs in public spaces is attacks on other dogs, and many such incidents go unreported.

There are also more status dogs in domestic homes, where young children sharing the same space are at risk of attack. Fortunately, such attacks are rare, but data show that the number of attacks by dogs in general and bull breeds in particular has been increasing. It is worth noting that any dog can be dangerous and any dog can attack, but the issue with status dogs is that the size, bite power and aggressive nature of many breeds is such that the damage they can do may be life threatening or life changing. Again, more research is needed.

The next chapter considers how the police and local authorities are responding to public concerns. It also examines the challenges of addressing the risks and implementing the legislation as well as some of the different practices now emerging across the UK.

Notes

[1] Chris Brooke, 'Man, 21, bled to death after Alsatians bit him 51 times', *Mail Online*, 4 February 2009, accessed 28 August 2011.

[2] BBC News, 'Post Union plea over dog attacks', 25 December 2008, http://news.bbc.co.uk/go/pr/fr/-/1/hi/uk/7799594.stm, accessed 30 August 2010.

[3] CWU ((2011) 'Time to change dog laws says CWU and RSPCA', Press release, 9 September.

[4] www.cwu.org

[5] CWU (2009) 'New dog laws – "What are you waiting for PM?", Press release, 13 July.

[6] Matt Watts, 'Lambeth council worker attacked by dog in Streatham Hill', *Epping Forest Guardian*, 25 November 2011, www.guardian-series.co.uk/ archive/, accessed 7 February 2010.

[7] Jamie Henderson, 'Student escapes jail after dog attacked mother-of-three in Sutton', *Epping Forest Guardian*, 19 January 2010, www.guardian-series. co.uk/archive/, accessed 7 February 2010.

[8] www.mercury-today.co.uk

[9] Stuart Winter, 'Horror of the pitbulls attacking guide dogs', *Sunday Express*, 16 January 2011.

[10] 'Essex Police horses on the men after dog attack', www.horseandhound. co.uk/news, 12 January 2011, accessed 21 January 2011. Two horses were injured in the attack in Chelmsford, Essex. Officers were thrown but uninjured.

[11] *Birmingham Mail*, 'West Midlands dog-fighting increase', 19 March 2009.

[12] *The Guardian*, 'Thousands of urban trees mauled and destroyed as "weapon dog" owners train animals for fighting', 12 August 2009.

[13] See note 12.

[14] See note 12.

[15] See note 12.

[16] Kevin Bradford, 'Dangerous dogs set loose on trees in East Barnet park, *Waltham Forest Guardian*, 28 August 2009, www.guardian-series.co.uk/archive/, accessed 7 February 2010.

[17] 'Southwark warns dog owners over damage to trees after 18 destroyed in just six months', www.southwark.gov.uk/news/article/225, accessed 7 July 2011.

[18] BBC News, http://news.bbc.co.uk/go/pr/fr/-/1/hi/northern_ireland, accessed 3 April 2009 (no longer available).

[19] *South London Press*, 'Library ground used to train fighting dogs', 16 October 2009.

[20] *South London Press*, 'ASBO and parks ban for man who terrorised with his dog', 14 August 2009.

[21] *Liverpool Echo*, 'Asbo for Liverpool teen who encouraged dog fights', 18 May 18 2009, www.liverpoolecho.co.uk

[22] *South London Press*, 'Mum savaged by dog while protecting kids', 24 April 2009.

[23] Telephone survey for GLA (2011) briefing. Summary of results survey work carried out by ICM research on behalf of the Greater London Authority in August 2010 based on 1,002 interviews (gender, age, tenure, working status and area of London lived in) to ensure data is representative. All demographic differences referred to are statistically significant a 95% confidence level.

[24] Only 36% think mugging/physical attack is a problem and 34% think drug use or dealing is a problem.

[25] R. O'Meara, 'Dangerous dogs on Britain's streets: the truth', *Dog Magazine*, 18 June 2009, www.dogmagazine.net, accessed 25 June 2009.

[26] Lawrence Conway, 'Dogs home is overrun by abandoned Staffies', *South London Press*, 5 August 2011.

[27] The Dogs Trust (2011) 'Number of UK stray dogs reaches eleven year high', Press release, 5 September.

[28] See note 27.

[29] The question is worded as follows: 'The media often refer to "status dogs" as those whose looks or breed type are thought to convey a particular impression of their owner – such as Bull breeds, Rottweilers, Akitas or Crosses of these. With this in mind, please answer the following (estimates are acceptable).'

[30] This figure differs slightly from the regional total in 7.2. This is because to maintain comparability with methods used in previous surveys, the national total is calculated separately from the regional totals. As a result, the individual regional figures do not always equal the reported UK total.

[31] Regions relate to 13 TV regions throughout the UK.

[32] The survey includes responses from 332 local authorities, including 261 in England, 27 in Scotland, 26 in Northern Ireland and 18 in Wales. The total number of local authorities is 404. This represents a response rate of 82%.

[33] Dogs Trust fashion dog research statistics, 6 September 2011, as provided by Dogs Trust Press Office in private email.

EIGHT

Responses to the issue of status dogs

Having established the nature of the phenomenon of status dogs and how it presents both risks and challenges for the public, we now look in more detail as to how these are being addressed by the statutory authorities, namely the police, the courts and local and regional government. The chapter also examines emerging good practice from animal welfare agencies that are now at the forefront of tackling this issue.

Setting the scene

In their review of the Dangerous Dogs Act (DDA) 1991 and the regulatory responses in the 1990s, Lodge and Hood (2002) report police enforcement as 'patchy'. After a 'short period of vigorous enforcement' tackling drug dealers, they claim police reprioritised the issue and focused attention elsewhere, although this was in relation to dangerous dogs rather than status dogs.

The issue now presenting in the 21st century is slightly different. First, requests to tackle status dogs have arisen not from the police but from local communities via Safer Neighbourhood policing panels and councillors' mailbags. Requests surfaced at local forums, council meetings, tenants' and residents' meetings and police community consultative groups and via the letters pages of the local press. Hallsworth (2011:400) contends that the police themselves have talked up the problem of status dogs 'to justify an ongoing flow of resources', although there is no evidence to support this and such a claim denies the reality of local people's experience.

Second, the increased visibility of bull breeds and status dogs in parks and open spaces has begun to present problems. Here again, local residents, friends of parks and dog walkers have raised concerns via user groups, dog wardens and park rangers.

Third, the role of status dogs and dangerous dogs has changed significantly from the 1990s. Now status dogs are increasingly linked to criminal elements in the UK and the US. In France, the number of dangerous dogs – *les chiens dangereux* (mainly pitbull-type dogs) – rose from around 2,000–3,000 in 1993 to around 30,000 by 1998. The deliberate use of weapon dogs on African immigrants in 1996 led to legislative revisions in France (Lodge and Hood, 2002).

Alongside the increased ownership of status dogs, and associated issues of criminality and perceived threats to public safety, there has been a rise in the number of status dogs relinquished to UK animal welfare agencies, kennel clubs and shelters. This is also evident at RSPCA animal hospitals and local veterinary surgeries.

Through local partnership working, pressure is being placed on authorities for action. In 2007, Liverpool City Council reacted to the death by pitbull attack of five-year-old Ellie Lawrenson by reviewing local procedures, including preventative measures and risk assessments. Hallsworth (2011: 400) contends that the government response to the issue of dangerous or status dogs, including the establishment of the Metropolitan Police Service (MPS) Status Dog Unit, is a 'manifestation of the punitive Security State', and denies it is a reflection of the concerns raised by practitioners and members of the public.

MPS Status Dog Unit

In July 2008, the MPS established the London Dangerous Dogs Forum with partners across the capital to support a London-wide strategy to address dangerous and status dogs. This forum established the first coordinated response to the issue, leading to widespread joint activity across London.

Increasingly, the MPS identified a rationale for creating a dedicated unit to address issues of aggressive dogs. For example, in 2008/09 a total of 719 dogs had been seized by the MPS and kennelling costs (averaging between £13.70 and £22.00 per dog, per day, was running at £1.342 million (including veterinary and transport costs).[1] By April 2010, this figure had risen to £2.65 million.[2]

On 2 March 2009, the MPS launched its new Status Dog Unit (SDU) as part of the existing Dog Support Unit. The SDU, established at a cost of £350,000, retains an inspector, a sergeant and five police constables. All officers are accredited dog legislation officers (DLOs). Processing of dogs within the unit is holistic, including dog welfare, kennelling and veterinary treatment alongside support for MPS colleagues acting as expert witnesses in prosecutions and working proactively to ensure cases are effectively concluded. The unit is both reactive and proactive, and has the capability to seize dogs. Importantly, it draws together all dog-related activity, reducing costs and creating a centre of expertise.

Following the involvement of aggressive and illegal dogs in the murder of Seyi Ogunyemi in April 2009 (see Introduction, this volume), the SDU established closer links with MPS divisions working on serious crime involving drugs, robbery and gangs. In July 2009, it undertook Operation Navarra, raiding the homes of 12 known gang members. The unit's Sergeant McParland acknowledged the link to gangs: "This operation is about targeting gang members using dogs in violence and crime"[3] (see Chapter Five).

Hallsworth (2011), who is vehemently opposed to the SDU and to legislated activity that euthanises bull breeds, criticises the unit, suggesting that 'seizing people's pets and picking up dogs who have bitten other dogs is low status work', and that the unit has recast its purpose by aligning itself to tackling gangs and organised crime, allowing it to 'assume a significance and status such activity otherwise lacks' (Hallsworth, 2011: 400). He further contends that 'by continually talking up the Pitbull menace, the Unit continues to justify its employment and the huge resources needed to fund its murderous activity' (p 400). This somewhat jaundiced critique denies the validity of public concerns regarding safety, as well as the data indicating a link to serious and organised crime (see Chapters Five and Six).

Intelligence about dangerous dogs and referrals to the unit come in many forms and commonly involve the police reporting a possible illegal dog. The main source of referrals is the Safer Neighbourhood teams (SNTs),[4] whose remit for patrolling local neighbourhoods brings them into regular contact with the owners/handlers of dogs that may be illegal, dangerous or out of control. Breed identification is not always possible. When challenged, young men often claim the dog is not a pitbull, but another legal breed. MPS officers, including police community support officers (PCSOs), are not trained to identify illegal dogs, so they must refer potential cases to the SDU, for example, by emailing a photograph of a suspected dangerous dog. This quick technique reduces the number of dogs seized unnecessarily. Other referrals to the SDU come from the drugs squad, murder squad or the Violent Crime Directorate.

The majority of public calls about incidents involving dogs come through the emergency 999 service. These calls range from immediate incidents (for example a child being savaged by a dog), to potential threats (a dangerous dog spotted in a park), to general concerns over neighbours breeding illegal dogs. From January to April 2010, the unit received 980 spontaneous calls to the MetCall emergency service from the public to report incidents or concerns about possible illegal dogs. Calls received by MetCall trigger an immediate response from a specialist dog van. Once at the scene, the dog handler determines the required level of response. The MPS SDU only gets involved if the dog is seized. Other referrals are made through partnership groups such as Safer Neighbourhood panels, community safety groups, residents' and tenants' groups, and local councillors.

Acting on intelligence reports, police are permitted to seize a dog in its domestic location, which is important in establishing ownership. If owners/handlers are challenged in more public places, they often claim to have found the dog wandering in the streets only moments before. Denial of ownership is more difficult, however, if the dog is discovered during a domestic raid. Dog food found in the kitchen makes denial of ownership more difficult.

The unit also receives intelligence and/or referrals from home care workers, health visitors and social services professionals, for example domestic violence workers or social workers visiting children on the at-risk register. Any cases that involve animal cruelty or neglect are referred to the RSPCA. Primary care trusts, social housing managers, local dog wardens and park rangers also make referrals. To address the volume of work in London, the SDU has prioritised boroughs[5] with each being allocated a DLO.

When the police receive notification of a possible illegal dog, a decision is made whether or not to obtain a warrant and seize the dog. Seizures are then made during planned raids. The police photograph and examine the dog before preparing case files for the Crown Prosecution Service (CPS). If the police decide to prosecute, officers will then act as expert witnesses at court.

MPS SDU officers may receive photographs of dogs via email along with requests for determining whether they fall into the category of dangerous dogs. Local officers obtain a warrant and SDU officers are required to execute the warrant. Warrants may be linked into other criminal activity such as drugs, firearms, stolen property or violence.

A number of outcomes have been achieved during the first two years of the SDU (March 2009–11):

- in 2009-10, the SDU seized 1,155 dogs; this figure fell to 1,023 dogs in the following year;
- SDU officers entered 526 premises under warrant;
- officers carried out more than 1,300 pre-planned operations to deal with dangerous dogs, including operations where the SDU was required to attend because it was thought a dog on the premises presented a danger;
- dog support officers responded to over 4,684 spontaneous calls;

- more than 859 prosecutions were brought (40% of seizures);
- more than 379 prohibited dogs were returned to owners under the DDA 1991.

In addition, the SDU collaborated with the RSPCA in numerous operations, and increased the level of policing at large-scale public events such as the Notting Hill Carnival, resulting in the presence of fewer dogs.

Seizure

Any operation involving seizure is intelligence-led. The MPS SDU does not proactively patrol the streets seeking to identify dangerous dogs and then seize them, although should CCTV operators identify young men with aggressive or dangerous dogs in a park, the MPS SDU may undertake a street-based operation in conjunction with local police to address the issue. This undermines claims by Hallsworth (2011: 397) who alleges that it is the creation of a dedicated MPS SDU that is responsible for the growth in the problem of dangerous dogs: 'the decision to create a specialist unit with a mandate to seize dogs and a policy shift to seize more dogs as opposed to fewer'. Hallsworth's claim overlooks the fact that seizing dogs posing a potential threat to public safety did not start with the creation of the MPS SDU; nor, indeed could any 'policy shift to seize more dogs' be identified. This accusation implies that dogs are seized at random from the streets, which is not the case. Hallsworth argues, unconvincingly and without evidence, that the MPS SDU talks up 'the pitbull menace' to 'justify its employment and the huge resources needed to fund its murderous activity' (Hallsworth, 2011: 400). On the contrary, an increase in the number of seizures has arisen from an increased number of such dogs referred or reported to the police, being used in the course of criminal enterprise, or being illegally bred/imported. Resources, such as they are, are used to ensure the welfare of the animal and the safety of staff and the general public. Legal delays undoubtedly have an effect on kennelling costs, but these arise from the unfamiliarity of the courts and the criminal justice system in dealing with animals in custody alongside an increase in the number of cases reaching court.

Any seizure has to be fully risk assessed for the potential threat it poses to police officers and the public before a warrant is sought or executed, as this research respondent indicated:

'If a drug dealer uses a dog to protect the stash, then this is fed into the risk assessment. The police then get a warrant, mindful of the dog. There is also the possible escape of the dog into the streets. The risk assessment takes this into account. If the primary case for the action is the drugs, then the warrant will be on drugs. This is best for the court. Some will be dog-specific. Others will be for drugs and dogs.' (Police officer, Tower Hamlets)

Officers from all forces interviewed identified that aggressive dogs, notably bull breeds, are used by drug dealers to slow the entry of the police into the premises:

'We had a raid yesterday, this family is engaged in criminality – five dogs were in the house. We had also taken a pitbull from them before, and they are literally used as a slowing tactic for the police. The family deal Class A drugs. They know for a fact our entry as police officers into that house is going to be so much slower due to the dogs. And it is a common occurrence, we get booked out to those instances all the time.' (Police officer, Merseyside)

Where seizures arise from police raids on premises, it is often because Class A drugs are stashed on site. Aggressive dogs must be tackled before officers can search the premises:

'Someone will put the door in and the dog team will come, riot shield, fire extinguisher and holding stick and we will go down the hall to drive the dog back into the back of the premises to then allow our search team access to the building quickly to the other guys in the room where the drugs might be, before they start to flush the drugs.' (Police officer, Merseyside)

In London, dogs may be seized by the local dog van if it comes across an incident as it happens or if SDU officers are unavailable. However, in approximately 90% of cases, SDU officers seize the dog themselves. Dogs identified as pitbull types may be at risk of being seized on more than one occasion unless they have been microchipped. In these circumstances, it is the preferred tactic to bring the dog in for full assessment so they can be formally assessed under the DDA 1991.

Protective kit

MPS officers attending seizures and dog incidents have access to specific kit. This includes a repellent spray called Bite Back and newly acquired electric shields that work in a similar way to tasers. Shields, which cost approximately £250 each, incorporate a membrane that can conduct up to 40,000 volts of electricity. The purpose of the shield is to scare or contain the dog until it can be effectively handled. It is typically used to fend the dog away on entering the premises, should, for example, the dog launch itself from the top of the stairs. On impact, the electric current is triggered, which momentarily shocks the dog, but it recovers almost as soon as the charge is terminated. The shields also have jack-plugs and triggers that act as a safety mechanism:

> 'We've used it a couple of times and the first time it was used was in a squat in the dark and with the crackling, the ozone smell, the noise and the lights and everything in the dark, the dog just turned around and ran and didn't go anywhere near the shield. And, that apparently 90% of the time is what will happen. It just another piece of kit for us'. (Police officer, MPS SDU)

Other equipment, such as handling poles, is also available. Similar kit is now available to other forces in the UK. Some people claim that the kit used makes the dog more agitated:

> 'Once the RSPCA come for your dog and bring out the big stick with a loop on it, it drives the dog mad anyway, they don't like it – makes the dog more aggressive. Two years ago my mate's house got raided. We were there when the police booted down the door and someone like Michelin man came in and went straight into the garden for the dog. He had a big stick, the dog was fine before but was now going mental. So now they said it was a dangerous dog, but it weren't at all.' (Professional UK dog fighter)

Dispatch by firearm

At the point of seizure, or when the dog is first viewed, the police dog handler makes an immediate assessment as to whether or not they can control the dog. If they consider they cannot, the duty officer will call the firearms team, which will assess the situation and shoot the dog.

This decision is only undertaken if there is a danger to public safety. A dog cornered in a yard, therefore, is unlikely to be dispatched, unless it breaks free into a public area. A dog may be dispatched, however, if it has caused significant injury and the risk assessment by the duty handler determines that no further duty officers should be put at risk. Dogs are usually dispatched with shotguns using 6ml x 9ml bullets. Between October 2009 and October 2010, this occurred on 13 occasions. When it does occur, the dog is taken to a vet, who conducts a post-mortem for the following reasons:

- to establish if there was anything medically wrong with the dog to determine or exacerbate its behaviour;
- to provide confirmation of the officer's account and establish if it died cleanly or suffered.

Strict protocols exist regarding how dogs are bagged, tagged and retained for forensic evidence.

Dogs in custody

Once a dog is in custody, it is further examined and formally assessed. This may be problematic as breed recognition can require the input of professionals, including court expert witnesses. Assessment is usually undertaken by a police DLO, and requires physical confirmation of breed. Temperament is partially considered to determine the most appropriate kennelling destination or the potential danger to police or kennelling staff. However, a formal assessment of temperament involving expert witnesses is reserved until the court is ready to determine the dog's breed and to decide whether or not it should be destroyed or returned to the owner under a section 4A of the DDA 1991. This is similar to a section 4B disposal which can be granted by application, as opposed to section 4A which is granted following prosecution. The court must be satisfied that the dog presents no public danger.

Once breed and temperament have been determined the SDU officers will liaise with the SNT response team or CID and consider which of the following three courses of action to pursue:

- prosecute the owner for the charge brought;
- apply to the courts under section 4B of the DDA 1991 to return the dog under the rules of exemption;

- obtain a disclaimer from the owner that signs the dog over to the police. In this case, all charges are dropped and the dog becomes the property of the police.

Section 4B applications (the civil route)

Under section 4B of the DDA 1991, a civil application may be made for the destruction of an illegal dog. As one potential outcome of this process is exemption, resulting in the dog being returned to its owner, many members of the public refer to this section as the 'legalisation' of their dog. Nonetheless, the application does give responsible owners the opportunity to have their dog returned subject to its being neutered, tattooed, microchipped, insured and listed on the exemption register. Such applications are dealt with in magistrates' courts.

The magistrate is duty bound to consider whether the dog is a danger to public safety. Some officers argue that the courts should have a presumption towards destruction and that this should take precedence over any favourable behavioral report required by the magistrate when making a decision.

How magistrates deal with owners with criminal convictions varies across the UK. In the West Midlands a benchmark agreement operates whereby police will not advocate on the owner's behalf if they have previous convictions for serious drugs offences, serious assault, weapons, firearms or gang-related offences. In this event, the case goes to court for prosecution. Again the magistrate decides whether or not the dog is returned under the exemption rules.

Where the dog is exempted the police will provide a court report noting that if the owner abides by the exemption register conditions the dog will not pose a threat to public safety. This implies that the owner will follow the exemption requirements closely. Officers acknowledge that it does not necessarily follow that an irresponsible or antisocial owner will have an antisocial dog:

> 'You'd be surprised how many perfectly sociable dogs, do not fall under that category, 'cos of the criteria we have and the owner can quite often have very sociable dogs but it is the owner who is not sociable.' (Police officer, West Midlands)

It is difficult to tell to what extent owners convicted under the DDA are affected by the loss of their dog, particularly as replacements are readily available. Some may switch breeds, perhaps to a cross-breed, although others see this as 'downgrading'. For some owners with criminal records it is likely that the removal of their dogs is viewed by them simply as an occupational hazard, similar to having to pay a court fine; in other words, it is a temporary interruption that does not interfere with their long-term criminal enterprises.

There are two potential impacts of civil applications. First, and in the public interest, the civil route offers a fast and relatively cheap opportunity for resolution, leaving the way clear for criminal courts to concentrate on prosecuting those with criminal convictions. Second, it may skew statistical data, because those who sign their dogs over to the police do not receive any sanctions: they cannot be subject to legal charge and cannot be banned from owning dogs. This presents a problem to those seeking to collate data on the number of incidents involving dangerous dogs. The police recognise that this is an issue and suggest that returned dogs be subject to control measures.

The use of civil applications clearly indicates that the police consider animal welfare as well as public safety in such cases, and that officers can and do advocate for some dogs to be returned to sociable conditions and responsible owners. This contrasts sharply with Hallsworth's (2011: 400) assessment that 'the disproportionate response to the rise of "dangerous dogs" ... can be understood as a direct manifestation of the Security Sate and the punitive turn in which it is engaged'.

Unlike in criminal proceedings, where the focus is on a single defendant and the courts prohibit acknowledgement of previous convictions, civil action enables the police to consider and then address the possibility of harm occurring to other family members within the household. A common issue arises when owners of illegal dogs attempt to use other family members to register their dogs or claim ownership of the animals. This is frequently done because the real owner of the animal has previous criminal convictions whereas the other family member may have none. However, under the DDA 1991 it is not possible to shift the responsibility for ownership to someone else. In addition, when preparing reports for the magistrate's court, the police will consider all aspects of the domestic environment to which the animal may be returned. Not only will this assess potential harmful environments, such as cramped or unhygienic conditions, poor security or boundary fencing, it will also verify the offending histories of all domestic residents.

Uncontested civil actions under section 4(B) cost less than those that are contested (often half as much), and are usually completed quickly. If multiple cases are on file at once, the police force solicitor may need to instruct counsel on additional costs. Expert witnesses called to determine the breed further increase costs. In 2010, the MPS SDU made 224 section 4(B) applications, of which 167 were approved. See Appendix D for further detail on costs.

Disclaimers

At the point of intervention (seizure), owners are informed that they may sign the animal over to the police. In this event, the owner receives a solicitor's letter, setting out the potential kennelling, veterinary and legal costs. Costs are typically in the region of £700 to £1,000. Although not previously the case, the police now always pursue these costs and any outstanding debts, and recovered assets are returned to the borough command unit.

Following seizure of any animals, police vans must be cleaned thoroughly to avoid the spread of possible canine infections such as parvovirus. Where whole litters of pups are seized, details of each individual dog are recorded. When it is signed over, a dog becomes police property; however, some owners are too emotionally attached to their dogs to relinquish them.

Owners may invoke a disclaimer when a dog has been involved in a biting incident or in cases where the owners do not realise that the dog is illegal and ask the police to euthanise it. Disclaimers may also be used when police seize breeding pairs with pups. In this scenario, the only legal recourse is to return them to the owner, as it is an offence to rehome them or give them away. However, if a court were faced with having to return breeding adult dogs with a large litter of pups to what were considered to be unsuitable living conditions, it could at that point issue a destruction order. In such a scenario, if the adult dogs were socialised and of good temperament, the police may agree to a disclaimer for the pups, and to return the adults only on condition they are neutered and microchipped in accordance with the exemption rules. Dogs that are not proscribed by the DDA 1991 can be rehoused.

Court standards

The prohibited breeds determination standards used in court cases brought under the DDA are derived from the stated case of *Regina v Knightsbridge Crown Court ex parte Dunne; Brock v DPP [1993]* 4 All

ER 491. Here Lord Justice Glidewell states that a dog is a pitbull if it approximately amounts to a sustainable number of characteristics of a pitbull as described by volume 1, issue 3 of the *Pitbull Gazette*, published by the American Dog Breeders Association (ADBA) in 1977.

Some experts maintain that this definition is not stringent enough by Kennel Club breed standards. But in comparison with the Kennel Club Illustrated Breed Guide it is actually far more descriptive of the dog itself. Expert witnesses (employed by the court) must be impartial and are required to work through the stated case explaining how form meets function, why the dog looks the way it looks and how that benefits or detracts from its fighting abilities. The decision by the expert witness is accepted by the CPS, other police forces/authorities and local authorities. The defence counsel may challenge a claim that a dog is illegal by calling its own expert witnesses, and even if its first witness agrees with the initial findings, counsel is entitled to seek a further opinion. However if their first expert witness agrees the dog is illegal then the counsel are entitled to seek a further opinion. Some expert witnesses use a points system to determine whether or not the dog is a pitbull. Others work on the basis of DNA.

Temperament is also assessed on a scale of 10 against ADBA standards for attitude. The DDA 1991 was aimed at prohibiting dogs bred for fighting, so fighting and wrestling ability is also considered against ADBA standards to determine how 'game' a dog is. The 10% marking seeks to determine how 'game' the dog was, how 'up for it' it was and how much it wanted to 'go for it'.

Merseyside

The police response in Merseyside is similar to that of the MPS, although there are some noticeable differences. In 2007, following the death of five-year-old Ellie Lawrenson in Liverpool, Merseyside police launched Operation Darceni, giving owners an opportunity to hand in illegal, dangerous or aggressive dogs. The local newspaper, the *Liverpool Echo*, termed this a dog amnesty, although it was not publicised as such. It resulted in numerous calls from owners concerned that the puppy they bought might be a pitbull or claiming they could no longer control their fully grown aggressive dog. Many pitbulls and other dangerous dogs were handed in and euthanised, although there are no detailed records pertaining to numbers. Many other dogs were exempted and returned to families. No other local authority has since replicated this scheme.

In 2009, following the death of four-year-old Jean-Paul Massey in a dog attack, Merseyside police established its own status dog team to provide a proactive response to status and dangerous dogs.

On Merseyside, as in London, from the moment of seizure the police are responsible for the dog. In the past, several different individuals were involved and at each stage operating costs were incurred, for example, seizure and transfer to kennels (£30); health check and injections at the kennel (£100); kennelling fee (£10 a night). The failure of a DLO to attend an assessment on the first night might have resulted in a £150 cost for a dog that might not even be illegal. This presented welfare and financial challenges.

To address this challenge, Merseyside initiated a triage system. Old kennels in police stations (used for stray dogs) were reopened and dogs are housed there pending assessment. Any dog requiring a full examination, such as a potential pitbull, is referred to outside kennels for a full examination. This means that potentially dangerous dogs are transferred direct to external kennels with the expertise to undertake immediate risk assessment, resulting in cost reduction, improved quality and accuracy of assessments and proactive management of dangerous dogs.

On Merseyside, initial responsibility for assessment is now undertaken by warden patrols for stray dogs. Until 2008, the responsibility for stray dogs lay with the police, before shifting to local authorities. Now each local authority employs three dog wardens, working from 8am to 5pm on weekdays. An out-of-hours service is provided by a private company. However, the partnership arrangements have still to address the fine points of detail and disputes can arise over responsibilities for lifting certain breeds and operating times. The police still receive requests to deal with strays, including dangerous dogs. Local residents often report dogs as dangerous even when they know this not to be the case, because they believe they will get a swifter response. Nonetheless, police recognise the imperative to act on such cases. As one Merseyside officer put it, "If you leave a stray out, it is only a matter of time before it chases another animal or a child or gets angry." Dealing with the stray will also prevent a future section 3(1) offence if the dog injures someone. Section 3(1) provides for the owner or handler to be guilty of an offence if they allow a dog of any breed to be 'dangerously out of control in a public place'.[6]

Operation Newberry

Another initiative to tackle dangerous dogs in Merseyside is Operation Newberry, a database that monitors dogs with deferred assessment (dogs too young to be formally assessed) and exemptions. The deferred assessment allows for a 'home till court' listing. The database lists young pups, normally under four months old. Assessment is deferred until the dog is approximately seven months old, when the police formally assess the breed. Retention at home reduces kennelling costs. This is important in case the dog is later assessed as having insufficient characteristics to formally determine it as a pitbull. In this case, the dog would be returned to the owners. In the past, such cases have incurred up to £2,000 in costs.

Adult dogs, however, are seized and assessed. In the past, young adult pitbulls were occasionally left at the owner's home until the court hearing and at the discretion of police, if officers deemed the home environment to be suitable; for example, if the owners had no previous criminal convictions and agreed to certain conditions, such as insuring and muzzling. Such arrangements were usually suited to mature couples with well-socialised dogs. However, Merseyside police claim that increasingly aggressive dogs are owned not by mature couples but by younger families and that families owning pitbulls and other aggressive dogs appear are likely to be criminally linked:

> 'These days, virtually every case – say 99% that our force solicitor is looking at – is involved in criminal activity, either from the owner or the owner's family.' (Police officer, Merseyside)

When police returned to the property to seize the dog, owners would often claim that the dog had run off or was being temporarily rehoused with friends. Others would abandon their dogs on the streets. Others would be abandoned onto the streets. Current risk assessment practices make it impossible to leave a dog with its owners once it has been identified as a pitbull or a dangerous dog. In Merseyside, the police prefer to tackle the issue through civil action. Dogs that are assessed as 'borderline', that is, they have many pitbull characteristics but are deemed suitably socialised, are microchipped to prevent them coming back into the system at a later date if referred again for assessment.

Exemption requires owners to ensure that dogs are fully insured with third-party insurance. Merseyside police find that owners commonly insure their dog for the first year before letting insurance slide. The insurance status of the exempted dogs is monitored via data supplied by insurance companies and the Department for Environment, Food and Rural Affairs (Defra). Owners failing to renew their insurance are prompted by three warning letters. If insurance is not provided, dogs that were once technically legal via exemption now become illegal, giving police the power of seizure. Owners with criminal convictions may be served with a warrant. There are approximately 250-300 exempted pitbulls in the Merseyside area; in 71 cases, owners have breached their exemption agreement by failing to insure. The Operation Newberry database allows proactive action by police to ensure that owners comply with legal requirements.

Police action to follow up breach of exemption through lack of insurance may not be straightforward, as this interviewee indicated:

> 'This guy shouldn't really have an exempted pitbull, he has criminal convictions and doesn't insure his dog. We visit with a warrant for power of entry but we are invited in. When we say we will take the dog, it all kicks off. The bobby ends up crashing through a glass door with the owner. The bobby has cuts to his hands; the subject has cuts to his back where he fell backwards through the door. He ends up fighting the police, rolling around on the living room floor with this dog biting him. Arising from that one incident we have assault of police; obstruction of police; breach of exemption for the pitbull and all the S.1 offences that come with that. These are some of the joyful characters that the team here deal with every day.' (Police officer, Merseyside)

Kennelling

The kennelling of status and dangerous dogs, including prohibited dogs that are effectively in custody, is a considerable challenge for police authorities. It requires careful management of the dog's welfare, but due to delays in the criminal justice system there is the potential for escalating costs.

The MPS SDU contracts with nine private commercial kennels, each sourced through European procurement contracts. They are assessed on service provision, quality of provision and pricing. When dogs become a police responsibility, they are kennelled in the cheapest accommodation unless their case presents special requirements. Dogs are sometimes circulated around different kennels as a welfare provision if they fail to thrive at one specific kennel. Some kennels specialise in kennelling different breeds, others in managing and improving dogs that are particularly difficult to handle/control or are excessively aggressive. Here dogs are leash walked and socialised. Kennels exercise a duty of care, with consideration to welfare provision. Illegal or dangerous dogs may also pose a risk to kennel staff if they are aggressive or dangerously aggressive. In 2007, a 52-year-old female kennel worker in Wiltshire was attacked by a 12-stone rottweiler found stray in the New Forest. In the 90-minute attack, the kennel worker suffered over 100 bite wounds and subsequently had her arm amputated.[7] The history of the dog was unknown at the time of its placing in the kennel and the animal did not initially display signs of aggression.

In London, the MPS has approved a kennelling budget of £10.6 million[8] for four years, triggering debates as to how to reduce kennelling costs. Kennelling costs for Merseyside were £332,146 for 2010-11, including vets and transport costs.[9]

Kennelling dogs provides a number of challenges for the MPS:

- Kennelled dogs are at risk of infection. In 2009, 60 dogs were lost in one MPS kennel to parvovirus.
- Kennels may be overcrowded. On 4 October 2010, the MPS held 370 dogs in kennels.
- A single court case can involve several dogs, all of which have to be kennelled; for example, one case in October 2010 included 16 dogs.
- Prolonged court cases, caused by appeals and judicial reviews for example, increase kennelling times. In one case, a dog had been kennelled for 18 months pending the court hearing.

The judicial process

To provide guidance on the legal and case management issues which arise during the processing of court cases involving dogs, HMCS, the Justices' Clerks' Society and Defra (2010) published *An introduction to the case management of dangerous dog cases.*[10] This procedural manual clarifies process both for courts and for agencies managing dogs in custody, setting out key timeframes for actions to reduce custody time for dogs and subsequent kennelling costs.

From the point of seizure, the MPS must undertake a full assessment of the dog (which is done within 24 hours), liaise with the officer involved in working on the case, compile a full expert witness report and return it to the case officer. This work may be complicated by officer shift patterns. Finally, an appointment is made with the CPS and the report is delivered. MPS SDU analysis indicates that this takes on average, 27 days. A further 99 days elapse on average until the first appearance of the case in court. This extends to well over 100 days if the case is escalated to the crown court. During this time, the dog remains kennelled. The delays in the court system have instigated ongoing debates and pressure for inventive resolutions, including consideration of a dedicated CPS lawyer for dog issues.

Further barriers to swifter processing of section 4B applications are evident among the courts themselves. It should be possible to make five or six applications to one nearby magistrate's court, as this remains within the jurisdiction of the central criminal court. However magistrates' courts are often reluctant to undertake work on behalf of other courts without formalised mandates from the local criminal justice board. Such localised formalities result in MPS SDU officers travelling extensively across London to different magistrates' courts. As a result, five officers may attend five different courts in one day.

Opportunities exist for improving the current system that will maximise the welfare of the animal and reduce costs. This is particularly relevant in view of the fact that 50% of the dogs may be returned to kennels and that the costs are seldom fully recovered. Possible improvements include:

- a dedicated CPS lawyer;
- an agreed mandate for a single court to process all section 4B applications;
- dedicated court sittings for grouped cases;
- three or four courts, (ideally one in each quadrant of London) with specific experience in handling such cases;
- strict adherence to shared protocols to expedite listings involving a dog in custody.

MPS SDU had undertaken 'familiarisation' workshops with over 100 London magistrates by the end of 2010 to raise awareness of issues regarding aggressive and dangerous dogs. This was partly because some police officers felt that the courts could on occasion 'play down' cases involving dangerous dogs because they felt their role was to focus on human criminality rather than animal-related issues. In addition, officers had experienced a general reluctance by CPS staff to bring charges for offences involving aggressive dogs as the CPS staff assumed this would result in the destruction of the animal. (Officers suggested that this was based on empathetic animal welfare views rather than the prospect of additional work.) In cases involving serious criminality, police officers are more cogniscent of the fact that it is important to retain charges for dog-related offences in case the more serious charges fail to secure a conviction.

The key legal challenge is the issue of listing the case in court. Cases regarding dogs are frequently not prioritised, taking second place to drug dealing or theft of a motor vehicle. This results in increased kennelling costs, so that, for example, a pitbull in kennel might cost the taxpayer £10 a day or more. These issues have been reported in both Merseyside and London, where police believe magistrates to be unsympathetic to cases relating to dangerous dogs. Here the police can wait up to 60 days for a hearing, which may then be adjourned. In addition, hearings may take place anywhere in the capital, so last-minute adjournments after officers have spent time travelling to court are particularly frustrating, not to mention expensive.

Court adjournments are frequent in cases involving dogs and may arise from unfamiliarity with the law pertaining to dogs. Moreover, there is a lack of appreciation of the fact that delayed proceedings means extended kennelling for dogs in custody. Unfamiliarity with procedure by legal teams also produces delays; for example, behavioural reports are often not undertaken until directed by the court. Improvements that would address these issues include:

- awareness-raising among members of the CPS in relation to dog-related offences;
- training of local magistrates via the Magistrates' Association;
- improved judicial procedures, for example by reducing the number of court adjournments through ensuring that any offending histories relating to drugs, violence or criminal associations which might be pertinent are collated in advance to prevent delays;
- block booking of court sittings to clear backlogs of cases.

In a further complication, the CPS may decline to pursue charges under the DDA 1991. In one case in Merseyside, a pitbull was seized during a raid on a young man's house under the Misuse of Drugs Act 1971. The defendant entered a guilty plea with regard to the drugs charge but the CPS declined to bring charges in relation to the dog lest it 'complicate the sentencing' and lead to the defendant changing his plea. The decision not to charge took four months. The police then converted the case to a civil matter. As a result of various delays, including an appeal, the dog (seized in June 2009) was finally destroyed (in March 2011). This case cost Merseyside police £8,000. A dog kennelled for such a length of time is unlikely to be suitable for return. Some officers believed the CPS had a poor understanding of dogs in custody and were solely focused on those issues they considered to be more serious, that is, those involving drugs and guns. MPS SDU officers point out, however, that it is important to bring charges for dangerous dog offences in case the substantial prosecution fails.

The costs of prosecution vary depending on the type of case. This makes budgetary management complicated. For further detail on the average costs of cases and how these vary, see Appendix D.

Judicial disposals

Police officers would prefer to see owners with criminal convictions deprived of their aggressive or illegal dogs. This does not always happen, as magistrates may place a dog on the exemption register regardless of an owner's criminal convictions. Police argue that this is often done by officials on lay benches rather than district judges. Some police officers suggest that there should be a presumption in law towards the destruction of any illegal dog.

> 'If someone has a former offending history for shoplifting – it's probably nothing. Won't affect the dog, place is secure, environment is secure, risk assessment is ok; generally reformed person. So we are not too bothered, then we would probably be ok. However, if it's violence or weapons, it shows the person loses control now and then and so are unsuitable to have a dog in the home.' (Police officer, Merseyside)

The MPS SDU has a wide range of potential disposals for dogs (see Appendix C for further details). In 2010, a total 1,236 dogs were subject to judicial disposal. Of these, 298 were destroyed on court order, and 153 destroyed on disclaimer. In addition, 167 civil applications for destruction were approved under section 4B.

Disposal of the dogs involved in the murder of Seyi Ogunyemi

After the murder of Seyi Ogunyemi (see Introduction), the judicial process for disposing of the dogs involved was not straightforward. Originally, the dog owners were charged under section 3 of the DDA 1991 for allowing their dogs to bite the victims. Johnson was also charged with an offence under section 1 of the DDA 1991, as his dog was a registered pitbull. It had already been through a formal court process the previous year. The barrister dealing with the case felt that listing the dangerous dog offences would 'confuse the jury'. Thus at the end of the trial there were no dangerous dog offences on the charge sheet to legally allow for judicial disposal.

The issue was finally resolved through the use of a deprivation order under the Criminal Sentencing Act 2000. This states that in cases where the defendant is found guilty of using an object in the course of committing a crime, the court may deprive the defendant of such item, for example, a car used in a ram raid. Menezes, however, had by this time requested the return of his dog. A subsection of the DDA 1991 was then used to request the judicial disposal of both dogs involved in the murder, as the MPS felt it inappropriate for these dogs to be returned to the community.[11] This is normally a straightforward application to the court, and defendants have the right to be present in court if their property is being considered for destruction. However, on this occasion the defence decided to contest the application, instructing a barrister to claim that the dog was not involved in the murder (despite the fact the dog's saliva was found on the victim's coat). The MPS in turn instructed a barrister to contest this claim, leading to further adjournments until a destruction order was finally granted in October 2010, some 18 months after the dog was seized.

Local authority, animal welfare agency and government responses

Local authority responses

The local authority is a key agency with statutory responsibility for addressing public and community safety. How a local authority addresses the issue of status or dangerous dogs varies considerably, depending on whether or not it perceives it to be a problem. Local politics often determines whether or not action is pursued, and how vigorously. While some authorities ignore the issues, others are developing responses and good practice is emerging. As with many community programmes, evaluation of responses or programmes is weak and partners should look to strengthen this aspect of their interventions.

One key challenge in addressing the issue of status dogs is that responsibility for this falls between a number of different teams: parks and environmental services, community safety, police, dog wardens and social housing services. In authorities where the predominant working style is for each department to work in isolation from other departments, effective partnership working may stall and be ineffective, In some areas, local authority byelaws may provide additional legislative support, for example, a byelaw banning dogs in grassed areas, communal areas of housing estates or children's playgrounds. It is possible to bring legal action in cases where owners fail to control dogs, and several authorities have moved recently to issuing antisocial behaviour orders (ASBOs) or acceptable behaviour contracts (ABCs) in relation to dog offences (Home Office, 2010). A number of London authorities have also used ASBOs as sanctions against those using dogs to intimidate neighbours or residents.[12]

The challenge for many local authorities is that some incidents do not necessarily constitute an offence, for example, young people congregating with bull breeds in public places; walking several bull breed dogs at the same time; walking a dog off the lead on a public footpath or highway; or allowing dogs to bark or growl at passers-by. Some local authorities are now keen to be proactive in addressing the issue; for example, the mayor of the London Borough of Newham has made it a contractual promise to take action against dangerous dogs.

Supporting legislation

Table 8.1 lists the legislative tools that exist to address the issues of status dogs and dangerous dogs. Different legislative powers are favoured or used by different partners. Section 8 of the Animal Welfare Act 2006 builds on the provisions of the preceding 1911 Act, and strengthens the legislative framework for addressing dog fighting. This section creates a specific offence of animal fighting as opposed to a general 'offences of cruelty'. These new provisions are not widely understood by agencies or the young people who chain roll their dogs. The new Act prohibits:

- causing an animal fight or attempting to do so (section 8, subsection 1a);
- receiving money, publishing a fight, training an animal to fight or take part in a fight (section 8, subsection 1b-i);
- being present at a dog fight (section 8, subsection 2);
- recording dog fights, or showing, publishing, supplying or possessing such recordings (subsection 93).

Young people who chain roll their dogs, gamble on such fights and record them their mobile phones to forward to friends or publish online would be guilty of multiple offences under the Act.

Table 8.1: Legislative powers available to address issues of status and dangerous dogs

Legislation	Relevance	Key implementing agency
Dangerous Dogs Act 1991	S1, S3	Police
Dogs Act 1871	Permits civil proceedings to be brought for irresponsible dog ownership and incidents of attacks on other animals	Police, local authority, members of the public
Animal Welfare Act 2006	S4 (unnecessary suffering), S8 (fighting) also entry and seizure powers under S19 and S22	Police, RSPCA
Control of Dogs order 1992	Collar and tag	Local authority
Byelaws	Various local prohibitions	Local authority
Housing Act 1996	Notice of seeking possession and injunctions for breaches of tenancy and serious nuisance	Local authority
Anti-Social Behaviour Act 2003	ABC or ASBO to those who cause alarm, harm or distress to others	Local authority/police
Clean Neighbourhoods and Environment Act 2005	Dog control orders	Local authority, enforcement by local authority and police
Policing and Crime Act 2009	Gang injunctions	Local authority

Other legislation used is the Dangerous Dogs Act 1989, the Metropolitan Police Act 1839, the Town Police Clauses Act 1847 and the Offences Against the Person Act 1861.

Local authorities also have sole responsibility for stray dogs under section 68 of the Clean Neighbourhood and Environment Act 2005. Some authorities issue fixed penalty notices under sections 55-67 of this Act to those who fail to adhere to dog control orders. Defra's guidance to enforcers, however, notes that local authorities should ensure 'effective wide-ranging consultation prior to the use of such orders' (Defra 2009: 7) and ensure adequate enforcement so that responsible dog owners do not feel they are being penalised for the problems of others. This guidance recommends the training of relevant officers, the development of practical skills in dog behaviour and handling, educational programmes and partnership working with local agencies.

Registered social landlords

Registered social landlords (RSLs) have begun to realise that there is a potential problem with status and dangerous dogs on their properties, although they are in a strong position to tackle problems through their powers to manage, grant and regulate tenancy agreements. Pertinent issues include breeding animals for profit in cramped and unsuitable conditions, abandonment and strays, chain rolling and dog fighting, intimidation of other tenants, and noise and welfare issues.

The Defra guidance to enforcers states that tenancy agreements should include 'a clear and positive policy towards dogs with sanctions and consequences if a tenant fails to adhere' (Defra , 2009: 7). Tenants usually require permission to keep a dog and may be restricted from owning dogs in flats. Some RSLs now offer free microchipping or require compulsory neutering of dogs in their properties while others limit permitted animals to one per property. Such policies help to reduce irresponsible dog breeding.

Brent: Operation BARK

The London Borough of Brent was chosen as the starting point for a localised policing and partnership responses to status dogs and dangerous dogs. Entitled Brent Action for Responsible Canines (BARK),[13] the project was set up in 2007 as a partnership between the MPS, the RSPCA, the Brent Housing Partnership, Brent Council and the Mayhew Animal Home. The partnership aimed to reduce antisocial behaviour linked to the misuse of dogs while addressing community safety and improving levels of responsible ownership. It established a work programme based on four elements:

- reassurance – including events for local people to keep them informed about key issues;
- information sharing among partner agencies;
- prevention – improved local signage, regular patrolling of parks and school and group educational visits;
- enforcement – regular multi-agency patrols and proactive interventions using all available legislation.

This successful formula has been adopted by other local authorities and the project has been renamed Borough Action for Responsible K9s.

Wandsworth Council

Since 2007, Wandsworth Council has been at the forefront of local authority responses to status and dangerous dogs. Since 2009, it has been the responsibility of tenants, leaseholders and the tenants of leaseholders to have their dogs microchipped. This has allowed the council to establish an active dog database of over 4,000 dogs at a cost of almost £70,000. Microchipping is free to social housing tenants but costs £10 for others. To date, over 2,000 dogs have been successfully microchipped. The council clearly states that responsibility lies with the person named on the tenancy agreement and that this tenancy may be at risk if the dog is not controlled at all times and raised responsibly. Tenants are given several opportunities – through correspondence and visits from housing officers and dog control officers who will microchip dogs on the spot – to comply, after which proceedings for eviction are initiated. Despite the success of this initiative, a similar planned project was dropped by Harrow Council after a public consultation.

Partnership action is clearly set out in an action plan identifying roles and responsibilities.[14] The council also promotes responsible dog ownership through 'Walk to School' weeks with school children, educational roadshows and talks to tenants and residents associations. The borough's Youth Offending Team (YOT) also established a series of two-hour workshops for young people in conjunction with Battersea Dogs and Cats Home (BDCH).

Southwark Council

The approach in Southwark is based on partnership working, with a key focus on communications. The Safer Southwark Partnership established a dog action group in April 2010, including the council community safety team, housing services, parks, waste management and communications services, alongside the RSPCA, MPS and BDCH. The dog action group operates its own version of BARK within the borough. It has also developed a dog action strategy that aims to tackle dangerous dogs and dogs out of control by promoting responsible ownership, tackling irresponsible ownership, tackling banned breeds and meeting national best practice for tackling stray dogs. There are four key elements:

- community involvement – encouraging positive behaviours and discouraging antisocial behaviour through a network of educational and community engagement programmes;
- early intervention – information sharing and improved reporting among partners;
- intensive support and intervention – provision of welfare support and advice;
- enforcement – intelligence-led enforcement action.

Lambeth Council

The London Borough of Lambeth faced particular challenges in tackling high numbers of stray dogs and numerous incidents of dog fighting and chain rolling. In 2009, it ranked highest of all London boroughs in terms of the volume of dangerous dog offences.[15] It also accounted for the highest number of stray dog arrivals at BDCH.[16] Table 5.2 in Chapter Five sets out local residents' perceptions of the prevalence of dog fighting in the borough.

Although it was initially slow to realise the extent of the problem, the Safer Lambeth Partnership has now has now developed a coordinated response to tackling the issue. This activity includes the creation of a dog control task group to identify and implement a range of responses, including the development of a dog action plan. A dogs scrutiny commission was also established and in May 2010 made 20 recommendations for improvement of service. The action plan for 2009-10 focused on:

- enforcement action – for example, Operation Navarra;
- neighbourhood-targeted operations in hotspots;
- use of statutory powers to tackle antisocial behaviour;
- use of Housing Act/tenancy powers to restrict the prevalence of dogs in social housing, for example through tenancy restrictions;
- use of environmental powers/byelaws;
- promotion of BARK to include microchipping and awareness-raising among young people;
- improved management and reporting of stray and nuisance dogs;
- effective media communications; and
- improved multi-agency partnership working.

The borough has since launched Dog Watch, which encourages dog owners and walkers to report suspicious behaviour or irresponsible dog ownership. Full evaluation of many of these programmes remains outstanding.

Welfare agencies

Animal welfare agencies are often on the front line in terms of working with status dogs and dangerous dogs. They are also at the forefront of developing credible and effective projects to encourage more responsible dog ownership.

RSPCA

The RSPCA was one of the first agencies to identify the increase in status dogs, reflected in its inspectors' workloads. It then raised the issue nationally through press releases and extensive media coverage. The charity hosted a status dogs summit in 2009 and 2010 to bring partners together and identify good practice (RSPCA, 2009). This early recognition of the topic and the good practice recommendations arising from these events underpins much of the good practice currently used by local partners. In addition, the society works daily on the issue of status and dangerous dogs, undertaking investigations into dog fighting, animal cruelty and abandonment.

People with Dogs Project

The People with Dogs Project was established in 2007 and is aimed at reducing intimidation and antisocial behaviour involving dogs on London streets. The project is a partnership between BDCH, Blue Cross, the RSPCA, MPS, the Greater London Authority (GLA) and Wandsworth Council. The project is aimed at educating young people aged six to 16 years about the effects and impact of irresponsible dog ownership. The project has produced an educational pack and a DVD showing young men chain rolling dogs and purchasing puppies from irresponsible breeders. The pack also contains teachers' notes that explore the topics raised in the film. The project aims to be inclusive of owners of all breeds and seeks not to exclude or alienate owners of bull breeds but rather to develop and build empathy and understanding.

Blue Cross

The Blue Cross is a charity dedicated to improving the lives of sick and unwanted pets. Operating since 1897, it runs two animal hospitals and approximately 20 UK animal adoption centers. In January 2011, the charity revealed an increase in the number of banned breeds being treated at its animal hospitals and welfare clinics in the previous five years.[17] The issue of status dogs and dangerous dogs has been raised by Blue Cross volunteers and educational officers in talks to primary schools and youth groups across the UK. In 2010, the charity delivered workshops to over 25,000 children in the UK.

Dogs Trust City Dogs Project

The Dogs Trust is the UK's largest dog welfare charity and rehomes over 16,000 abandoned dogs every year. The trust created the City Dogs Project[18] at the end of 2009 to address the issues of young urban dog owners with status dogs. The project provides essential practical advice to those young people, mainly aged 14-24 years, who are often new to dog ownership and possibly lack the experience to train or look after their dogs. The project offers neutering, flea and worming treatments, working with youth organisations and local councils to engage young people in local parks. Key elements of the project are that the service is available to young people at times suitable to and defined by them. The service is confidential and there is 'no pressure' to take up services.

The Dogs Trust also has 10 full-time educational officers who attend primary schools in inner-city areas addressing status dog ownership through workshops. One aspect of the project in London focuses on population control of bull breeds. The trust has also provided more than 10,000 free microchips to London councils and RSLs to support their events and activates. The trust has been leading a national campaign for compulsory microchipping.

Regional government

In addition to local government, regional government has formulated responses to status dogs. The issue of status dogs and dangerous dogs as a concern for the public was identified and actioned early on by the regional GLA. Despite being subject to some unfair criticism, the GLA was influential in raising the issue of status dogs in London. It then played a central role in coordinating regional agencies and local government to work in partnership to tackle the issues of both status and weapon dogs.

In November 2009, the GLA raised the issue for central government and London councils by hosting a dogs summit involving the MPS, animal welfare charities, housing organisations and local authorities. At the summit, a discussion paper entitled *Weapon dogs: The situation in London* (GLA, 2009), established the concept firmly as a policy issue and reported on the impact of weapon dogs on Londoners. The report identified key areas for joint partnership focus, including:

- the development of standard procedures and policies for tenancy agreements by the Tenant Services Authority;

- continued partnership working and development of joint guidance with a view to changing the current dangerous dog legislation. The GLA established and hosted the London Dangerous Dogs Forum, which initiated multi-agency working in London;
- a proposal for local authorities to work with trading standards and tax and benefit agencies to explore how to tackle illegal breeding and improve effective enforcement;
- proposals for local authority Youth Offending Teams to work with young people via animal welfare charities to identify and develop universal and targeted educational programmes;
- the promotion of discounted neutering and microchipping programmes;
- joint events with the London Tree Officers Association to develop good practice regarding safeguarding the environment;
- improved data sharing;

The GLA and the MPS SDU have also supported training on status dogs and dangerous dogs to magistrates and court staff to improve their knowledge and understanding of the issues and to recognise the need to deal with them more efficiently and effectively through the court system. Thus far training has been given to around 100 staff.

National government

England

Central government intervention has revolved largely around proposed legislative changes to the DDA 1991, for example, the creation of local authority authorised officers. This would remove powers from the police to act with regard to dangerous dogs. It is doubtful that such proposals would improve the current situation as fiscal restraints on local government are already leading to cuts in dog warden and park ranger services. Such proposals would only lead to further confusion among members of the public about how to report incidents and would provide patchy responses from councils.

Some animal welfare agencies have lobbied publicly to repeal the Act. Others have called only for repeal of section 1 of the Act, which bans certain breeds (often termed breed-specific legislation). In 2009, the RSPCA joined these calls for repeal and was supported by groups such as DDA Watch and the Coalition for Improved Dog Ownership Standards. Many organisations, kennel clubs and welfare charities believe that the DDA 1991 has failed to protect the public or to eradicate the pitbull terrier in the UK, and has led to the needless euthanising of many dogs on the basis of breed and on looks. Several like-minded agencies formed the Dangerous Dogs Act Study Group,[19] administered by the Kennel Club, which has lobbied for changes to the Act for a number of years.

In 2009, Liberal Democrat peer, Lord Redesdale, tabled a private member's bill on dog control in the House of Lords, aiming to abolish breed-specific legislation, criminalise attacks on private property and increase the emphasis on behaviour of the dog and its owner. The bill will be reviewed further in 2011/12, but as a private member's bill, it is uncertain whether it will receive royal assent. Various amendments and alterative proposals are being drafted by agencies. The bill and the consultation by Defra have kept the issue politically alive, although there appears to be less consensus on some of the issues than many had thought (see Appendix E for the details of the consultation and the results).

At present, it appears that central government is struggling to replace the DDA 1991 and its 1997 amendments with something that places responsibility more on the owners than on the breed. At this stage, different interest groups and professionals are taking different principled positions with regard to outcomes of the proposed bill. Currently, the primary dog welfare charities and agencies, the Dogs Trust, Kennel Club and RSPCA, oppose breed-specific legislation, with the Dogs Trust and Kennel Club keen to scrap both section 1 of the DDA 1991 and breed-specific legislation.

More recent proposals involving the Association of Chief Police Officers (ACPO) and the RSPCA leave breed-specific legislation intact. ACPO presently supports the bill, which was drafted by a working group of police, local authority dog wardens and the RSPCA. Specifically, the bill aims to:

- further public protection by extending legislative powers to include any incidents occurring 'within private property';
- improve early intervention with the use of dog control notices and orders, enabling officers to place any of a wide spectrum on conditions on irresponsible/status dog owners;
- increase public reassurance through robust implementation of these measures;
- ensure cost savings by reducing kennelling and prosecution costs.

Should these provisions operate in similar ways to improvement notices under the Animal Welfare Act (monitored by the RSPCA with a high rate of compliance), they would provide authorities with a suitable point of intervention and be more effective in safeguarding public safety. The serving of an improvement notice/control order would prevent the need to engage the costly court process. A high level of compliance with these requirements would naturally bring about the necessary sea change in social attitudes towards key breeds of dog. As a result, within a few years breed-specific legislation could be rescinded.

The Home Office also provided £20,000 to ACPO to help police forces train dedicated dog legislation officers and to better equip the police to address issues of dangerous and status dogs. Defra provided a similar award in 2009. Defra has also funded Liverpool University to undertake a meta-analytical study to investigate the risk factors for aggressive dog–human interactions.

Scotland

The Control of Dogs (Scotland) Act 2010, enforceable from 26 February 2011, adopts a 'deed not breed' approach to tackle irresponsible dog ownership, making the dog owner fully responsible for the actions for the dog. The Act, passed unanimously by the Scottish Parliament, aims to close a loophole in the DDA 1991. It ensures that dog owners can be held to account if the dog attacks or if they fail to control the dog if it becomes dangerous. Dogs deemed 'out of control in a private or a public place' can result in issue of a dog control notice (termed dog ASBOs by the media). Owners failing to comply with the notices can be forced to keep their dogs leashed at all times, have it neutered, attend training courses to make them more responsible dog owners or be fined up to £1,000. The Act saw 693 investigations being undertaken from February to December 2011, with 67 dog control notices being served.[20] Calls have often been made for similar approaches to be tried in England. In 2010, Professor Reilly, President of the British Veterinary Association (BVA), stated that the current provision of banning certain breeds such as pitbulls failed to protect people from aggressive dogs, and he called for the introduction of dog ASBOs to place the responsibility on the owner.[21]

US anti-dog-fighting programmes

Just as the US has a large number of people engaged in illegal dog fighting of bull breed dogs, it has numerous local projects and programmes to address illegal dog fighting, for example the award-winning youth intervention programme, Knock Out Dog Fighting.[22]

There are also numerous programmes aimed at owners of bull breeds and tackling irresponsible dog ownership. Given the long-standing role that the American pitbull terrier (APBT) has played in the American psyche, there are many respectable and responsible owners of APBTs who remain vocally loyal to bull breeds, putting in considerable energy to try to improve the image of the dogs. 'Bully shows', for all bull breeds, are common across the US and showcase bull breeds in a positive light. Weight-pulling competitions are common and are established, some say, in an attempt to permit owners to demonstrate the abilities of the dogs while resisting the temptation to use them for fighting. Such events, however, are marketed to owners in ways that reinforce the aggressive traits and reputational characteristics of the bull breeds. They are also attended by owners involved in dog fighting and used as networking opportunities for fighters and breeders, despite their apparently innocent family-oriented appearance. *AtomicDogg* magazine provides show listings and has many positive features about responsible ownership and breeding. However, at the same time the publicity values and styling seem to be at odds with those of 'traditional' APBT owners seeking to recapture the 'noble qualities' of the breed within the family as opposed to the urban street context.

In addition, there exist a number of programmes largely for urban or street youth established by the Humane Society of the United States, local kennel clubs and welfare agencies[23] such as Battle Against Dog-fighting and YMCA Humane Education and Leadership Program.[24]

The Knock Out Dog-fighting programme is a donation-driven programme run by volunteers and has been working for 10 years to stop dog fighting.[25] It aims to address underlying reasons for young people engaging in dog fighting by developing positive role models and using a host of celebrity and professional boxers, fitness experts, dog trainers and martial artists to promote responsible dog ownership.

The programme focuses on choices, consequences and overcoming issues of status and reputation by building personal self-esteem. It runs several successful show events alongside a youth intervention programme for schools, community centres and juvenile detention facilities that includes school assembly presentations, weekly classes and workshops. Programmes are also linked to gang violence, with targeted programmes for gang hotspots using behaviour modification techniques for those identified as being at risk. The programmes have established a formula of not preaching to young people or telling them not to fight their dogs; rather, they work to stop abuse of animals by offering healthy alternatives. A younger version of these programmes, called For Pits Sake, runs for younger aged children. Programmes in the US that target young people, children or gang-affiliated young people mix interactive and experiential learning using peer mentors.

Community-based programmes also operate, focusing on local education of adults and addressing links to child violence, domestic violence and animal cruelty. Faith and community organisations are actively engaged, and programmes emphasise empowering local people, particularly young mothers, to speak out against dog fighting and animal cruelty. Successful local programmes also develop through grassroots community organising and local multi-agency partnership working. Some programmes link to local sports teams or to work with service dogs, guide dogs and people with disabilities. Some welfare agencies run Prevent a Litter programmes, aimed at reducing irresponsible and prolific back-street breeding.

All successful anti-dog-fighting programmes advocate bull breeds as part of the family, raise empathy and seek to improve the image of the bull breed dogs by stressing pro-social traits, training and responsible behaviour of owners and dogs.

Conclusion

Status dogs and dangerous dogs can present numerous challenges for all agencies. This is especially so for the police, who navigate a complicated set of legislative arrangements. It is clear animal welfare is central to their operations, but this must be set alongside the issue of public safety. Police are critical of, and often frustrated by, the workings of the criminal justice system, which at times seems to mitigate against good practice and animal welfare, notably in the issues of timings of proceedings and of kennelling.

Local authorities and animal welfare agencies are increasingly alert to the issue of status dogs and dangerous dogs and a variety of good practice is certainly emerging. It is likely, however, that practice is patchy across the UK as a whole. While animal welfare and educational programmes are available in some locations, access to such programmes may be patchy in other locations. Moreover, evaluation of these programmes is limited and if such schemes are unable to demonstrate impact they may be subject to funding cuts. While programmes aimed at developing responsible dog ownership are central to tackling the issue of status dogs, questions arise as to the sustainability of such programmes over coming years.

It must also be recognised that solutions from central government, at least in England and Wales, still seem remote and now lag behind the actions of other governments. It is likely that sustainable improvement will only finally come with legislative change.

Notes

[1] MPS SDU interview, 4 October 2010, for this research.

[2] Presentation on the MPS SDU by Inspector Trevor Hughes, GLA Dangerous Dogs Enforcement Seminar, 29 March 2011.

[3] Gilani, N. , 'Police crackdown on "dangerous dogs" in South London', *South London Press*, 13 July 2009.

[4] MPS Haringey Dangerous Dogs Operation, 20 July 2011. Bruce Grove Safer Neighbourhood team is leading Haringey's response to dangerous dogs, after it became the first such team in the borough to have dangerous dogs set as a ward priority in response to concerns raised about dog behaviour in Lordship Recreation Ground and Downhills Park in Tottenham, http://content.met.police.uk/news/Dangerous-dogs-operation/1260269311750.

[5] As of October 2010, these are Lambeth, Lewisham, Southwark, Hackney, Haringey, Tower Hamlets, Waltham Forest, Ealing.

[6] Section 10(3) defines 'dangerously out of control' and section 10(2) defines 'public place'.

[7] Laurie Hanna, 'Kennel maid gets £500K payout for Rottweiler attack', *Daily Mirror*, 8 March 2011.

[8] MPS SDU interview, 4 October 2010, for this research.

[9] Merseyside Police Dogs Unit interview, 11 March 2011, for this research.

[10] Now published on the HMCS website.

[11] Section 4B 1(6) states: 'Where a dog has been seized under S.5(1) or 5(2) of the DDA – under a warrant or in the street (which applied in this case); the person has been or is to be prosecuted or the dog cannot be given back without contravening S.1, the Court may destroy the dog and shall do so unless it's satisfied that it doesn't present a danger to the public.'

[12] Neeta Dutta, 'Trio used their dogs to intimidate neighbours', *Ealing Times*, 22 November 2007.

[13] www.brent.gov.uk/eh.nsf/animal%20welfare/LBB-60

[14] www.wandsworth.gov.uk/Home/EnvironmentandTransport/Dogs/default.htm

[15] Lambeth Council, 'Action to tackle crime and ASB associated with 'status dogs': update', Report by Adults and Community Services, 22 March 2010.

[16] See note 14

[17] www.bluecross.org.uk

[18] www.dogstrust.org.uk

[19] Members include Battersea Dogs and Cats Home, Blue Cross, Dogs Trust, MPS, the Kennel Club, Wandsworth Borough Council, Wood Green Animal Shelter.

[20] BBC News Scotland, '"Good start" for new dog asbo law', 24 December 2011.

[21] Louise Gray, 'Vets call for "dog ASBOs"', *The Telegraph*, 17 February 2010.

[22] www.knockoutdogfighting.org/index.html

[23] www.safehumanechicago.org, www.barriodogs.org, www.safetyarounddogs.org; www.humanesociety.org

[24] www.madacc.com

[25] See note 22

NINE

Conclusion

The reasons for writing this book were numerous. Initially, it was the murder of 15-year-old Seyi Ogunyemi in Lambeth in 2009 during my research into gangs in Brixton and Stockwell that alerted me to the issue of gangs using status dogs. I quickly wanted to establish if this incident was isolated or extensive. My gang research had already alerted me to issues of urban dog fighting among youths and how young men paraded their aggressive bull breed dogs to gain status among their peers. There was a need to understand this phenomenon by getting behind the media headlines and scare stories to see where the truth lay. Second, there was a need to explore the links with antisocial behaviour and criminal activity and to identify motivations for using dogs to convey status. This involved a search for the facts, which itself proved more difficult and challenging than I had imagined. It also led me to the conclusion that status dogs are now an inclusive and visible element of the UK urban landscape. Lastly, there was a need to place this phenomenon on record and to collate and contextualise the available data.

By linking certain groups of young people to issues of public safety and dog ownership, the book offers a unique contribution towards understanding the motivational complexities of using dogs to convey status. Throughout the book I illustrate the various strands of this phenomenon demonstrating that these strands do not exist in isolation from one another. This issue is much more multifarious than simple arguments about deed or breed and involves complex interrelationships that are key to any understanding.

My investigations illustrate that the status dog phenomenon is recent, but is a current reality in the UK. It is also a highly complex issue due to:

- the subjective nature of definitions of status or weapon dog;
- widespread varying opinions on the purpose and efficacy of legislation;
- lack of agreement on the seriousness of the issue;
- lack of suitable or available data;
- poor data quality or evident data inconsistencies;
- complex methodological difficulties involved in researching ownership;
- lack of previous academic research, notably UK research;

- the traversing nature of the topic, spanning as it does, the interdisciplinary nature of the topic;
- lack of collated knowledge by any single agency.

These challenges make the topic complex and difficult to research, but also difficult for agencies to address. As an issue of social policy, it is currently homeless and is yet to be properly situated within a contemporary social policy context. Nevertheless, there are several important points worth making in conclusion.

The phenomenon of status dogs

The term 'status dog' is both new and pejorative and although it is increasingly recognisable, its social currency is still developing. What is now little contested is the noticeable, if yet unquantifiable, rise in the number of aggressive bull breeds on UK streets. This rise, paralleled in other western countries such as the US, is clearly no urban myth.

As with any emergent phenomenon, views are divergent as to the real nature of the issue. For many, this concerns the potential risks posed by aggressive bull breeds and whether it is the animal or the owner that poses the risk. One major concern is irresponsible back-street breeders who mass breed dogs for financial gain. Some dogs are bred for aggression and pose a potential threat to the public and crucially have the physical ability and strength to inflict damage.

Pitbulls are often the dog of choice for owners seeking a dog to convey status. This questionable accolade is due to the pitbull's legendary loyalty, malleability and notorious gameness to continue fighting. Pure-bred dogs seldom pose a problem. However, irresponsible or back-street breeding frequently results in poor quality-dogs. These are a potential threat to the public for the following reasons:

- they may have been bred for dog–dog aggression or dog–human aggression;
- they are easily aroused and can remain highly aroused;
- they show few or no warning signs before they attack;
- they have the physical ability and strength to inflict damage;
- they can inflict considerable tissue damage, causing life-changing injuries.

When irresponsible socialisation, aggressive or cruel training is coupled with unhealthy or irresponsible breeding, there are credible concerns and risks to the public. Despite the many myths surrounding pitbulls, and setting aside arguments that they are genetically predisposed to aggression, it is clear that there are established facts that make pitbulls a legitimate cause for concern regarding public safety. The Greater London Authority, the police and animal welfare agencies are right to focus energy on this issue.

The media

In the US, the pitbull has undergone a public transformation from noble, hard-working frontier dog to a maligned breed negatively associated with guns, gangs and the emergence of 'subterranean values' of the 'feral underclass' (and its US association with ethnicity and race). Critically, this is indicative of shifts in the contemporary accepted norms of human–animal relationships, notably increased commodification. While media misrepresentation, pejorative imaging and associated myths have undoubtedly played a role in this journey, signifying 'otherness', the dog still retains qualities with enduring appeal to certain owners. Yet it is these same qualities that effectively seal its fate.

This transformative journey has been assisted by the media's role in the social construction of the concept of status dogs and weapon dogs, in the US in the 1980s via the so-called 'pitbull panic' and in the UK in the early 1990s, creating the preconditions for the hurried introduction of the controversial Dangerous Dogs Act (DDA) in 1991. Some elements of moral panic can be noted in contemporary mediated messages, although this is most likely the media acting as early receptor of a shift in cultural/social norms and values regarding dogs and their role in society. While media reporting has not facilitated understanding of the issue, it is clear that there are legitimate fears from numerous quarters relating to the appearance of aggressive bull breed dogs in our open spaces.

Motivations for ownership

Motivational reasons for status dog ownership may appear at first obvious, but in reality are more complex. My research indicates multiple motivations, ranging from protection or fashion to establishing money-making breeding machines, to image creators and identity makers. Motivations vary depending on the social field of the owner, permitting some dogs to remain household pets in loving environments, while others are traded up/down, abandoned or turned into fighting dogs. Motivational factors arise from the complex web of macro and micro socioeconomic issues affecting those in deprived urban environments.

This is particularly the case for those seeking to maximise reputation and respect within the social field of the violent urban street gang. While this includes fragile masculinities and physicality, the overriding factor remains an imperative for young men to generate street capital to provide enduring reputational advantage that then elevates their status, providing new opportunities to generate economic capital, respect and advancement.

How do status dogs convey status?

For young men seeking to build a reputation, a bull breed dog is an ideal mechanism by which to attain this – much more so than the latest trainers or downloaded music track. Acquiring a status dog becomes a strategy for self-improvement. The goal of the acquisition is first to build a reputation, then to obtain respect. By acquiring a status dog, this reputation can be enhanced though:

- initial novelty value;
- demonstrating that you are a 'player', that is, you understand your own environment and what gains respect;
- demonstrating knowledge of the dog/breed;
- 'kitting out' the dog with leather harnesses and chains;
- amplifying the physique and musculature of the dog, so it appears bigger/more aggressive;
- building further social capital through interactions now focused on both owner and dog;
- dictating group action by including the dog in activities. This improves the owner's standing within peer groups, providing opportunities for dominating or advancement.

These reputational advantages then become routes to 'distinction' within the group. This conveys status. Owning a status dog provides sufficient enduring reputational advantage for young people to overcome other fluctuations in their reputational status. This includes new bonding opportunities with peers of higher rank who may also have status dogs. The dog then becomes your 'passport' for mutual conversations above your rank, or across groups.

For many young people, especially those affiliated to gangs, the dog itself comes to represent the habitus. The dog with its muscular physique becomes a physical reflection of the young men, mirroring the paramount attributes of their habitus: being hard, aggressive, tenacious, full of energy and ready for the fight; having stamina and a lust for life; and not backing off or backing down. The canine attributes and characteristics make the dog the physical embodiment of the habitus. Those sharing the habitus or social field understand this implicitly without explanation and thus the status dog is welcomed without question. The bull breed is the logical dog of choice. Anyone acquiring such a dog demonstrates a commitment to the habitus and the neighbourhood. Others will perceive this and this gains approval among peers. Status dog acquisition fast-tracks reputations and owners assume the brand characteristics of their acquired brand. Such fast-tracking often appeals to those who have few other routes to build a reputation. Reputational advancement is then progressed by using the dog functionally for chain rolling and impromptu dog fights. Additional reputational qualities are acquired, such as:

- increased confidence
- influence over other members
- opportunities for breeding/selling
- bragging rights
- improved image building by posting images on social networking sites
- visibility – maintaining a high neighbourhood profile.

Status dogs are used to defend established reputations – a social imperative regarding 'respect'. Owners sporting a bull breed in a full harness are unlikely to experience casual disrespect. This reduces prospects of casual violence, ensuring that status dog owners incur fewer challenges from rivals (although rivals may seek back-up from another animal). Status dog owners refer to this as having the dog for protection (from other youths/ rival gangs). As challenges occur daily, so a status dog is considered good protective insurance.

Challenges are also formally settled by using the dog to 'square off' with a rival's dog. In a gang, this may protect young men from being stabbed during fights. Dogs are then chain rolled to settle the score for low-level altercations. Status dog ownership reduces the possibility of social exclusion in many socially deprived neighbourhoods where the fear of isolation, exclusion or victimisation often leads young people to reluctantly join gangs (Pitts, 2008). However, if this function ceases to be relevant, the dog may be discarded, neglected or abandoned. This may result because of a reputational shift in the owner (because he cannot control the dog, the dog becomes a burden, an embarrassment or a liability and leaves him subject to ridicule or stress) or in the dog (it becomes seen as a liability, unfit for purpose, and fails to live up to expectations of the owner or the group).

Cultural factors

The status dog, as represented by bull breeds and in particular the pitbull, is now a firm fixture in the cultural identity of the US and the UK and is a firm cultural fixture in deprived urban neighbourhoods. In contemporary Britain, the pitbull has acquired a certain level of appeal that is beginning to mirror that of the US where increased visibility leads to increased cultural resonance. As pitbulls become more visible in our open spaces and our lives, they take up a recognisable position and shared meaning in our cultural landscapes. It was not by mistake that Sarah Palin touched on this widespread cultural positioning when she made her famous quote about pitbulls at the US Republican national conference in 2008: "You know what they say the difference between a hockey mom and a pitbull is? Lipstick." So accepted are the reputational characteristics of pitbulls that this quote not only had resonance with a worldwide audience, but also had the effect of associating her with the characteristics of tenacity, loyalty, strength, protection and aggression.

Overarching this is a cultural domain of hip hop, now adopted as the cultural motif and aural wallpaper of ghettoised communities. Within this world, the status dog occupies its new home as a fully fledged 'homie'. As with the music, status dogs and bull breeds have become cultural signifiers that speak volumes to those from public housing projects and deprived estates.

Increasingly, status dogs are associated with marketing that reinforces the reputational qualities of the dogs, branding them as the perfect dog for survivalists, gangs and urban warriors.

The evidence

My research indicates a universal lack of academic and policy research on this issue, coupled with limited availability of data. Generating the true UK picture of status dogs is further complicated by misrecognition of dog breed and type, and failure to record/collate data. Available data are often of poor quality. This holds true across all public sectors, from hospital A&E departments, which fail to record the nature or severity of bites, to those police forces that fail to prioritise the issue. The Home Office and Defra have recently both declined opportunities to conduct further research into status dogs.

Notwithstanding the above points, I set out to capture for the first time the views of practitioners, professional and owners of status dogs. This research study proved complex and lengthy, with multiple ethical and methodological challenges. On occasion, I felt personally threatened, by either a dog or its owner. Nonetheless, the evidence presented indicates the reality of the phenomenon. The evidence supports the concept of using dogs to convey status as a reality for some young people.

The links between status dogs, weapon dogs and criminal activity are evidenced here for the first time and the evidence is compelling. The Association of Chief Police Officers should now conduct further research into owners' offending histories, generating profiles to further demonstrate these links. It is indeed worrying that some dogs are used as criminal adjuncts, facilitators and weapons. This role, for which the pitbull is now the new standard bearer and poster dog, builds on the physical and reputational characteristics of the dogs, often cruelly twisting them into amplified, super-aggressive hood hounds to suit the functional requirements of those in status deficit. This is furthered, sometimes knowingly, sometimes unwittingly, by those irresponsible breeders seeking to profit from current popularity. Despite this somewhat bleak finding, it is worth remembering that it is only a minority of dog owners who use their animals in such a way.

Dog fighting

The issue of dog fighting is also linked to status and dangerous dogs and remains significantly underresearched in both the US and UK. Where dog fighting exists in urban rather than rural areas, issues of social deprivation and links to gambling are prevalent.

Recent US research evidences the strong links between dog fighting and criminal networks. Again in the UK, such issues remain unresearched and unquantified. While dog fighting is on the radar of agencies such as the RSPCA, several challenges prevent quantification and agency intervention:

- underreporting of fights
- neutralisation techniques employed by those involved
- secrecy
- the spontaneous nature of chain rolling
- the normalisation of dog fighting as part of the habitus
- the challenges of gathering evidence

- the reluctance of witnesses to come forward and the culture of not grassing.

Current UK evidence suggests that involvement in dog fighting matches the typology established by the Humane Society of the United States (HSUS), with chain rolling by youths being the most prevalent form at present in the UK. Research indicates a potential for graduation from street chain rolling to hobbyist fighting to professional-circuit dog fighting. Addressing this presents a challenge to UK animal welfare agencies. They may need to shed what is frequently a cuddly and fluffy public image and develop some real urban grit and realism if they are to reach youths involved in urban street dog fighting and prevent it from escalating in frequency and severity.

The concerns for public space

Prolific breeding and increased ownership of status dogs has significantly increased the visibility of aggressive bull breeds in our open spaces. This in turn has generated general public anxiety and fear, leading some people to change the way they use public space. Specific anxieties and safety implications exist for young children and families, postal staff, working guide dogs and park users.

Fatal dog attacks are mercifully rare. While any dog can be dangerous, bull breeds invariably have the potential to inflict life-changing and life-threatening damage. As such, any proliferation of such dogs in public must be carefully managed and monitored.

Responses to the issue of status dogs

Status dogs and dangerous dogs present specific and challenging problems for UK public agencies, not least that:

- control measures are confused and irregularly applied;
- police and local authority responses vary considerably and are inconsistent;
- there is a lack of national public information campaigns that raise awareness of the issue;
- efforts to ban breeds while allowing some to keep their pitbulls via an exemption index create confused/mixed messages;
- there is a lack of information available in community languages;
- local byelaws, such as the ability to ban pitbulls from parks, are underutilised.

Animal welfare agencies and local authorities are increasingly engaging with the issue of status and dangerous dogs in both policy and projects. However, projects are often localised and short term, with limited, if any, evaluation.

The fiscal costs of this issue remain undetermined by Defra. Recent economies in public expenditure have not created any noticeable imperative to reduce kennelling costs, hospital admissions and so on. It is possible that accurate cost calculations would impel politicians to expedite resolutions regarding legislation. The NHS is reportedly spending upwards of £2.7 million annually treating the victims of dog bites[1] (not including days lost from absence from work). Veterinary treatments for mistreated status dogs and the practice of euthanising banned breeds add to the costs, as do effective policing, long-term kennelling of dogs in custody, court costs, judicial delays and the employment of expert witnesses. If these policing and judicial costs are extrapolated across all 44 forces in England, Wales and Northern Ireland, and added to NHS treatment costs and employers' costs of work days lost through absence, it is possible that the total expenditure for addressing issues of dangerous and status dogs is considerable and probably sits in range of £50 million to £100 million.

Legislation

Any discussion in the UK regarding status dogs and dangerous dogs quickly turns to legislation, notably the widespread perception of the failure of the DDA 1991. Some key questions about the Act jump to the fore:

- Has it led people to switch breeds? The evidence suggests that it does.
- Has it led people to specifically seek out ownership of illegal dogs? Probably not, but there is no evidence either way.
- Has it led to irresponsible breeding to get round the Act? Yes, leading to many dogs, notably pitbulls, being bred irresponsibly and a proliferation of cross-breeds.

Deed-not-breed and breed-specific legislation remain touchstone issues for many people. At present, breed-specific legislation inevitably ensures that sociable dogs are taken into custody. The key reason given for retaining breed-specific legislation is that irresponsible dog ownership persists. It seems to be incontestable that the pitbull, above all other dogs, is subject to cruelty and abuse by humans – by those breeding irresponsibly and by those using it as a weapon. Given this situation, at what point do you say that this breed of dog is suitable and available for all members of the public? Perhaps we are not at that place yet.

While the goal remains that of responsible dog ownership, this cannot be achieved by legislation alone. Currently, the abuse of certain dog breeds and types (notably the pitbull) persists and is apparently increasing. Society seems to be further away from a point where breed-specific legislation can be removed. As such legislation remains a main tool for authorities maintaining public safety, it seems appropriate to retain it until such time as society's outlook has changed with regard to these dogs. In an ideal world, breed-specific legislation would not be required but removing it before any significant shift in how societies interact with these breeds may weaken the ability of authorities to contain dog fighting, chain rolling, weapon dogs and the use of dogs for criminality. The breed-specific element in the legislation (section 1, DDA 1991) remains a useful tool for public safety. For example, where dog fighting is suspected but there is insufficient evidence to authorise a warrant under the Animal Welfare Act, the police have no power to enter premises, but section 1 of the DDA 1991 allows for entry if the dog in the yard can be identified as a pitbull.

While the removal of breed-specific legislation should be society's goal, pre-emptory removal of this tool would inhibit the work of authorities and agencies to address the issues raised in this book. A review of the legislation should be welcomed following a concerted campaign to change social attitudes towards these dogs, to one where general dog ownership is more responsible and better managed.

Solutions

This book is primarily concerned with placing the issues on record rather than an in-depth search for solutions. However, it may be useful to formulate some propositions to drive forward the debate. Websites are replete with personal views and ideas on how to resolve the DDA 1991 and each animal welfare agency has its own position. During 2011, greater consensus has appeared across these agencies about the reality and seriousness of the status dog issue. Should this lead to a consensus of proposals followed by real and effective legislative change, improvement to the current situation might be possible. However, given the surprising variety of responses to the Defra (2010) consultation, there is still some way to go. The only point with full consensus is the need for reform of the current legislation. There is not room here to fully explore all possible solutions, so instead I suggest some areas for consideration:

- more targeted programmes to reach gang-affiliated young people and those with criminal links, using innovative techniques such as dog-care and welfare programmes for incarcerated offenders;
- the development of a coordinated, national multi-agency publicity campaign to recast the image of the dogs – not as aggressors, but as companions;
- a refreshed legislative focus on risks to public safety and potential to cause harm;
- licensing for breeders to reduce irresponsible and unhealthy 'scatter breeding' of dogs;
- tighter restrictions on social housing tenants regarding ownership and breeding of bull breeds;
- abolition of the prohibited list of prescribed dangerous dogs, including the Index of Exempted Dogs (if the intention is to breed out the pitbull, it seems contradictory to permit some individuals to continue to own these dogs);
- shifting enforcement from the dog's behaviour to that of the owner, possibly using a three-category offence rating from minor to intermediate to serious. In this way any dog involved in a minor offence is immediately designated as being potentially harmful, requiring the owner to take preventative action, such as muzzling, repairing or improving the enclosure for the animal, or licensing the dog;
- compulsory microchipping of all dogs;
- compulsory third-party insurance for all dogs, with premiums banded to reflect potential danger to the public. This would require additional health research into bite rates and types of injuries;
- compulsory registration for all dogs with animal welfare agencies;
- policing through fines for dogs not chipped or insured;
- expedition of criminal justice procedures to reduce kennelling costs and provide swifter justice;
- adoption of the HSUS typology for dog fighting.

An issue for social policy

The lack of a clear policy framework on the new phenomenon of status dogs has resulted in the issue being diluted or relegated in terms of social policy to one that concerns only 'animal lovers'. Evidence suggests that it is a more serious and profound phenomenon requiring both improved understanding and coordinated partnership action.

Increasingly, good practice is emerging, but evaluated programmes are scare and funding for new programmes even scarcer. Crucially, the issue must be rapidly situated in current social policy. Solutions must include multi-agency work involving youth services, health services, public education, criminal justice agencies, animal welfare agencies, registered social landlords and local authorities. The issue may be best situated in community safety and criminology. Links to criminality need further exploration, as do links between poverty and using dogs for social advancement or income generation. There is a need to tackle the human issues of status deficit and poverty while removing dogs from the equation. Local agreement and regional leadership on the nature of the problem is key. Clarity is required regarding effects on neighbourhoods, communities and young people, with a need to address the factors that create the environments and generate the motivational need for young men to use and abuse dogs in the search of status. While localised solutions and actions will help, it is only by engaging with young people, and addressing these macro socioeconomic factors, especially poor education, that we will ever be able to fully ensure that this intriguing but disturbing social phenomenon is tackled, reversed and put back 'on the chain'.

An alternative perspective

To sum up the complex argument for owning a status dog, it is perhaps best to view the proposition from the perspective of the owner.

Owning a status dog may be considered an intelligent adaptation to the daily challenges faced by those living in dangerous, neglected and disadvantaged communities or involved in 'street life'. It reduces the likelihood of being disrespected. It offers opportunities for status advancement and to control personal/social space. Ownership builds cultural and personal authority, offering a credible threat of violence. Status dogs bring their own frightening and well-documented reputations, providing a seductive image of masculinity and physicality. They offer opportunities for making money and keeping money already made. They provide a way of intimidating and of conveying silent messages. They reaffirm male identity and link into an illegal underworld of drugs, gambling, guns and gangsters, offering associations of valour, street jousting, chivalry and secret codes. They are suggestive of being street savvy and urban contemporary, conveying power, control, 'bling' and action. Status dogs offer untapped energy, unpredictability and an antidote to boredom. They offer an easy way to attack rivals without using guns or knives, thus reducing the chance of arrest.

They offer opportunities for impromptu street fights and the allure of breeding champions and establishing bloodlines. They offer the chance for owners to be the envy of peers in pubs nationwide. They are 100% loyal, they will not snitch on you and you can mould them to your command. They demand respect, provide safety and convey the message 'I am not be fucked/messed with.' Above all, they convey – and ensure – status. Looked at from this perspective, the question we should perhaps ask is not 'Why do people have status dogs?' but 'Why don't they?' For gangs and young men living 'on the streets', if status dogs did not already exist, they would have had to be invented.

Note
[1] Rowenna Davies, 'Beware of the law', *The Guardian*, 28 September 2011.

Afterword

Reception of the first edition

I spent many months researching links between hip hop culture and 'dangerous' dogs, exploring their centrality both to gangster culture and to the music and cultural imagery that so powerfully characterises this world. I became more familiar with the lyrics of certain hip hop starts than I ever thought possible, and identified artists whose lyrical inclusion of certain types of dog (notably pitbulls) indicated an acceptance of these dogs into a gangster lifestyle, suggesting that these dogs were, in fact, animal embodiments of the personal, physical and mental characteristics of gang members. While the lyrics were both violent and expressive, they perfectly illustrated how pitbulls had been embraced into gangs (particularly in the US). The music publishing houses that own the rights to the lyrics, however, thwarted my sociological musical trip, and following even further months of telephone calls to Los Angeles, Chicago, Miami and Detroit, months of valuable research had to be axed.

Suffice to say, I now know that rap and hip hop tracks are penned by several different people sitting around in a room, presumably getting stoned and/or drunk, then subsequently falling out before all claiming credit for different lines and lyrical content. And once each artist signs up to a different publishing house this means, of course, that one publishing house will own, for example, 12% of the track, another 8%, another 17% and so on. No one can advise who owns the remainder, or how they can be contacted. As a result, this exercise defeated me, and to evidence the links between hip hop, gangster culture and the ownership of 'dangerous' dogs could no longer be included without such fully licensed permission.

Following publication of the first edition, the reception to *Unleashed* has largely been positive, although criminology and sociology remain fairly insouciant to issues of animal welfare. The media, in its various guises, are both tantalised by the prospect of pitbulls, providing as they often do, much needed visual content for 'Poverty Porn' exposés of a life on benefits, while also providing opportunities to rally the campaigning masses with lurid headlines and details of the latest fatal attack by a dog. This has, in fact, made me wonder whether I should have made more of the issues of the class structure of dogs and their owners in the original book.

The book has received considerable interest from those working in animal welfare, veterinarians, dog behaviourists, dog wardens, policy officers, animal charities and so forth, and publication has resulted in a busy round of seminars, lectures and conference papers. It appears that there remains a real interest for professionals as well as for lay people, to build an understanding of why this phenomenon is happening, how it has presented itself and what can be done about it. It seems that the issue is now placed firmly into the social policy context (although it has yet to be clearly situated and to find a suitable home), that the research undertaken has clarified the different groups involved in this phenomenon and the motivations behind these groups. It has also clarified the evidential shortcomings of data collection from all agencies alongside the stasis of central government in addressing the challenges posed by this phenomenon.

I now want to demonstrate that this topic is not just a passing fad, but one that will be with us for a while, pointing as it does to a wider range of issues relating to human–animal relations. To do this I briefly examine the currently topicality of 'status' dogs and 'dangerous' dogs, consider some recent incidents and examine any new data that is now available.

Addressing reviews received about the book

Entering the world of dogs and dog lovers has been an eye-opening experience. I have been both impressed and heartened by the passions and emotions I have encountered from those who hold valuable their relationships with dogs. Perhaps the world of criminology has become too inured to crime and sociologists too detached and dispassionate, but this level of hot-blooded passion and debate has been refreshing for me.

I have also learned that none of the nine million dog owners in the UK agree with one another as to what constitutes either the issue or the policy response to the issue. I have learned much more about the class structure of dog ownership and how this can be replicated in the kennel clubs and animal welfare charities that service this multi-million pound industry. This has, in fact, made me wonder if I should have made more of the issues of class structure of dogs and their owners in the original book. One review called *Unleashed* a 'thinly veiled excuse for class hatred', despite the reviewer stating that they had not read it but had only listened to the discussion of the book on BBC Radio 4, 'Thinking Allowed', with Laurie Taylor. Although some have suggested that the issue of status dogs and dangerous dogs is purely one of class, and I can certainly see their point, I think on balance that it is slightly wider than that.

A further issue identified post-publication is that the book appears to have had 'cross-over' appeal. It was originally conceived and penned for an academic audience of criminologists and sociologists, and was written from this perspective. But such is the lack of research into this field, that those addressing issues of animal welfare and status dogs on a daily basis – namely, veterinarians, animal welfare specialists, dog behaviourialists, dog charities and so forth, have also found the book of interest. However, again, as with all books with 'cross-over' appeal, they can seldom please everyone, as people will interpret the book from their own disciplinary perceptive. It is worth recalling, however, that the book was written from a sociological perspective to place the issue firmly into social policy and not from a dog behavioural perspective as some may have wished.

My introduction to the world of reviews has shown me that they naturally reflect the diverse range of opinions held by readers. Some are flattering, some just plain inaccurate or wrong, but the most disconcerting are those that have misunderstood you. More worryingly still are those that seek to distort your claims for their own political or personal advantage. One such review was provided by a well-known animal behaviouralist who sought to condemn the book for not supporting what I consider to be their pathological hatred of pitbulls, and for failing to cite the work of a close friend, Merrit Clifton.[1] *Unleashed* was not a book about the merits, or otherwise, of pitbulls; it was to place on record the emergence of an issue for social policy that thus far has not been properly addressed. I also came under criticism for failing to support the argument for heritability of behaviour abnormally aggressive dogs. I did actually raise this point in the book, and have considerable sympathy for this view, although I leave the animal welfare and dog experts to argue in more depth over this point. Clearly more research is needed into this aspect of dog behaviour.

It is clear that 'punish the deed, not the breed' arguments are central to the debates on bull breed dogs and status dogs in the UK, and my research indicates a need to move on from this unhelpful binary to also consider issues of harm, public safety and the damage that can be caused by dogs. And it is here that all dogs differ – while all dogs can bite, not all can cause the same level of harm or damage.

Carri Westgarth undertook what I consider to be a more useful review for *Veterinary Record* (22 December 2012). While it was broadly positive, I am criticised for using the terms 'status', 'aggressive', pitbull', 'bull breed' and 'Staffordshire Bull Terrier' almost interchangeably, although both the critic and I share the view that such is the dearth of research in this area that any lack of clarity is understandable. There was also a reference to a need to provide greater clarity in identifying which statements were my personal beliefs, which were anecdotes and which were from 'renowned experts'. And in a world of many 'experts', this point is probably well made. Should space allow for a future publication, this point will be firmly addressed.

One thing I have learned is to ensure that any media appearances on radio, or more importantly on television, should be carefully managed. Specifically, it is critical to ensure you are given the correct title when appearing on any of the television news channels. I now think that some criticism directed towards me was the result of mislabelling, as one early appearance had me listed as a 'dangerous dog expert', and this is not a label I subscribe to. It is suggestive of being a dog behaviourist, veterinarian or dog welfare specialist, labels I would quickly deny.

After this happened to me on Sky News, I received a number of communications challenging this (unwanted) nomenclature. The most acerbic of these came from ... Canada – such is the global reach of pitbulls!

Westgarth suggested there was a weakness in the book in terms of addressing the issue in 'isolation from the wider context of dog ownership', pointing out that status is part of the dog world per se, regardless of income. The review continued, stating that *Unleashed* provided a:

> ... rather simplistic portrayal of a dichotomy between a new phenomenon of 'irresponsible' owners who own and breed certain dog types just for status, and traditional 'responsible' owners that have these same breeds as pets.

In truth I tried to convey that this widely adopted binary of 'irresponsible' versus 'responsible' is, in itself, too simplistic, although it provides a useful jumping off point for a more in-depth exploration of the issues. There are many 'hooded' young men who care deeply about their dogs – it's just that by choosing an aggressive pitbull, this choice says more about their precarious social positioning than if had they selected, for example, a Labrador. I had hoped that I moved on to say that the issue is as much about branding of canine attributes and issues of supply and availability as anything else. From a sociological perspective, the concept of status takes on different degrees of importance depending on which social field or social milieu one operates within. For unemployed young men in deprived estates, it is the generation of street capital that is of the greatest importance; however, this defining logic only pertains to those inhabiting such street environments. Here the logic of the street world dictates that status is achieved through what might be termed 'inverted' qualities, namely, violence, aggression, cruelty, not backing down, loyalty, grit and invincibility. Where such inverted qualities match the branded attributes of a dog, then the match appears supremely conceived. In the day-to-day world of your average dog lovers, or the more exclusive world of pedigree dogs and world-class breeding, such issues are simply non-existent as a different logic pervades these worlds. For those occupying this privileged world their status is displayed and achieved through a wide variety of different means and not simply through aggression, or physical violence or via brands that speak to those methods.

This point perhaps runs to the heart of the matter, and it is certainly key in raising the emotional temperature of the issue of dangerous and status dogs, so that many people feel righteously aggrieved when the issue is raised in the media. Specifically, many are keen to point out that the media are not talking about them. Dog lovers become audibly upset on radio chat shows as they believe that they are being criticised and lumped together with 'irresponsible' dog owners. Families who own loving and nurturing 'Staffies' (Staffordshire bull terriers) get angry when Staffies are described as aggressive or dangerous. People quickly jump to defend their own treatment of dogs, seeking to distance themselves from the 'Others'. I am told by news production teams that their studio phone lines all but burn out with calls from 'angry dog lovers' whenever a storyline is run about dangerous dogs, each quickly stating that they have a pitbull, a Staffie or an Akita, and that their dog 'does not behave like that' or their dog is 'well cared for and loved'.

Again, we are talking here about different social fields, social domains and backgrounds. This is reminiscent of a discussion about alcoholics when the phone lines start buzzing with people saying 'I have a glass of wine a week and I'm perfectly fine', 'I'm not an alcoholic so stop saying that people who drink are alcoholics'. I am, however, overstating the point to illustrate the type of responses that can be typically viewed in online commentaries run by both broadcast and print media following a story. Literally hundreds of communications can be posted as discussion threads, the majority of which are effectively disclaimers, insisting that they are not like those portrayed in the news piece. And I have no doubt of their honest sincerity; however, by their very engagement in such discussion forms and by displaying an active interest in the topic of animal welfare, such communications and contributions place the writer/caller in the camp of both dog-loving and engaged citizens who are by their nature less likely to engage in cruel or violent behaviour towards their animals. In short, we are back to the conundrum I found in undertaking the research – no one is going to call up or write in to admit that they got a dog because they were suffering from status deficit!

Herein lays the challenge of trying to obtain a balanced view of this issue – more research is needed, even though such research is difficult to undertake.

Without doubt, the issues raised in *Unleashed* remain valid and pertinent in 2014, suggesting that it is not a short-lived trend. In the past two years newspapers, television and radio media have all extensively covered stories of status dogs and dangerous dogs. Radio chat shows, such as London's highly popular LBC, regularly have jammed phone lines whenever they cover such stories.

Key issue persists

For the general public, it is the media that ensures the issue of status dogs and dangerous dogs remains in the public eye. Central to this is the level of dog attacks on humans that continue to be widely covered in the media. Since the publication of *Unleashed*, several of these have been high profile in regional or national press. For example:

- Five police officers were attacked by a pitbull in Newham, East London, after they raided the owner's address in March 2012. The owner was convicted of three offences of owning a dog dangerously out of control in a public place, jailed for 22 months and banned from owning a dog for five years. The owner was later acquitted of one of the charges against him as the judge ruled that the dog had attacked one of the police officers in the owner's garden, which was 'private property'.
- A 22-year-old man was jailed for 12 months after admitting 10 counts of owning a dog dangerously out of control in a public place. His Staffordshire bull terriers escaped from his East Sussex home in July 2012 and went on to attack 10 people, three of whom needed plastic surgery.

A Staffordshire bull terrier attacked two-year-old Kieron Guess in Swindon in the garden in June 2012. Kieron was placed in an induced coma for a week and underwent 10 separate operations to save his sight and to rebuild his face following the attack.

- More than 30 police officers in riot gear and two armed officers were called on to contain two bull mastiffs at a house in Lancashire after they mauled 19-year-old Daniel Boardman. The operation lasted 30 hours until the dogs were tranquilised and then euthanised, and it is estimated to have cost £30,000.

Most high profile of all, however, has been a series of fatal attacks on humans. These include the deaths of four people in 2013 ranging in age from just 4 to 79, the two highest profiles being the death of Jade Anderson, aged 14, and Lexi Branson, aged 4. Many of these issues have highlighted the inability of authorities to bring prosecutions when the incidents occur on privately owned property. Table AF1 at the end of this chapter provides a grim tally of 18 fatal incidents since 2005.

Campaigns for action

A number of high-profile public campaigns have been initiated following these tragic incidents. In Scotland the *Daily Record* newspaper is leading the way with its 'Stop Danger Dogs' campaign, providing extensive coverage of recent incidents, including the near-fatal attack on eight-year-old Brogan McCuaig in Glasgow in October 2012. The campaign, including an online petition that the newspaper intends to present to Holyrood Parliament, states that 'too many children have been scarred emotionally and physically because current laws are not robust enough'. It calls for:

- the return of dog licensing, with stringent tests for prospective dog owners;
- dog wardens to police the new system, funded through the cost of licensing;
- mandatory microchipping of all dogs;
- a Holyrood debate on extending additional safety measures such as muzzling.

The Scottish First Minister, Alex Salmond MSP, has recently met with victims of dog attacks including Veronica Lynch, whose daughter Kellie (aged 11) was savaged to death by two rottweilers on a beach in Ayrshire in 1989, and who supports the newspaper's campaign.

Following the death of Jade Anderson in March 2013, Jade's parents backed a campaign to cut the risk of dog attacks, aiming at encouraging owners to be responsible and to control their dog's behaviour. It has support from Wigan Council, Blue Cross charity, Wigan and Leigh

Housing and Greater Manchester Police. Such campaigns are useful in raising awareness and increasing debate, and also in generating local free microchipping provision. However, my own interaction with Wigan Borough Council following the fatal attack suggests that it is still far behind in addressing issues of dangerous dogs in its communities, let alone being proactive. A Freedom of Information (FOI) request for details of what action it was taking as a result of this incident failed to generate a single report, debate, listed council minute, action plan, strategy or commissioned research. Moreover, the Council's Community Safety Team appeared bemused that such an issue might fall within their remit. Such lackadaisical approaches by local authorities must be addressed, and good practice, such as that from the London Boroughs of Lambeth, Wandsworth, Lewisham and Brent, should be more widely circulated. The peculiar nature of dog attacks and dangerous dogs means that as an issue of public policy it continues to fall between policy stools, and while it is clearly an issue for Community Safety Partnerships it seldom finds a logical home in this policy domain, which is possibly why some councils appear to have taken no serious steps to preventing such attacks.

The incidents of attacks on postal workers have also become increasingly high profile over recent years, with 5,500 attacks on postal workers since April 2011, some resulting in permanent disablement.

Following these incidents, the Royal Mail Group's chair, Donald Brydon, commissioned an independent inquiry into dog attacks that was undertaken by former High Court judge, Sir Gordon Langley. The report, published in November 2012, highlighted the legal loophole in England and Wales that provides limited legal protection for anyone attacked by a dog on private property. At present, approximately 70% of dog attacks on postal workers occur on private property.[2] Noting that under such conditions legal sanctions are largely limited to action against the dog, the Langley report called for the compulsory microchipping of all dogs within three years. Following publication of the report the Royal Mail agreed to take a more robust approach to suspend deliveries where dog attacks had occurred, and to pursue legal action against the owners of dangerous dogs. These proposals have been actively welcomed and supported by the Communication Workers Union that has been campaigning via their 'Bite Back' campaign for five years to have such issues addressed. Royal Mail has spent over £100,000 on awareness campaigns and the purchase of 'posting pegs' for its postal staff (plastic tongs that grip the letter and are then used to insert it through the letterbox so that human digits are not at risk of dog bites). While between 3-4,000 postal staff are attacked annually by dogs (of which only some are classified as dangerous dogs), successful campaigns such as a 'Dog Awareness Week' and 'Bite Back' achieved a 20% reduction in dog attacks in the summer of 2012 compared with that of 2011.

Following the recommendations from the Langley report and more proactive action by the Royal Mail Group, postal services will now be suspended as a result of dog attacks or the threat of dog attacks. In 2013 in Sheffield postal deliveries were suspended twice in two months following dog attacks on workers, and in Reading in the same year, 40 families did not have their mail delivered for seven months following a safety dispute with Royal Mail over an 'aggressive dog'.

Further contributions to the debate

A further indication of the enduring nature of the issue of dangerous dogs, status dogs and weapon dogs is its growing focus for academic research. Earlier in the book I bemoaned the dearth of academic research and writing on this topic. Since the book was written, however, there has been a slight improvement, the most significant of which is the RSPCA-funded study undertaken by Cardiff University[3] entitled, *Status dogs, young people and criminalisation: Towards a preventative strategy.* Frustratingly I became aware of this report just as my own book went to press, and thus it was not possible to review it at that time. It is a useful and significant contribution to the discussion, and worthy of inspection by anyone seeking to advance their knowledge of this topic. As with *Unleashed*, it seeks to set the issue into a social policy context, with an emphasis on moving the debate towards a more preventative strategy.

As the report is funded by the RSPCA one does have a sense that its primary audience is perhaps the RSPCA itself, which has lagged behind other animal welfare agencies in addressing the issue of status dogs despite a range of early conferences and reports that helped place the issue on the public radar in 2009/10. Since then, however, charities such as Blue Cross, Dogs Trust and Battersea Dogs and Cats Home have actively sought to develop preventative programmes and outreach projects to young people and communities faced with the immediate social challenges of addressing status and dangerous dogs. Indeed, page 17 of the report offers a moment of self-criticism for the RSPCA when it notes that proactive commitment to 'prevention' of animal abuse has been a marginal concern for the RSPCA's enforcement and protection work. Critics might opine that the RSPCA retains a solidly middle-class hauteur that has constrained its ability to react quickly to the emergence of a societal (and some might say class) shift in the audience it requires to address to tackle status dogs and dangerous dogs. Or a more forceful critic might suggest that despite coming into contact with the issue (and the owning clientele) of status dogs and dangerous dogs through prosecutions and in animal welfare hospitals, the RSPCA has largely been caught unawares, unable to reach out to working-class men and communities that have not joined 'cosy' kennel clubs. As such an inability to adapt to changing social conditions may have affected the ability of the RSPCA to address these new challenges. Indeed, a recently leaked report suggests that such issues of a change in policy direction have been actively debated within the RSPCA.[4] That, however, is a debate for another time.

On a positive note the RSPCA/Cardiff University research report confirms the fact that the issue of status dogs and dangerous dogs is a real one for communities. It also confirms many of my own findings: the paucity and inaccuracy of data; issues of image equating to respect and status; that dogs are used for fighting and as weapons; the role of the dog in the gang world; the role of backstreet breeding; and that young men feel humiliated if they don't have the 'right' dog. The findings noted that dogs may be robbed from young people and that young men also have the dogs for personal safety (whereas my research found it was mostly young women and older mature men who used status dogs this way). The research also noted a significant link to criminality for owners of status dogs and significant use of the dogs as weapons. Interestingly, the report noted that companionship was a key motivational factor (which suggests, perhaps, that the dog is less of a commodity). It also stated that the youths interviewed supported law enforcement against 'bad' owners, but despite the harsh, cruel and negative training techniques used on their dogs, none of the owners considered themselves to be 'bad' owners. These are useful findings.

I would disagree, however, with the report's claim that 'public concern over status dogs developed out of anxiety from the police and the RSPCA over negligent ownership and breeding of illegal and prohibited dog breeds by young people' (page 9). I propose instead that public concern was ignited due to the visual impact of seeing such dogs in local parks and high streets alongside the rise in dog attacks and the subsequent high-profile media furore that followed. I am certainly aware of the mailbags of local councillors filling up with requests for action on this topic years before any RSPCA interest.

The report also commented on the importance of owners retaining an 'exclusive bond' with their dogs – this was not a significant finding for me, and I doubt if this would hold in gang situations where shared dogs are not uncommon. Similarly the report challenged the 'claim that banned breeds are responsible for the majority of dog attacks' (page 12), and that these are stranger-attacks by dogs on the street (as suggested by the official version of the status dogs problem). While this might well be the case, I am unclear what the authors mean by 'the official version of the status dog problem'.

As valuable and as worthy a contribution as this research report from the RSPCA is, its contribution is somewhat weakened by the methodological problems of accessing the very respondents it sought to report on: only two young people were interviewed in Manchester and five in London. The researchers found that negative stereotyping of young people and dogs prevented access to young people with such dogs. I do sympathise with this predicament. However, it also appears that the gatekeepers used to access the young people possibly over-influenced in their mediating role, a fact not fully considered in the report.

While the report does offer some tantalising bones, several issues are raised that were not highlighted as significant or were under-developed as findings or themes, including:

- reports from respondents about the 'inevitability' of getting a dog due to the local hostile environment;
- the authors largely failed to appreciate the brand values being reported by respondents, and to then link this to motivations of obtaining a dog and the roles performed by bull breeds;
- the differences between respondents thinking of themselves as 'responsible' owners but actually displaying 'negative training techniques' that identify them as highly irresponsible;
- the transference of (mostly negative) training techniques among youths was noted, but its wider significance was not picked up and addressed. I would describe this as attempts by the young people to generate street capital by claiming knowledge and seeking to position themselves as authoritative. Alongside this comes the received wisdom dispensed to youths that it is not 'big' or 'cool' to attend formal dog training classes;
- the 'secret world of Staffordshire bull terrier and pitbull terrier owners' is alluded to, but not developed;
- best practice is not identified or evaluated;
- claims that money made from breeding is demand-led, with size, colour and potential of the dog as the most important. This results in mixes that could, if unchecked, lead to increased levels of aggression. This point seems to me to be key to the issue of status dogs, and yet again remained undeveloped.

Part of the RSPCA/Cardiff study included research undertaken by The Campaign Company (TCC), once again funded by the RSPCA. The TCC undertook research into the motivations of young people owning status dogs. Again the TCC research confirms many of the findings from *Unleashed* and from the RSPCA/Cardiff study. However, yet again the research suffers from a low level of research participation and methodological weaknesses.[5] Despite these shortcomings the TCC research usefully identifies that some owners of bull breed dogs may decline to use available services because of the fear of their dogs being seized by the authorities.

Tinkering with the legislation

In the absence of any formal overhaul of the Dangerous Dogs Act (DDA) 1991, the UK government is continuing with its piecemeal tinkering of the legislation. While much of this relates simply to post-hoc issues such as harsher sentences after any event has taken place, some recently adopted proposals by both the UK and the Welsh governments requires all dogs to be microchipped by 2016 in England and by March 2015 in Wales. In 2014 the UK government will publish new regulations on dog microchipping.

Another aspect of legislation is the sentences given to those whose dogs are out of control and who attack either humans or other dogs – these can appear unduly lenient or may vary considerably.[6] To address such regional variations which, to the public, appear inexplicable, the Sentencing Council undertook a consultation on draft guidance for dangerous dog offences in December 2011. It stated[7] that in 2010 sentences for dangerous dog offences were mainly conditional discharge (33%) and fines (32%).[8] In August 2012 the Council published its definitive guidelines in response to the consultation, stating that its proposed changes were aimed at reducing the number of discharges and raising the number of offenders receiving either custodial sentences or community orders. Factors that increase the seriousness of offences can now include if the offence was committed against a person 'providing a service to the public' (for example, a postal worker). Moreover, criminal compensation orders can be made up to a maximum of £5,000.

The issue of backstreet breeding, however, remains in the background – the issue of status dogs and dangerous dogs can only really be tackled effectively when this issue is addressed with improved legislation.

Further legislative amendments were inserted into the new Anti-social Behaviour, Crime and Policing Bill that was presented to Parliament in May 2013. In this omnibus Bill, Section 7 makes provision for amending the DDA 1991. Importantly it seeks to extend the current legal provision to make it a criminal office to have a dog dangerously out of control on private property. Protection will be given to family members, postal workers and professionals visiting the home alongside exemption from prosecution for those householders whose dogs attack trespassers while in or entering a home. New measures for the police and local authorities to take preventative action will also be included to require dog owners to take reasonable steps to address their dog's behaviour, such as attending training classes or repairing boundary fencing.

In October 2013 the Department for Environment, Food & Rural Affairs (DEFRA) published *Proposed changes to maximum penalties for dog attacks: Summary of responses and way forward.*[9] In the Summary, DEFRA report that 3,180 people and organisations completed the online survey, noting that 91% of respondents recommended that maximum penalties should be increased.[10]

Following this consultation the UK government proposes to increase the maximum penalties for aggravated offences under Section 3 of the 1991 Act in England and Wales. This will provide for:

- 14 years' imprisonment for a fatal dog attack
- 5 years' imprisonment if a person is injured by a dog attack
- 3 years' imprisonment if an assistance dog either dies or is injured by a dog attack.

Scotland – legislation with teeth?

The Scottish government has sought to move forward under its own steam to address the issues of dangerous dogs and public concerns following a series of high-profile incidents, including:

- 8-year-old Brogan McCuaig, mauled for six minutes by two American bulldogs in Glasgow in October 2012;
- 11-year-old Aiden Gallacher, attacked by a Japanese Akita in Coatbridge in October 2013;
- 14-year-old Jade Wilson, attacked by a Staffordshire bull terrier in Glasgow in August 2013;
- 18-month-old Millie McCue, savaged by a Staffordshire bull terrier in Glasgow in February 2013;
- 7-year-old Jude Kier, attacked by a Staffordshire bull terrier in Hamilton in 2011;

- 10-year-old Rhianna Kidd, savaged by two rottweilers in Dundee in August 2010.

Each of these attacks caused significant injury requiring surgery, and in the last incident cited above, the owner of the dogs responsible was jailed for one year. In addition, bull breed dogs have been cited in the Scottish media regarding several 'weapon dog' attacks. In one case, Derek Duncan used his Staffordshire bull terrier, which he was using for breeding as a stud dog, to attack a friend, causing injury. Duncan, from Dundee, was jailed for three-and-a-half years in May 2013, and banned from keeping a dog for 10 years.

The Control of Dogs Act Scotland 2010 was introduced in February 2011. The key plank of this was the introduction of dog control notices (DCNs).

A local authority officer can issue DCNs to an irresponsible dog owner if their dog is deemed to be out of control as defined by the Act, or causing a 'reasonable' sense of alarm to any individual reporting it. They also effectively permit anticipatory action to be addressed. The issuing of a DCN is a civil matter, but its breach then becomes a criminal offence. Since the introduction of the 2010 Act in February 2011, approximately 3,200 investigations have been conducted into dogs that could be considered potentially out of control, and 230 DCNs have been issued. Provision of a DCN includes both flexible and compliance measures, for example, it might include muzzling, neutering or a training component, but all DCNs issued require the dog to be microchipped within 14 days of the notice. Failure to comply with a DCN (often nicknamed a Doggie ASBO) can result in a fine of up to £1,000, or in extreme cases, a prison sentence or destruction of the dog. The Act has been described by dog control officers as of great assistance in preventing dangerous dogs from causing harm to the public.

Table AF2 below shows the number of offences involving Dangerous Dogs recorded by the police in Scotland from 1998-99 to 2012-13. There is a noticeable reduction in the number of recorded offences involving dangerous dogs from 2010-11 to 2012-13. While the total number of offences has dropped to 1,012, the lowest figure for 10 years, the majority of this figure (945 offences) is made up of the offence of failing to keep dogs under control, which has increased significantly since 2010-11. This suggests greater reporting of incidents, greater confidence in reporting and also greater vigilance by the authorities.

The figures of DCNs issued indicate their use increased from 92 issued in the period 27 February 2011-26 February 2012 rising to 147 in the period 27 February 2012-26 February 2013. However, these figures mask considerable variance among local authorities in terms of investigations and also DCNs issued. For example, Fife Council issued 47 DCNs, Aberdeenshire Council 17 and West Lothian Council 40. Conversely, the Councils of Angus, Moray, North Lanarkshire and South Ayrshire all issued no DCNs between 27 February 2011-26 February 2013. Most curious of all is Dundee City Council that, despite undertaking 141 investigations over this period, has yet to issue a single DCN. This fact is curious, as the city has been the location of multiple dog attack incidents over the past five years.

Table AF3 provides some additional data on people convicted for dangerous dog offences in Scotland. This data illustrates that only four convictions have arisen following the breach of a DCN under the Control of Dogs (Scotland) Act 2010, Section 5(1) (that is, the criminal as opposed to the civil element). It is perhaps still too early determine of overall efficacy of the new DCN legislation and the impact it will have on the overall number of offences.

In a further recent development the Scottish government has undertaken an extensive public consultation on licensing and microchipping of dogs. Aimed ostensibly at reducing the number of dog attacks, the consultation will run until 31 March 2014. Proposals under consideration include:

- Compulsory microchipping – to help authorities identify owners and hold them to account for their animal's behaviour and to maintain welfare standards. Similar schemes are already in place in Northern Ireland, and also in France, Canada and Denmark.
- Compulsory muzzling – at present this applies only under the DCN legislation to those animals that are deemed to be out of control or at risk of behaving dangerously. This would therefore be an extension of this measure to include all dogs. The potential benefits and challenges of compulsory microchipping are comprehensively set out.
- Dog licensing – the last dog licensing scheme in the UK was abolished in 1987 when licenses cost approximately 37p. At the time only about 50% of dog owners bothered to obtain one.

While this consultation will have to run its course, I analysed almost 400 online commentaries posted in a discussion thread and submitted to BBC News Scotland on 27 December 2013 over a 24-hour period. These commentaries from the public are suggestive of the likely responses to the consultation. Approximately one third were in favour of the proposals, one third were unclear in their commentaries as to how they might vote and one third rejected the proposals offered.

However, in truth, many would accept compulsory microchipping but would reject muzzling or licensing, with some even recommending 'chip the dogs, muzzle the owners'.

Most recently one Scottish MSP has called for the dog control legislation to be tightened even further with the creation of a List of Restricted Breeds, such as German shepherds, rottweilers and Rhodesian ridgebacks. These dogs have been identified and entered onto the Restricted List largely due to their physical strength and capacity to do considerable damage if they do attack. Under these proposals special conditions would apply to those owning such dogs; for example, owners would need to ensure only those aged over 16 could walk the dogs. Those owning a Restricted List dog might also be subject to further assessment to ensure they were both responsible and capable owners. Such proposals follow the Irish model of rules relating to certain dog breeds legislated under the Control of Dogs Regulations 1998 (S1 No 442 of 1998). Under this legislation, 11 breeds[11] (and strains/cross-breeds) of dog are subject to restrictions:

- they must be kept on a short strong lead by someone aged over 16 who is capable of controlling them;
- they must be muzzled whenever they are in a public place;
- they must at all times wear a collar bearing the name and address of the owner.
- This process is supported by on-the-spot fines.

Clearly such proposals offer a possible way forward in this debate, but it seems extraordinary that the UK government or DEFRA has not already looked at these existing measures. Of course such proposals raise questions of enforceability, not least when so many dog wardens have been the victims of local government spending cuts. The appropriate sanctions for non-compliance would need to be carefully established, as would systems for monitoring and enforcement. Such proposals do have the potential to suddenly increase the number of abandoned dogs, however, and should be carefully considered. Notwithstanding such challenges, it does appear that the establishment of a Restricted List (to sit alongside the current UK list of four prohibited dogs) might well be a valuable way forward to both limit the proliferation of these dogs and to ensure a certain baseline of responsible ownership and welfare. In an attempt to move away from the 'deed, not breed' binary, establishing a Restricted List based on weight, physicality and bite power might have some currency with the public.

Proposals to address the issue

It is clear that more preventative measures are needed to address this issue. I am convinced, more than ever, that this is a serious issue of public policy affecting communities and neighbourhoods throughout the UK, and not, it must be emphasised, just those in social housing. At its heart this is mostly an issue about public fears and community safety.

To summarise, I revisit some key recommendations below:

- Compulsory microchipping – these can be easily and cheaply inserted harmlessly into the dog. They hold considerable information (which must be updated) and can be easily scanned by handheld scanners, although it should be noted that this measure alone will not be sufficient, and nor is it a panacea for dog control.
- Dog licensing – I remain of the view that we should return to dog licenses. At present this is operated successfully in several countries, for example, Northern Ireland, Eire, New Zealand and Australia. I believe that licensing would foster a greater sense of responsibility for pet ownership and permit an improved focus on animal welfare. Certainly the critique can be made that only responsible dog owners will participate in any such requirement, but the advance of IT since 1987 provides improved opportunities for compliance, monitoring and uptake should this be reintroduced. Any national UK introduction would also provide an opportunity to overhaul the DDA 1991 while undertaking a national campaign to highlight responsible dog ownership with a view to changing public perceptions of animal welfare and improving education. Links to pet insurance should also be considered.
- Compulsory dog insurance, details of which can be available on the dog's microchip. Failure to have current insurance would mean the removal of the dog by the authorities.
- DCNs appear to be working effectively in Scotland and could perhaps be introduced in England and Wales to good effect.
- There could be free dog training programmes and animal welfare programmes available locally to communities.
- An Animal Welfare Proficiency Certificate could be developed for primary schools.
- Public education should be targeted, specifically at disengaged youth, and delivered in suitable local venues.
- A national publicity campaign could be set up, possibly using national sports stars and celebrities to endorse responsible behaviour.

- The role of schools and youth clubs is central to the implementation of educational and preventative programmes on animal welfare.
- There needs to be improved partnership work through Community Safety Partnerships including auditing, policy development, action planning, community events etc.
- There must be improved data collection and data sharing by local agencies, local authorities and most importantly, by health trusts and Accident and Emergency departments; for example, at present dog bite data by breed is not recorded by health trusts.
- A national data set could be created. While this might best be done by the RSPCA, they have as yet not led the way in this aspect.
- Dogs on social estates should be audited – Registered Social Landlords and local authorities should audit the number and type of dogs in social rented accommodation with a view to quantifying the issue and informing policy.
- There should be tighter policy development and controls in housing management, for example, tenancy controls on certain breeds of dog (that is, those that might be on the Restricted List).
- Animal abuse is not a recordable offence in so far as the police do not compile official crime statistics reports. It is time to consider if the police should, in fact, record such incidents.
- Sale of dogs on the internet should be restricted.
- There needs to be improved preventative measures regarding breeding legislation.
- There should be tougher enforcement action against those found guilty of having their dogs out of control, including the removal of the dogs and injunctions preventing them from simply replacing dogs removed by authorities (at present, banning orders can be for as little as six months). In addition, offenders should be required to pay the vet bills of those animals injured in any dog-on-dog attack.
- A comprehensive costing exercise of the costs to the public purse of the whole issue of status dogs and dangerous dogs is needed. This crucial data is missing from current policy debates.
- It would be helpful to have increased research funded by animal welfare charities and by central government, including evaluation of DCNs in Scotland.
- These above measures should be consolidated in a revised Dangerous Dogs Act for England and Wales.

Notes

[1] Merrit Clifton is an investigative journalist based in the US who has assembled an impressive array of findings relating to dog attacks and dog bites. Notably, he argues that his evidence indicates that pitbulls are, by some measure, not only aggressive, but also the dog most likely to be involved in fatal attacks.

[2] *Inquiry into dog attacks on postal workers*, Report of Finding and Recommendations (November 2012) by Sir Gordon Langley, commissioned by the Royal Mail Group.

[3] Hughes, G., Maher, J. and Lawson, C. (2011) *Status dogs, young people and criminalisation: Towards a preventative strategy*, RSPCA and Cardiff University.

[4] In 2013, in a leaked document, the Deputy Chair of the RSPCA, Paul Draycott, cautioned that the RSPCA might lose sponsorship from some of its wealthy patrons if it was seen to be too political, for example, in proactively prosecuting issues such as fox hunting or badger culling.

[5] The research interviewed only 5 status dog owners alongside 50 school/college students and some professionals (unstated number).

[6] For example, in December 2012 one man in Angus, Scotland, whose illegal pitbull dog savaged the family pet of an elderly local woman, was handed a £70 fine and banned from keeping dogs for 70 weeks.

[7] Sentencing Council (2012) *Analysis and Research Bulletin 2012*.

[8] The average fine was £228.

[9] See www.gov.uk/defra

[10] In addition, 83% of respondents recommended an increase in sentencing for injury occurring to an assistance dog or blind person, and 69% for the death of an assistance dog and 76% for the death of a person.

[11] This Restricted List includes: American pitbull terrier; English bull terrier; Staffordshire bull terrier; bull mastiff; Doberman Pincher; rottweiler; German shepherd; Rhodesian ridgeback; Japanese tosa, Japanese akita; and bandog.

Table AF1: Fatal dog attack victims in the UK since 2005

Date	Victim	Age	Location	Dog involved	Comments
Feb 2014	Ava-Jayne Corless	11 mths	Blackburn	American pitbull terrier	Fatal attack by dog in house as baby slept in upstairs room
Dec 2013	Emma Bennett	27 years	Leeds	American pitbull terrier	Pregnant mother of four killed by two American pitbull terriers
Oct 2013	Lexi Branson	4 years	Mountsorrel, Leics	Bulldog	Lexi was mauled to death by her pet dog. Her mother stabbed the dog to death to free Lexi
May 2013	Clifford Clarke	79 years	Liverpool	Bull mastiff/ bandog cross	Clifford was attacked and died when he opened his back door and was confronted by the dog. The dog was shot dead by the police. Two local women were arrested on suspicion of offences under the DDA and manslaughter
March 2013	Jade Anderson	14 years	Wigan	2 bull mastiffs; 2 Staffordshire bull terriers	Jade was attacked by the dogs at her friend's house
Nov 2012	Harry Harper	8 days	Ketley, Shropshire	Jack Russell	Harry was attacked in his cot at home by the family pet and possibly killed by a single bite to the head
Oct 2012	Gloria Knowles	71 years	Morden, London	2 French mastiffs; 2 American bulldogs; 1 mongrel	Gloria was attacked in the garden by her daughter's five dogs when she went to feed them, and suffered a fatal heart attack
Jan 2012	Leslie Trottman	83 years	Brentford, London	Pitbull terrier	Leslie was killed in his garden when his neighbour's dog escaped and attacked him
Dec 2010	Barbara Williams	52 years	Wallington, Surrey	Neapolitan mastiff	Miss Williams' landlord's dog burst out of its cramped cage and attacked her. It was contained by police riot shields then shot dead. The dog's owner pleaded guilty to failing to ensure the dog's welfare and was also charged in possession of another illegal fighting dog
April 2010	Zumer Ahmed	18 months	Crawley, West Sussex	American bulldog	Zumer's uncle bred and sold dogs from his garden shed. Zumer was killed when the uncle's bulldog entered the house. The uncle was arrested for manslaughter; the charge was dropped. There was no prosecution under the DDA as the attack was on private property. The uncle was charged under the DDA with possessing a pitbull terrier dog bred for fighting. He was banned from keeping dogs for five years; 15 months later the uncle was fined £765 for breaching his ban and for keeping five dogs at his home

Date	Victim	Age	Location	Dog involved	Comments
Nov 2009	John Paul Massey	4 years	Wavertree, Liverpool	Pitbull terrier type	John Paul was killed at his grandmother's home by his uncle's dog. The police shot the dog dead. The uncle (aged 21) was jailed for four months for three charges under the DDA
May 2009	Andrew Walker	21 years	Blackpool	2 alsatians	Andrew was savaged to death in his garden by two alsatians owned by his friend who had been allowed to raise them despite earlier convictions under the DDA 1991
Feb 2009	Jaden Mack	3 months	Caerphilly, South Wales	Staffordshire bull terrier; Jack Russell	The dogs took the child from a dining table and then attacked him at his grandmother's home after his grandmother fell asleep. The dogs were later destroyed
Jan 2009	Stephen Hudspeth	33 years	Bishop Auckland	Staffordshire bull terrier	Stephen died from blood poisoning after an attack by a Staffordshire bull terrier
Jan 2008	James Redhill	78 years	Plaistow, London	Rottweiler	James' own pet attacked him in the street
Dec 2007	Archie-Lee Hirst	1 year	Wakefield	Rottweiler	Archie-Lee was attacked at his grandparents' house by the 10-stone family pet that snatched him from his seven-year-old aunt. The police shot the dog dead
Jan 2007	Ellie Lawrenson	5 years	St Helens	Pitbull terrier type	Ellie was attacked at her grandmother's home by her uncle's dog. The uncle (24 years) had been warned that the dog was dangerous. He was jailed for eight weeks for owning an illegal breed
Sept 2006	Cadey-Lee Deacon	5 months	Leicester	2 rottweilers	The child was taken from her cot while her mother was otherwise distracted, by two guard dogs belonging to her mother's new partner. The attack happened in the Rocket Inn pub
Nov 2005	Liam Eames	1 year	Leeds	American bulldog	Liam was attacked by the family pet as his mother and he had played in their garden

Table AF2: Offences involving dangerous dogs recorded by the police in Scotland, 1998-99 to 2012-13

Year	Dangerous dogs, failure to control, supervise, destroy[1,2]	Failure to keep dogs under proper control, contravention of an order[3]	Dogs bred for fighting[4]	Total
1998-99	669	187	8	864
1999-2000	490	239	16	745
2000-01	397	257	17	671
2001-02	330	284	16	630
2002-03	355	360	8	723
2003-04	403	433	13	849
2004-05	529	618	16	1,163
2005-06	531	517	19	1,067
2006-07	532	623	21	1,176
2007-08	557	587	13	1,157
2008-09	567	604	25	1,196
2009-10	624	653	32	1,309
2010-11	624	668	29	1,321
2011-12	236	941	11	1,188
2012-13	67	945	13	1,025

Source: Annex 1 – data on dangerous and out of control dogs in *Promoting responsible dog ownership in Scotland: Microchipping and other measures,* Scottish Government, December 2013.
[1] Consists of offences under the Civic Government (Scotland) Act 1982, Section 49.
[2] Most out of control dogs are now dealt with directly by local authorities following the introduction of the Control of Dogs (Scotland) Act 2010, implemented in February 2011. The authority will consider issuing a DCN when a dog has been out of control.
[3] Consists of offences under the DDA 1991, Sections 3 and 4.
[4] Consists of offences under the DDA 1991, Sections 1 and 2.
All figures provided by local authorities.

Table AF3: Scotland: people convicted for dangerous dogs offences[1]

Offence	2006-07	2007-08	2008-09	2009-10	2010-11	2011-12	2012-13
Dogs Act 1871, Section 2	65	50	73	70	85	28	0
Civic Government (Scotland) Act 1982, Section 49(1)	19	11	7	12	13	11	20
Civic Government (Scotland) Act 1982, Section 49(4)	2	0	5	2	1	1	3
Dangerous Dogs Act 1989, Section 1(3)	0	0	0	1	0	0	0
Dangerous Dogs Act 1991, Sections 1(2) and 1(7)	0	1	0	0	0	1	0
Dangerous Dogs Act 1991, Sections 1(3) and 1(7)	0	0	3	2	3	5	4
Dangerous Dogs Act 1991, Section 3(1)	43	38	62	45	81	88	93
Dangerous Dogs Act 1991, Section 3(3)(a)	4	2	2	2	1	2	0
Dangerous Dogs Act 1991, Sections 3(3)(b) and (4)	3	2	1	0	1	0	0
Control of Dogs (Scotland) Act 2010, Section 5(1)	0	0	0	0	0	0	4
All	136	104	153	134	185	136	124
People convicted under the Control of Dogs (Scotland) Act 2010, Section 5(1)1							
Offence by result	2012-13						
Community payback order	1						
Admonished	1						
Dog disposals	1						
Compensation order	1						

Note: [1] Where main offence.
Source: Scottish Government Court Proceedings database

Bibliography

Agnew, R. (1998) 'The causes of animal abuse: a social psychological analysis', *Theoretical Criminology*, vol 2, no 2: 177-209.

Aldridge, J. and Medina, J. (2007) *Youth gangs in an English city: Social exclusion, drugs and violence*, ESRC end of award report, RES-00023-0615, Swindon: Economic and Social Research Council.

Allen, T. (2007) 'Petey and Chato: the pitbull's transition from mainstream to marginalised masculinity', Unpublished thesis, University of Southern California.

Anderson, E. (1990) *Streetwise: Race, class and change in an urban community*, Chicago, IL: Chicago University Press.

Anderson, E. (1999) *Code of the streets: Decency, violence and the moral life of the inner city*, New York, NY: W.W. Norton and Co.

Arluke, A., Levin, J. Luke, C. and Ascione, F. (1999) 'The relationship of animal abuse to violence and other forms of anti-social behaviour', *Journal of Interpersonal Violence*, vol 14: 963-75.

Ascione, F.R. (2005) *Children and animals: Exploring the roots of kindness and cruelty*, West Lafayette, IN: Purdue University Press.

Ascione, F.R., Weber, C.V. and Woods, D.S. (1997) 'The abuse of animals and domestic violence: a national survey of shelter for women who are battered', *Society and Animals*, vol 12: 1-17.

Baktin, M. (1984) *Rabelais and His World*, Bloomington, IN: Indiana University Press.

Baldry, A. (2003) 'Animal abuse and exposure to interparental violence in Italian youth', *Journal of Interpersonal Violence*, vol 18, 258-81.

Barnes, J.E., Boat, B.W., Putnam, F.W., Dates, H.F. and Mahlman, A.R. (2006) 'Ownership of high risk ("vicious") dogs as a marker for deviant behaviour: implications for risk assessment', *Journal of Interpersonal Violence*, vol 21, no 12: 1616-34.

Baudrillard, J. (1988) *Selected writings*, Cambridge: Polity Press.

Bauman, Z. (1992) *Intimations of postmodernity*, London: Routledge.

Becker, H. (1963) *Outsiders: Studies in the sociology of deviance*, New York, NY/London: Free Press/Collier-MacMillan.

Belk, R. (1996) 'Metaphoric relationships with pets', *Society & Animals: Journal of Human-Animal Studies*, vol 4, no 2.

Ben-Yehuda, N. (1986) 'The sociology of moral panics', *Sociological Quarterly*, vol 27, no 4.

Beverland, M.B., Farrelly, F. and Ching Lim, E.A. (2008) 'Exploring the dark side of pet ownership: status and control-based pet consumption', *Journal of Business Research*, vol 61, no 5: 490-6.

Bhattacharjee, C., Bradley, P., Smith, M., Scally, A.J. and Wilson, B.J. (2000) 'Do animals bite more during a full moon?', *British Medical Journal*, 321, 23 December.

Bourdieu, P. (1979) *Algeria*, Cambridge: Cambridge University Press.

Bourdieu, P. (1986) 'The forms of capital', in J.G. Richardson (ed) *Handbook of theory and research for the sociology of education*, 241-58. New York, NY: Greenwood Press.

Bourdieu, P. (1987) *Choses dites*, Paris: Editions de Minuit.

Bourdieu, P. (1990) *The logic of practice*, Cambridge: Polity Press.

Bourdieu, P. (1991) 'Le Champ Litteraire. Actes de la recherché en sciences sociales 89' (September): 4-46, cited in Swartz, D. (1997) *Culture and power: The sociology of Pierre Bourdieu*, Chicago: University of Chicago Press.

Bourdieu, P. and Wacquant, L.J.D. (1992) *An invitation to reflexive sociology*, Chicago: University of Chicago Press.

Brand, D., Brown, S., and Hallanan, B. (1987) 'Behavior: time bombs on legs', *Time Magazine*, 27 July.

Brooks, A., Moxon, R. and England, G.C.W. (2010) 'Incidence and impact of dog attacks on guide dogs in the UK', *Veterinary Record*, vol 166: 778-81, doi: 10.1136/vr.b4855.

Bullock, K. and Tilley, N. (2002) 'Understanding and tackling gang violence', *Crime Prevention and Community Safety*, vol 10: 36-47.

Campbell, B. (1993) *Goliath: Britain's dangerous places*, London: Methuen.

Clifford, D.H., Green, K.A. and Watterson, R.M. (1990) *The pit bull dilemma: The gathering storm*, Philadelphia, PA: Charles Press.

Cloward, R. and Ohlin, L. (1960) *Delinquency and opportunity*, New York, NY: Free Press.

Cohen, A.K. (1955) *Delinquent boys: The culture of the gang*, New York, NY: The Free Press.

Cohen, J. and Richardson, J. (2002) 'Pit bull panic', *The Journal of Popular Culture*, vol 36, no 2: 285-317.

Cohen, P. (1972) 'Subcultural conflict and working-class community', *Working Papers in Cultural Studies No 2*, Birmingham: CCCS, University of Birmingham.

Cohen, S. (1980) 'Symbols of trouble', in S. Cohen (ed) *Folk devils and moral panics* (2nd edn), Oxford: Martin Robertson.

Cohen, S. (2002) *Folk devils and moral panics*, 30th anniversary edition, London: Routledge.

Cohen, S. and Young, J. (1973) *The manufacture of news*, Beverly Hills, CA: Sage.

Collier, S. (2006) 'Breed-specific legislation and the pitbull terrier: are the laws justified?', *Journal of Veterinary Behaviour*, vol 1: 17-22.

Connell, R.W. (1987) *Gender and power: Society, the person and sexual politics*, Cambridge: Polity Press.

Connell, R.W. (1995) *Masculinities*, Oxford: Blackwell.

Daley, K. (2010) 'Street-level dog fighting in Chicago – exploratory research', Paper presented at Fighting Dogs Conference, League Against Cruel Sports, July 2010.

Daly, M. and Wilson, M. (1988) *Homicide*, New York, NY: De Gruyter.

Defra (Department of Environment, Food and Rural Affairs) (2003) *Types of dogs prohibited in Great Britain: Guidance on the recognition of prohibited dogs in Great Britain*, London: Defra .

Defra (2009) *Dangerous dogs law guidance for enforcers*, London: Defra.

Defra (2010) *Public consultation on dangerous dogs*, London: Defra.

Degenhardt, B. (2005) *Statistical summary of offenders charged with crimes against companion animals, July 2001-July 2004*, Report by Chicago Police Department.

DeGue, S. and DiLlo, D. (2009) 'Is animal cruelty a "red flag" for family violence? Investigating co-occurring violence toward children, partners, and pets', *Journal of Interpersonal Violence*, vol 24, no 6: 1036-56.

Delise, K. (2002) *Fatal dog attacks*, Manonville, NY: Anubis Press.

Delise, K. (2007) *The pit bull placebo: The media, myths and politics of canine aggression*, Manonville, NY: Anubis Press.

Delise, K. (2008) 'The media: a reliable source of information on dog attacks?', National Canine Research Council (www.nationalcanine researchcouncil.com/).

Diesel, G. (2008) 'Staffordshire bull terrier ownership', Epidemiology Division, Royal Veterinary College, Hatfield.

Dobson, R. (2003) 'Dog bites are no more frequent at full moon', *British Medical Journal*, 326, 17 May.

Dunne, P. (2009) 'The rise of the urban status dog', www.animalwardens.co.uk.

Dunning, E. Murphy, P. and Williams, J. (1988) *The roots of football hooliganism*, New York, NY: Routledge & Kegan Paul.

Evans, K. (2010) 'Identifying and dealing with offenders', Paper presented at Fighting Dogs Conference, League Against Cruel Sports, July 2010.

Evans, R., Kalich, D. and Forsyth, C.J. (1998) 'Dogfighting: symbolic expression and validation of masculinity', in L. Kalof and A. Fitzgerald (eds) (2007) *The animals reader: The essential classic and contemporary writings*, Oxford: Berg: 209-18.

Fairclough, N. (1995) *Critical discourse analysis: Papers in the critical study of language*, London/New York, NY: Longman.

Ferrell, J. and Hamm, M. (eds) (1998) *Ethnography at the edge: Crime, deviance and field research*, Boston, MS: Northeastern University Press.

Ferrell, J. Hayward, K. and Young, J. (2008) *Cultural criminology*, London: Sage Publications.

Flynn, C.P. (2000) 'Why family professionals can no longer ignore violence toward animals', *Family Relations*, vol 49, no 1: 87-95.

Flynn, C.P. (2011) 'Examining the links between animal abuse and human violence', *Crime Law Social Change*, 55: 453-68.

Forsythe, C.J. and Evans, R.D. (1998) 'Dogmen: the rationalization of deviance', *Society and Animals: Journal of Human Animal Studies*, vol 6 no 3, 203-18.

Foster, J. (1990) *Villains*, London: Routledge.

GfK NOP (2011) *Stray Dog Survey 2010: A report for the Dogs Trust*, London: GfK NOP Social Research.

Gibson, H. (2005) 'Dog fighting: detailed discussion', Animal Legal Historical Center, Michigan State University College of Law.

Giddens, A. (1976) *New rules of sociological method*, London: Macmillan.

GLA (Greater London Authority) (2009) *Weapon dogs: The situation in London*, London: GLA.

GLA (2011) *Dangerous dogs: Headline trends of multi-source data*, DMAG Briefing, London: DLA.

Gladwell, M. (2006) 'Troublemakers: what pit bulls can teach us about profiling', *The New Yorker*, vol 81: 38-43.

Goffman, E. (1967) *Interaction ritual*, New York, NY: Free Press.

Goffman E. (1971) *Relations in public: Microstudies of public order*, London: Allen Lane.

Goode, E. and Ben-Yehuda, N. (1994) *Moral panics*, Oxford: Blackwell.

Hagedorn, J. (2008) *A world of gangs*, Minneapolis, MN: University of Minnesota Press.

Hall, S. and Winlow, S. (2007) 'Cultural criminology and primitive accumulation', *Crime, Media, Culture*, vol 3, no 1: 82-90.

Hallsworth, S. (2011) 'Then they came for the dogs!', *Crime, Law and Social Change*, vol 55: 391-403.

Hallsworth, S. and Duffy, K. (2010) *Confronting London's violent street world: The gang and beyond*, London: London Metropolitan University.

Hallsworth, S. and Young, T. (2008) 'Gang talk and gang talkers: a critique', *Crime, Media, Culture*, vol 4, no 2: 175-95.

Hardiman, T. (2009) HSUS (Humane Society of the United States) (www.humanesociety.org/issues/dogfighting).

Harding, S. (2010) 'Status dogs and gangs', *Safer Communities*, vol 9, no 1: 30-5.

Harding. S. (2012) *The role and significance of street capital in the social field of the violent youth gang in Lambeth*, Published thesis, University of Bedfordshire, Luton.

Hayward, K. (2004) *City limits: Crime, consumer culture and the urban experience*, London: GlassHouse.

Henry, B.C. (2004) 'Exposure to animal abuse and group context: two factors affecting participation in animal abuse', *Anthrozoos*, vol 17, no 4: 290-305.

HMCS (Her Majesty's Courts Service), Justices' Clerks' Society and Defra (2010) *An introduction to the case management of dangerous dog cases*, London: HMCS.

Hobbs, D. (1988) *Doing the business*, Oxford: Oxford University Press.

Hobbs, D. (1994) 'Professional and organised crime in Britain', in M. Maguire, R. Morgan and R. Reiner (eds) *The Oxford handbook of criminology*, Oxford: Clarendon Press.

Hobbs, D. (1995) *Bad business*, Oxford: Oxford University Press.

Home Office (2010) *ASB Focus*, no 8, February, London: Home Office.

Home Office/Scottish Office/Welsh Office/Department of the Environment (1990) *The control of dogs*, London: Home Office.

Hood, C., Rothstein, H. and Baldwin, R. (2001) *The government of risk: Understanding risk regulation regimes*, Oxford: Oxford University Press.

Hope, T. (2001) 'Crime victimisation and inequality in a risk society', in R. Matthews and J. Pitts (eds) *Crime, disorder and community safety*, London: Routledge.

Hughes, G. and Lawson, C. (2011) 'RSPCA and the criminology of animal abuse', *Crime, Law and Social Change*, Special Issue.

Jacobs, B.A. and Wright R.(1999) 'Stick-up, street culture and offender motivation', *Criminology*, vol 37, no 1: 149-73.

Jessup, D. (1995) *The working pit bull*, Neptune, NJ: TFH Publications.

Jewkes, Y. (2004) *Media and Crime*, London: Sage Publications.

Kasperson, M. (2008) 'On treating the symptoms and not the cause, reflections on the Dangerous Dog Act', *Papers from the British Criminology Conference*, vol 8: 205-25.

Katz, J. (1988) *Seductions of crime*, New York, NY: Basic Books.

Kintrea, K. (2008) *Young people and territoriality in British cities*, York: Joseph Rowntree Foundation.

Kimmel, M, (1996) *Manhood in America*, New York, NY: Free Press.

Klaasen, B., Buckley, J.R. and Esmil, A. (1996) 'Does the Dangerous Dogs Act protect against animal attack: a prospective study of mammalian bites in the Accident and Emergency department', *Injury*, vol 27, no 2: 89-91.

Klein, M. (1971) *Street gangs and street workers*, Englewood Cliffs, NJ: Prentice-Hall.

Klein, M.W. and Maxon, C. (2006) Patterns and policies, Oxford: Oxford University Press.

Lambeth Council (2010) *Lambeth Dogs Scrutiny Commission*, London: Lambeth Council.

Lodge, M. and Hood, C. (2002) 'Pavlovian policy responses to media feeding frenzies? Dangerous dogs regulation in comparative perspective', *Journal of Contingencies and Crisis Management*, vol 10, no 1.

LTOA (London Tree Officers Association) 2010 *Bark better than bite: Damage to trees by dogs*, London: LTOA.

Maher, J. and Pierpoint, H. (2011) 'Friends, status symbols and weapons: the use of dogs by youth groups and youth gangs', *Crime Law and Social Change*, vol 55: 405-20.

Majors, R. (1986) 'Cool pose: the proud signature of black survival', *Changing Men*, vol 17: 5-6.

Majors, R. and Billson, J.M. (1992) *Cool pose: The dilemmas of Black manhood in America*, New York, NY: Simon & Schuster.

Matza, D. and Sykes, G. (1961) 'Juvenile delinquency and subterranean values', *American Sociological Review*, vol 26, no 5: 712-19.

Maxson, C.L. (1998) 'Gang members on the move', *Juvenile Justice Bulletin 10*, Washington, DC: US State Department of Justice.

McRobbie, A. (1994) 'Folk devils fight back', *New Left Review*, no 203: 107-16.

Merseyside Police (2010) 'Seizing dangerous dogs', Briefing paper for chief officers, September, internal report for Superintendent Krueger concerning dangerous dogs (costs).

Merton, R. (1938) 'Social structure and anomie', *American Sociological Review*, vol 3: 672-82.

Merz-Perez, L. and Heide, K.M. (2004) *Animal cruelty: Pathway to violence against people*, Walnut Creek, CA: AltaMira Press.

Merz-Perez, L., Heide, K.M. and Silverman, I. (2001) 'Childhood cruelty to animals and subsequent violence against humans', *Comparative Criminology*, vol 45: 556-73.

Messerschmidt, J.W. (1993) *Masculinities and crime: Critque and reconceputalisation of theory*, Oxford: Rowan and Littlefield.

Messerschmidt, J.W. (2000) *Nine lives: Adolescent masculinities, the body and violence*, Oxford: Westview.

Messner, M. (1989) 'Masculinities and athletic careers', *Gender and Society*, vol 3, no 1: 71-88.

Morgan, D. (1992) *Discovering men*, London: Routledge.

MPS (Metropolitan Police Service) (2007) *MPS response to dangerous dog offences*, Report No 5, London: MPS.

MPS (2009) *MPS response to dangerous dogs*, Report No 8, London: MPS.

Nast, H. J. (2006) 'Loving....whatever: alienation, neobliberalism and pet-love in the twenty-first century', Paper for the International Studies Program, DePaul University, Chicago, IL.

Netto, W. and Planta, D. (1997) 'Behavioural testing for aggression in the domestic dog', *Applied Animal Behaviour Science*, 52: 243-63.

Ortiz, F. (2010) 'Making the dogman heel: recommendations for improving the effectiveness of dogfighting laws', *Stanford Journal of Animal Law and Policy*, vol 3: 1-75.

Palmer, S. and Pitts, J. (2006) 'Othering the brothers', *Youth and Policy*, vol 9: 5-22.

Parsons, T. (1937) *The structure of social action*, New York, NY: McGraw Hill Book Company.

Pearson, G. (1983) *Hooligan: A history of respectable fears*, Basingstoke: Macmillan.

Philo, C. and Wilbert, C. (eds) (2000) *Animal spaces, beastly places*, New York: Routledge.

Phineas, C. (1973) 'Household pets and urban alienation', in *Journal of Social History* 7: 338-43

Pitts, J. (2003) *The new politics of youth crime: Discipline or solidarity*, Lyme Regis: Russell House Publishing.

Pitts, J. (2008) *Reluctant gangsters*, Cullompton: Willan Publishing.

Pitts, J. (2010) 'Mercenary territory: are youth gangs really a problem?', in B. Goldson (ed) *Youth in crisis? 'Gangs', territory and violence*, London, Routledge.

Power, E. (2008) 'Furry families: making a human–dog family through home', *Social and Cultural Geography*, vol 9, no 5: 535–55.

Presdee, M. (1994) 'Young people, culture and the construction of crime', in G. Barak (ed) *Varieties of criminology: Readings from a dynamic discipline*, London: Praeger.

Presdee, M. (2000) *Cultural criminology and the carnival of crime*, London: Routledge.

PSPCA (Pennsylvania Society for the Prevention of Cruelty to Animals) (2000) *Animaldom*, vol 70, no 7.

Puttnam, R. (2000) *Bowling alone*, New York, NY: Simon & Shuster.

Ragatz, L., Fremouw, W., Thomas, T. and Mccoy, K. (2009) 'Vicious dogs: the antisocial behaviours and psychological characteristics of owners', *Journal of Forensic Sciences*, vol 54: 699-703.

Randour, M.L. and Hardiman, T. (2007) Creating synergy for gang prevention: taking a look at animal fighting and gangs, in D.L. White, B.C. Glenn, and A. Wimes (eds) *Proceedings of persistently safe schools: The 2007 National Conference on Safe Schools*: 199-209, Washington, DC: Hamilton Fish Institute on School and Community Violence, The George Washington University.

Rawstorne, T. (2009) 'The "weapon dog" bringing terror to our streets and parks – and who are the hoodies "new status symbol"', *Mail Online*, 8 June, www.dailymail.co.uk/news/article-1191445.

Robins, D. (1992) *Tarnished vision: Crime and conflict in the inner cities*, Oxford: Oxford University Press.

Rojek, C. (1995) *Decentring leisure: Rethinking leisure theory*, London: Sage.

Roll, A. and Unshelm, J. (1997) 'Aggressive conflicts amongst dogs and factors affecting them', *Applied Animal Behavioural Sciences*, vol 52: 229-42.

Rosado, B. Garcia-Belenguer, S., Leon, M. and Palacio, J. (2007) 'Spanish Dangerous Animals Act: effect on the epidemiology of dog bites', *Journal of Veterinary Behavior*, vol 2: 166-74.

RSPCA (Royal Society for the Prevention of Cruelty to Animals) (2007a) *Briefing on dangerous dogs*, January, Horsham: RSPCA.

RSPCA (2007b) *Measuring animal welfare in the UK*, Horsham: RSPCA.

RSPCA (2008) *Position paper on status dogs*, Horsham: RSPCA.

RSPCA (2009) *RSPCA Status dogs summit 2009: Report of proceedings*, Horsham: RSPCA.

RSPCA (2010a) *Five years of measuring animal welfare in the UK 2005-09*, Horsham: RSPCA

RSPCA (2010b) *Prosecutions Department annual report*, Horsham: RSPCA.

Sager, M. (1987) 'A boy and his dog in hell', *Rolling Stone*, 2 July (Republished in *Wounded Warriors* by Mike Sager, Da Capo Press, 2008).

Sanders, B. (2005) *Youth crime and youth culture in the inner city*, London: Routledge.

Sanders, C. (1999) *Understanding dogs: Living and working with canine companions*, Philadelphia, PA: Temple University Press.

Semencic, C. (1984) *The world of fighting dogs*, Neptune, NJ: TFH Publications.

Semincic, C. (1991) *Pitbulls and tenacious guard dogs*, Neptune, NJ: TFH Publications.

Semyonova, A. (2006) 'Aggressive dog breeds' in *Heritability of behavior in the abnormally aggressive dog*, The Carriage House Foundation.

Sherman, C.K., Reisner, I.R., Taliaferro, L.A. and Houpt, K.A. (1996) 'Characteristics, treatment, and outcome of 99 cases of aggression between dogs', *Applied Animal Behaviour Science*, vol 47: 91-108.

Shover, N. (1996) *Great pretenders: Pursuits and careers of persistent thieves*, Boulder, CO: Westview Press.

Soloman, R.F. (2008) 'No curs allowed: exploring the subculture of dogmen', Unpublished thesis, Graduate School, University of North Carolina.

Spergel, I.A. (1964) *Racketville, slumtown and haulberg*, Chicago, IL: University of Chicago Press.

Stahlkuppe, J. (2000) *The American pitbull terrier handbook*, New York, NY: Barron's Educational Series, Inc.

Sternberg, S. (2003) *Successful dog adoption*, Indiana, IN: Howell Book House.

Swartz, D. (1997) *Culture and power: The sociology of Pierre Bourdieu*, Chicago: University of Chicago Press.

Sykes, G.M. and Matza, D. (1957) 'Techniques of neutralization: a theory of delinquency', *American Sociological Review*, vol 6, no 22: 664-70.

Tolson, A. (1977) *The limits of masculinity*, London: Tavistock.

Toy, J. (2008) *Die another day: A practitioner's review with recommendations for preventing gang and weapon violence in London in 2008* (www.lemosandcrane.co.uk/resources/forum/218/dieanotherday.pdf).

Twining, H., Aruke, A. and Patronek, G. (2000) 'Managing the stigma of outlaw breeds', *Society and Animals: Journal of Human-Animal Studies*, vol 8, no 1: 25-52.

University of Chicago Survey Lab (2008) *Dog fighting in Chicago: Exploratory research: Final report 2*, Chicago, IL: University of Chicago.

van Dijk, T.A. (1993) *Elite discourse and racism*, Newbury Park, CA,: Sage Publications.

van Dijk, T. A. (2001, 2003) 'Critical discourse analysis' in D. Schiffrin, D. Tannen and H. Hamilton (eds) *The Handbook of Discourse Analysis*, Oxford: Blackwell Publishing.

Velaquez, N. (2007) 'City Attorney Delgadillo launches new effort to target LA gang members who misuse and abuse dog', Office of the City Attorney press release, Los Angeles, 3 May.

Wacquant, L. (1998) 'Inside the zone: the social art of the hustler in the Black American ghetto', *Theory, Culture and Society*, vol 15, no 2: 1-36.

Wandsworth Council (2007) *Anti-social behaviour by youths with dogs*, Wandsworth: London.

Wandsworth Council (2009) *Report by the Director of Leisure and Amenity Services on the results of the public consultation on the proposal to introduce dog control orders to replace existing dog related bye-laws on public highways and footpaths and in parks and other open spaces*, Paper 09–175, 14 September, London: Wandsworth Council Environment and Leisure Overview and Scrutiny committee.

Winlow, S. (2001) *Badfellas: Crime, tradition and new masculinities*, Oxford: Berg.

Wolch, J. and Emel, J. (eds) (1998) *Animal geographies: Place, politics, and identity in the nature-culture borderlands*. London: Verso

Dangerous dog legislation, controversies and debates

Dangerous Dogs Act 1991

In the late 1980s and early 1990s, the topic of large aggressive dogs increasingly became a public issue in the UK. The concept of threats to public safety were cemented by two or three high-profile media attacks on members of the public, children and postal workers. However, rottweilers rather than pitbulls were the key breeds mainly referred to in the press. Through media pressure and supported by discussion on newly established breakfast TV channels, there began calls for swift government action to address what was described as a growing public menace, now referred to as dangerous dogs.

In 1991, following public and then political pressure, the Conservative government under John Major devised the Dangerous Dogs Act (DDA) 1991 to regulate the perceived problem.

As the RSPCA often reminds us, any dog can be dangerous. In the UK, under the DDA 1991 legislation a dangerous dog is defined as 'any dog that is dangerously out of control ... on any occasion on which there are grounds for reasonable apprehension that it will injure any person, whether or not it actually does so ...' (section 10(3)). In addition to defining when dogs can be considered dangerous, the government sought to prohibit specific breeds. Four dog types are prohibited under section 1: the pitbull terrier, Japanese tosa, dogo argentino and fila brazilero. The DDA 1991 bans ownership, breeding, sale, exchange and advertising for sale of these specified breeds of fighting dogs. Cross-breeds of those dogs are also covered by the legislation, while the Animal Welfare Act 2006 requires that owners are responsible for the behaviour of their pets. Table A1 sets out the UK dangerous dog legislation.

None of the prohibited dogs belongs to a recognised breed in the UK and thus the word 'type' is used. Section 1 therefore applies both to 'pure-bred' pitbull terriers and to any dog of the type known as a pitbull terrier. Assessment is undertaken depending on the characteristics, both physical and behavioural, of the prohibited type (Defra, 2003).

Table A1: UK dangerous dogs legislation

Incident	Most relevant Act	Offence	Penalty action
Owning a prohibited dog	Dangerous Dogs Act 1991, s1	Criminal offence	Maximum penalty: fine of £5,000, or 6 months' imprisonment, or both
Breeding, selling, or abandoning a prohibited type dog	Dangerous Dogs Act 1991, s1	Criminal offence	Maximum penalty: fine of £5,000, or 6 months' imprisonment, or both
Dog attack in a public place or a place where the dog is not allowed to go	Dangerous Dogs Act 1991, s3(1) or s3(3)	Criminal offence	Maximum penalty for aggravated offence: two years' imprisonment and/or an unlimited fine
Dog causing someone to reasonably believe they could be attacked, including during a dog-on-dog attack – in a public place or a place where the dog is not allowed to go	Dangerous Dogs Act 1991, s3(1) or s3(3)	Criminal offence	Maximum fine: £5,000 and 6 months' imprisonment where injury has been caused.
Dog attack in a private place	Dogs Act 1871	Civil remedy	Dog destroyed or control order put on dog by court. Owner can be disqualified from keeping a dog
Using a dog as a weapon/setting a dog on another person	Offences Against the Persons Act 1861, s20	Criminal offence	Maximum penalty: 7 years' imprisonment
Keeps or trains a dog for use in connection with an animal fight	Animal Welfare Act 2006, s8	Criminal offence	Maximum penalty: fine of £20,000, or 6 months' imprisonment or both

Source: Crown copyright

Section 3 of the Act address dogs 'dangerously out of control in a public place'. This refers to any dog that may be seized and kept in custody, with the owner fined or imprisoned for up to six months. If the dog then inflicts injury, the owner may be liable for up to two years' imprisonment. Controversially, the Act does not cover private places.[1]

Initially, over 8,000 dogs were placed on the Index of Exempted Dogs (IED) in 1991. From early 1992 to 1997 it was prohibited to add dogs to the index. Since the 1997 Dangerous Dogs (Amendment) Act courts can add dogs to the IED by court order. The number of dogs added to the IED has been low until recently as illustrated in Table A2. Data suggest some regional variation in the way courts proceed with such orders. In London, the number of dogs prohibited by section 1 of the DDA 1991 added to the IED in 2003 was nil; in 2004, it was five; in 2005, nil; in 2006, five; and in 2007, 71 (of these 17% of requests were for the London Borough of Lambeth).[2]

Table A2: Number of dogs added to the Index of Exempted Dogs

Date	1997	1998	1999	2000	2001	2002	2003	2004	2005	2006	2007	2008	2009
Certificates of Exemption status	9	36	26	15	4	7	0	6	1	6	141	255	314

Source: Hansard written answers on 1 December 2010: column 1325W, www.publications.parliament.uk/pa/cm201011/cmhansrd

In 1997, the Dangerous Dogs (Amendment) Act abolished automatic destruction orders of proscribed breeds and offered magistrates discretion regarding disposal either by destruction or by placing a dog on the IED. Prohibited dogs may be added to the index if the necessary requirements are met, that is, microchipping, tattooing, neutering, and keeping the dog leashed and muzzled in a public place. Dogs may only be added to the index once the court has issued a certificate of exemption.

The number of people prosecuted for offences under sections 1 and 3 the DDA 1991 are shown in Tables A3 and A4, respectively.[3] Figures indicate an initial flurry of court proceedings in the first couple of years of the Act that then tailed off in the mid-1990s. The number of court proceedings begin to rise again with the emergence of the Dangerous Dogs (Amendment) Act 1997. The Dogs Act 1871[4] begins to be used less frequently. The tables indicate the numbers of those found guilty in all courts from 1997-2006 and show a steady rise in the number of those found guilty of section 3(1) offences.[5] Convictions rates for section 3 offences are above 50% on all counts. Section 1 offences show lower overall numbers of proceedings and convictions. Proceedings against those selling or abandoning a fighting dog are very few, and from 1997-2006 no one was found guilty of selling a fighting dog.[6]

From 1997-2006, 90 were prosecuted for possession of a proscribed dog and only 43 were found guilty. During this period, only 26 individuals were found guilty of breeding fighting dogs. Such numbers as are currently available indicate low levels of prosecutions based on section 1, contrary to the views of some academics (Hallsworth, 2011). These figures should be set against aggregate figures of prosecutions between 1997-2006. During this time there were 4,993 prosecutions under DDA 1991 and 1,147 prosecutions under DDA 1989 and the Dogs Act 1871 (section 2).

Criticisms of the DDA 1991

The DDA 1991 has been the subject of much criticism from the public, the practitioners, the media and the police. The main criticism is that it allows certain proscribed dogs to be destroyed on the basis solely of breed – an inflammatory issue for dog lovers and animal welfare agencies such as the RSPCA, who claim that this labels the dog 'dangerous' purely because of its looks and reputation albeit that few, if any, of the interested agencies have fully addressed the observational points assembled by breed experts regarding genetics and aggression. Others believe the Act is ineffectual as it is easily circumvented by:

Table A3: Number of persons proceeded against at Magistrates Court for offences relating to section 1 of the DDA 1991, and the Dogs Act 1871 in England and Wales, 1997–2006

		1997	1998	1999	2000	2001	2002	2003	2004	2005	2006	
DDA 1991 s1(2)(a)	Breeding or breeding from a fighting dog	1 (0)*	6 (5)	1 (0)	2 (0)	1 (0)	6 (3)	4 (2)	15 (14)	3 (1)	2 (1)	Out of 41, (26) were found guilty = 63%
DDA 1991 s1(2)(b)	Selling, exchanging, offering, advertising, or exposing for sale a fighting dog	0	0	0	1	0	0	0	0	0	0	(1) found guilty
DDA 1991 s1(2)(d)	Allowing a fighting dog to be in a public place without a muzzle or lead	12 (8)	7 (2)	11 (6)	9 (6)	4 (2)	3 (2)	2 (0)	2 (1)	3 (3)	1 (0)	Out of 53, (30) were found guilty = 56%
DDA 1999 s1(2)(e)	Abandoning or allowing to stray, a fighting dog	3 (2)	0	2 (1)	0	0	1	0	0	1	0	Only 3 found guilty
DDA 1991 s1(3)	Possession, without exemption, of a PBT, tosa, or other designated fighting dog	15 (9)	23 (8)	12 (5)	5 (2)	4 (2)	6 (2)	1 (1)	5 (2)	11 (7)	8 (5)	Of 90 proceeded against (43) found guilty = 48%

Note: * Numbers in brackets = defendants found guilty

Source: Court Proceedings Database – Office for Criminal Justice Reform – Ministry of Justice, ref: 014-08. Note that data are compiled from numerous sources and noted limitations.
From *Hansard* written answers for 16 May 2007 (pt0011) request from Mr Drew (122351) and response from Mr Coaker; also *Hansard* written answers 2007 re Mr Bill Wiggin (177714) requesting and reply from Mr Jonathan Shaw

Table A4: Number of persons proceeded against at Magistrates Court for offences relating to section 3 of the DDA 1991, and the Dogs Act 1871 in England and Wales, 1991–2006

Statute	Offence description	1991	1992	1993	1994	1995	1996	1997	1998	1999	2000	2001	2002	2003	2004	2005	2006
DDA 1991 s3(1)	Owner or person in charge allowing dog to be dangerously out of control in a public place injuring any person	0	310	349	286	259	221	259 (121)*	434 (239)	449 (262)	458 (260)	490 (285)	537 (300)	560 (302)	597 (350)	645 (403)	703 (458)
DDA 1991 s3(3)	Owner or person in charge allowing dog to enter a non-public place injuring any person	0	20	36	25	22	18	22 (5)	28 (13)	34 (19)	48 (32)	50 (31)	38 (30)	52 (33)	48 (25)	44 (25)	54 (29)
DDA 1991 s3(1)	Owner or person in charge allowing dog to be dangerously out of control in a public place, no injury being caused	0	388	307	196	189	162	175 (88)	248 (125)	254 (126)	266 (130)	278 (157)	284 (150)	329 (171)	290 (167)	278 (168)	278 (160)
DDA 1999 s3(3)	Owner or person in charge allowing dog to enter a non-public place causing reasonable apprehension of injury to a person	0	30	21	8	18	4	10 (4)	12 (8)	9 (5)	24 (13)	20 (14)	18 (7)	20 (10)	11 (5)	24 (9)	19 (11)
DDA 1989, Dogs Act 1871, s2	Failure to comply with an order to keep a dog under proper control etc. dangerous dog not kept under proper control	1,031	889	609	551	510	513	492 (98)	454 (106)	401 (101)	462 (84)	374 (101)	336 (105)	335 (128)	352 (128)	306 (139)	232 (108)
Total		1,031	1,637	1,322	1,066	998	918	958	1,175	1,147	1,258	1,212	1,213	1,296	1,298	1,297	1,286

Note: * Numbers in brackets = defendants found guilty (from 1997)

Source: Court Proceedings Database – Office for Criminal Justice Reform – Ministry of Justice. ref: 014-08. Note that data are compiled from numerous sources and noted limitations.

From *Hansard* written answers for 16 May 2007 (pt0011) request from Mr Drew (12235l) and response from Mr Coaker. Also *Hansard* written answers 2007 re Mr Bill Wiggin (177714) requesting and replay from Mr Jonathan Shaw.

- breed switching: Barnes et al (2006) suggest that one outcome of the Act was to make pitbulls more attractive to the 'wrong' people. While this may be true, the evidence to prove it is elusive;
- reclassifying (for example, as American Staffs, American bulldogs, Irish SBTs or traditional Staffordshire bull terriers);
- cross-breeding: Dunne (2009) reports that crossing pitbulls with other bull breeds arises as people try to circumvent the law producing a dog outside the pitbull standard. It is difficult to do this, however, as the legislation prohibits all dogs, including cross-breeds, that appear 'to be bred for fighting or to have the characteristics of a type bred for that purpose' (Dunne 2009: 5).
- kennelling: if breed is not immediately identifiable, banned breeds must be seized and kennelled. In the UK, in the absence of dog licenses and registration, anyone can obtain a dog. It is not therefore possible to calculate numbers of particular breeds. In attempts to circumvent the legislation, many dogs are cross-bred to prevent them from being seized.

Dissenters claim that enforcement of the legislation is problematic. Moreover, there are no statistics relating to the number of legally classified dangerous dogs in the UK and whether or not this figure is increasing. Others deny there is any problem and view the Act as arising from a moral panic (Hallsworth, 2011; see also Kasperson 2008), undertaken for political expediency with no evidence of any existing social problem. Hallsworth (2011: 394) argues the Act provides 'a legal mandate for the entire destruction of the pitbull breed' based on genetics, which he describes as 'pre-emptive criminalisation with a vengeance'. Such views ignore the assembled evidence of inbred aggression in some breeds, notably bull breeds, and dismiss public anxiety over safety.

One common argument is that the Act is a 'sledgehammer to crack a nut'. This refers to the introduction of breed-specific legislation (BSL), which is strongly opposed by many, including the Dogs Trust, Kennel Club and RSPCA. It should be noted that the Act was introduced to offer some form of protection to the general public with respect to an increase in aggressive dogs but was also intended to address issues of irresponsible breeding by ultimately breeding out dogs such as pitbulls.

For many, the DDA 1991 is totemic of knee-jerk populist legislation that creates more problems than it claims to resolve. Detractors cite the fact that BSL or 'canine genocide' (Hallsworth, 2011: 391), has failed to address the proliferation of pitbulls in the UK. In addition, many opponents of BSL have questioned the issue of dangerousness of the breeds deemed illegal. In the UK, arguments regarding dangerousness have been taken up by Kasperson (2008), who, having reviewed the available epidemiological literature on dog bites, finds that 'dangerous breeds' do not bite more frequently than German shepherds and thus it is unjustified to direct legislation towards these breeds. This proposition, however, negates the ability of some bull breeds to inflict considerably more damage than a snap from a German shepherd dog. Kasperson argues that BSL treats the symptoms (pitbulls and other 'dangerous breeds') rather than the causes (dog owners). Kasperson (2008: 221) is on strong ground when she says we should focus attention on the causes of aggressive dogs, that is, the owners, who should be made responsible for their actions. This ground is far less secure when she claims that 'by abolishing breed bans the attraction of the pitbulls for the "wrong" kind of owners will diminish, rather than increasing it as the outlawing of certain breeds does' (Kasperson, 2008: 221). There is at present no evidence to support this.

Kasperson (2008) argues that if the Act were successful, pitbulls would all have died out by now. This fails, however, to take into account prolific back-street breeding and importation of pitbulls. Nor does it address the issue of hybridation and proliferation of cross-breeding. Kasperson (2008) cites Klaasen and colleagues (1996) as illustrating that the DDA 1991 appeared to achieve little in terms of protecting the public from pitbull bites. Rosado and colleagues (2007) found that 'dangerous breeds' contributed to only a few incidents of dog bites in Spain and argue that BSL is discriminatory and a less useful predictor of aggression than environment, learned behaviour and physical and mental wellbeing. Again, the experts are in conflict while public anxiety persists.

Any repeal of the DDA 1991 would, however, abolish section 1 – the section that allows the police to seize prohibited dogs unless they have been placed on the IED. A key tool for the police in responding to public safety concerns, section 1 seizures are a form of affirmative action that some police officers believe should be retained. Regardless of this, pitbulls remain a concern for the public. Moreover, bull breeds and large mastiffs are now commonplace throughout the UK, further ensuring that the new phenomenon of status dogs is central in the public mind. Furthermore, the issue of status dogs and dangerous dogs remains problematic for many people, and is unlikely to go away or to be resolved without legislative action and a change in social attitudes.

The dissenters of the DDA 1991 summarise their argument as one of 'deed not breed' – a belief that the dog owner should be punished for the deed it allows the dog to do, rather than punishing the breed for what it is. The police, who are tasked with ensuring public safety, often view the DDA 1991 as a practical tool and the basis on which the issue of dangerous dogs can be addressed effectively through the criminal justice system. They further note that the upswing or cultural shift in ownership towards illegal or status dogs is primarily responsible for the massive upswing in numbers rather than any failure of the Act per se (see Chapter Eight for a discussion of current government responses to the Act).

Notes

[1] There are no data that can be presented to indicate which breeds are responsible for most attacks or injuries to the public. Any data indicating levels of injuries or propensity for certain breeds to cause injury would also correlate to their proportionality in the UK dog population. If there were a surge in the UK population of Staffordshire bull terriers, one could surmise that they would statistically be more present in data of injuries by nature of the fact that there are more of them. Similarly accurate identification of breeds has always proven to be problematic.

[2] *Hansard* written answers, 22 January 2008, column 1986W. Mr Hands requesting and Mr J. Shaw responding.

[3] Data are provided on the basis of a principle offence. The Ministry of Justice notes that it makes every effort to ensure that figures are accurate and complete. However, it notes that data are extracted from large administrative data systems generated by police forces. As a result, care should be taken to ensure that data collection processes and their inevitable limitations are taken into account when those data are used.

[4] Under section 2 of the Dogs Act 1871, any person can petition a magistrate regarding a dog that is dangerous and not under control. This applies to both public places and private property. Dangerousness can be towards people or animals. Proceedings are civil in nature. The court is empowered to destroy the dog or order it to be kept under proper control using muzzles or leashes in a public place.

[5] Data for those found guilty are not available prior to 1997.

[6] DDA 1991, section 1(2)(b)

Status dog data from **RSPCA**, **MPS** and research findings

Table B1: Complaints received by the RSPCA in specific areas of the UK concerning status and dangerous dogs

Area	2006	2007	2008	Total
London	87	176	145	408
West Midlands	38	42	48	128
West Yorkshire	9	47	25	81
Merseyside	24	16	12	52
Gtr Manchester	14	17	14	45
Nottinghamshire	7	24	10	41
South Yorkshire	9	18	10	37

Note: Reports of dog fighting, notably chain rolling among youths, had also increased.

Source: RSPCA (2009)

Table B2: RSPCA dangerous dog statistics, April 2009

Location	Year	Organised dog fighting	Attacks on animals	Youths and dogs	Impromptu fights	Total
London	2006	9	14	35	29	87
	2007	21	19	47	89	176
	2008	8	15	45	77	145
						408
South Yorkshire	2006	3	2	3	1	9
	2007	6	4	1	7	18
	2008	3	1	1	5	10
						37
Merseyside	2006	5	4	6	9	24
	2007	2	3	2	9	16
	2008	5	2	1	4	12
						52
Birmingham	2006	17	4	8	9	38
	2007	4	7	6	25	42
	2008	7	6	7	28	48
						128
Newcastle-upon-Tyne	2006	0	2	0	1	3
	2007	1	1	1	0	3
	2008	0	3	0	0	3
						9

Note: Data for Greater Manchester and West Yorkshire were not available.

Source: www.rspca.org

Table B3: Number of dog-fighting incidents reported to the RSPCA by the public, 2004–09

Area	2004	2005	2006	2007	2008	2009
Dog fighting	24	36	137	358	284	204
% relating to street fighting	38	42	48	37	66	55

Source: www.rspca.org

Table B4: Dogs coming in to the MPS SDU by London borough, 2010/11

	Jan 11	Feb 11	Mar 11	Apr 10	May 10	Jun 10	Jul 10	Aug 10	Sep 10	Oct 10	Nov 10	Dec 10	Total
Barking & Dagenham	14		4			1	2	1	2	3	5	1	33
Barnet	5	2	4	1	2	2	2	3	5	2	2		30
Bexley						1	2					2	5
Brent	4		1		4		1		5		1	1	17
Bromely	2		1	3	2	9	4	2	1	3	4	1	32
Camden				2	1	2	1		1		1		8
Croydon	4	1	5	6	11	3	1	4	1	4	2		42
Ealing	1	10	13	4	1	2	6		5	2	5		49
Enfield	4	4	7	1	2	1	5	8	3	12	2	2	51
Greenwich	4	2		7	3	1	1		2	1		1	22
Hackney	5	2	2	4	11	6	3		5		4		42
Hammersmith	3		1	7	6		7	6	1	3			34
Haringey	4	2	8	1	13	11	5	2	1	4	3	2	56
Harrow	3	7	15	3	1	4	10	3	3	7	1	2	59
Havering	4	2	1	1	1	2	4	1	2	1	1	1	21
Hillingdon	2	2	4		3	3	3	3	7	5	5	1	38
Hounslow		3		1	5	2			2	4			17
islington	1		4	3		4	5	3	5	7	4	5	41
Kensington & Chelsea	1		3					12	1	1			18
Kingston					1	1	1	1		2		1	7
Lambeth	2	1	8	5	7	4	3	1	2	5	11	3	52
Lewisham	4	5	14	9	5	16	3	7	6	2	12	2	85
Merton	3	2		2			5	1		2	2		17
Newham	2	2		1	2	2	3	14		1	2	4	33
Redbridge	5	2	1	3	5	2	2	2	11	2	1		36
Richmond						2		1		2			5
Southwark	9	3	1	3	3	5	4	20	2	6	4	4	64
Sutton			1	2	4					3		1	11
Tower Hamlets	4	5	2	4	8	5	13	2	2	2	3	4	54
Waltham Forest	2			4	4		1	3	1		1	4	20
Wandsworth	2	4		2	3	5	4	3	9	14	5	3	54
Westminster			1	1	4	2	2		1	4	3	1	19
Total all BOCUs	94	61	101	84	108	98	103	103	85	105	83	47	1,072

Table B5: MPS SDU – section 3 by breed type, 2010

	Jan 10	Feb 10	Mar 10	Apr 10	May 10	Jun 10	Jul 10	Aug 10	Sep 10	Oct 10	Nov 10	Dec 10	Total
Pitbull	4	2	1	3	15	5	4	14	2	6	9	4	69
Staffordshire (and X)	4	3	2	5	2	10	5	7	9	5	5	2	59
American bulldog	3			1	1				4		2		11
Rottweiler	1	4	5	3			2		2				17
Bull mastiff		3	2	3	1			1	1		1		12
GSD		1	2		2	1	1	1	1	1			10
Mongrel			4	4	3	5	9	3	1	3	1		33
Akita			4						1		1		6
English bulldog			1		1		1			1			4
Husky X					7								7
Chihuahua												1	1
										Total S3 seizures			229

Table B6: Summarised findings from owners handlers of large/aggressive breeds

Function	No of interviewees	Females	Pitbull	Staffie/pitbull cross	SBT	Akita	Rott-weiler	Bull mastiff	AM bulldog	Alsation/AM bulldog cross	Staffie/akita cross breed	No of dogs
Pet	2	1	1		1							2
Status	18	5 (all aged under 18)	3	7	4			1	2	1	1	19
Status/ protection	1			1								1
Protection	7	5 (all aged 28-60)		1	7		1		1			10
Breeding	1				1							1
Breeding/ status	2				2	1						3
Breeding/ dog	1		5									5
Dog fighting	1				1							1
Total	33	11	9	9	16	1	1	1	3	1	1	

APPENDIX C

Disposals of status dogs by Metropolitan Police Service

Table C1 illustrates the disposals adopted for 2010 shows numbers and types of disposals undertaken by the MPS in 2010. An explanation of terms used, and the circumstances in which they are applied is listed below. For brevity I have included only terms that are not obvious and require a detailed explanation.

PTS (put to sleep) for other reasons: a typical example might be a pitbull abandoned in a stolen car. Any occupants arrested deny knowledge of the dog. Any uncaptured occupant, deemed to be the owner, cannot be traced. The owner's family also denies knowledge of the dog. However, the police must retain the dog in kennels for an indeterminate period, possibly up to a year. From an animal welfare perspective, this is deemed inappropriate, so the dog is euthanised. Police will examine the dog and take photographs and do an examination. Under the DDA 1991, it is not possible to give the dog to others. Such incidents are often time consuming. As the police are experienced in such incidents, the dog in this scenario is usually only retained for two weeks.

Died: refers to dogs that have died in kennels. Dogs live for eight or nine years on average. Kennelled dogs may be subject to viruses circulating in kennels. In 2009, the MPS lost 60 dogs to parvovirus in one kennel.

Restored: applies to dogs examined, found not to be a pitbull and returned to the owner.

4A order post-conviction (section 1): a dog convicted under section 1 of the DDA 1991 of being a pitbull where the court allows the dog to be registered back to the owner and placed on the IED.

4A order post-conviction (section 1 and section 3): a dog convicted of being a section 1 dog (e.g. a pitbull) under the DDA 1991 that has bitten someone (section 3 DDA 1991) and the court have asked for it to be registered on the IED.

4B applications: those who have not been prosecuted but who have applied to court for a decision on the dog or for exemption under 4B of the DDA 1991.

Table C1: MPS SDU disposals, 2010

DOGS OUT 2010	Jan	Feb	Mar	Apr	May	Jun	Jul	Aug	Sep	Oct	Nov	Dec	
Destroyed on court order	23	13	41	39	50	30	16	17	24	13	23	9	298
Destroyed on disclaimer	3	8	4	17		12	30	35	16	18	6	4	153
Shot		2											2
Died	1	1		1	4	1							8
Rehomed		4	3	5	1		3	11	1	9	2	2	41
Restored:													
Examined not pitbull	7	4	10	8	5	15	13	6	14	8	11	6	107
Pups not type	8		3	2									13
Registered PBT committed offence			1										1
Restored by Court (eg unmuzzled)	3		1	1						1			6
PTS other reasons							5	25	29	29	22	11	112
Restored after CPS error	1	1	2										4
4A order post conviction (S1)	5	7	4		12	10	12	14	10	15	15	2	106
4A order post conviction (S1 + S3)		2	1					2	1				6
4A order post conviction (S3)		6	1	8	6	4	3	5	6	5	5	7	56
4B approved	3	11	15	17	14	22	14	25	17	10	8	11	167
CPS refuse charge or NFA	1				5	1	2	7	6	6	5	4	37
S2 Dogs Act 1871	1					5	1	2			4	1	14
Found not guilty S1	2		1	3				1	2	1	1	2	13
Found not guilty S3		1					2	3	1	3			10
Found not guilty S1 + S3						1							1
Found not guilty cruelty									2				2
Prisoner's dog rehomed/restored	1		1	2		5	14		2		5	1	31
Cruelty restored or to RSPCA		1				1		9					11
S3 restored by Court no order made				6	1	1		1	1	5	1		16
Stray		1								2			3
Formal caution					1			1	1		1		4
Confidential operation				2									2
Evidence in GBH restored					1								1
In cannabis factory restored					1	1							2
Stolen dogs recovered restored					7								7
Restored humanitarian grounds						1							1
Quarantined											1		1
Total	59	62	87	112	108	109	116	163	133	117	108	62	1,236

Section 3(4A): invoked by the court when a dog is found guilty of biting. The court can apply restrictions such as neutering, muzzling in a public place or containment on a leash, or can request that the dog be euthanised. Some dogs will be destroyed for section 3 offences.

Section 2, Dogs Act 1871: police may sometimes make an application under this Act as it provides a useful legislative tool in a wide range of circumstances with regard to dangerous dogs.One advantage is that it applies regardless of where the incident occurs, for example in and around private dwellings; as a result it is often used by postal workers. This legislation provides a civil remedy to which the civil standard of proof is applied and proceedings can be taken even when a criminal offence has not been committed.

Found not guilty, section 1: unproven charges brought under section 1. There may be insufficient evidence to bring a charge, in which case the dog will be returned to its owner.

NFA (no further action): applies to other offences, such as a cruelty offence. If the owner receives a caution, the dog may be returned.

Prisoner's dog rehomed or stored: rehoming or kennelling in cases where an arrested and imprisoned owner has sole responsibility for a dog. This category may also apply to dogs seized during raids on cannabis factories. In these circumstances, the police keep the dog for two weeks and serve a tort notice under the Interference with Goods Act 1977 on the owner. This gives owners 28 days to collect the dog before it becomes police property. If the dog is claimed by a family member and is not illegal, for example, a rottweiler, it may be returned.

APPENDIX D

Legal costs

The following costs tables have been established as examples and averages by Merseyside Police (2010).

Table D1: Non-complicated case

Seizure of pitbull and owner prosecuted under section 1, DDA 1991, dog placed on the exemption register*	£
Transport costs: £30 per journey (taken in and back home)	60.00
Vet's fees (check-ups, vaccinations, tattooing)	300.00
Kennel fees (nine months at £10 per day)	2,700.00
Expert witness (DLO to counter defence expert DLO)	500.00
Total excluding court costs,** legal aid, wages of police (overtime) and CPS	3,560.00

Notes: * Merseyside Police, response to points raised by Lord Granchester concerning the issue of dangerous dogs, 4 July 2010.

** The decision to pursue a criminal prosecution is often taken by the CPS.

Table D2: Complicated section 1 case

	£
Transport costs: £30 per journey (multiple trips to vet/DLO exams)	180.00
Vet's fees (check-ups, illness, vaccinations, neutering)	500.00
Kennel fees (13 months at £10 per day)	3,900.00
Expert witness (DLO to counter defence expert DLO)	500.00
Total excluding court costs,* legal aid, wages of police (overtime) and CPS	5,080.00

Note: * The decision to pursue a criminal prosecution is often taken by the CPS.

Table D3: Non-contested (non-complicated) section 4B case

	£
Transport costs: £30 per journey (taken in and returned)	60.00
Vet's fees (check-ups, vaccinations, neutering)	300.00
Kennel fees (2 months at £10 per day)	600.00
Court costs (application for non-contested civil hearing)	200.00
Total excluding police wages	1,060.00*

Note: * For Merseyside Police, the average costs of a dog dealt with under section 4B where the process time is approximately three months, is only £1,300.

Table D4: Complicated section 4B case

	£
Transport costs: £30 per journey (inc to behaviorist exam)	180.00
Vet's fees (check-ups, illness, vaccinations, neutering)	360.00
Kennel fees (four months at £10 per day, including appeal)	1,200.00
Court costs (application for contested civil hearing)	500.00
Total excluding court costs,* legal aid, wages of police (overtime) and CPS	2,240.00

Note: * The decision to pursue a criminal prosecution is often taken by the CPS.
The cost of civil cases raised by Merseyside Police in the financial year 2010-11 was £39,275.00. The number of cases where costs were awarded in its favour against the owners was 67. In total, almost £2,000 was recouped through such awards.

APPENDIX E

Defra consultation, 2010

In 2010, Defra launched a public consultation[1] on various proposals to review and streamline current legislation to improve public safety, improve enforcement and stop cruelty to dogs. The consultation considered:

- repeal of the Dangerous Dogs (Amendment) Act 1997 to avoid further necessity for the Index of Exempted Dogs (IED);
- repeal of section 1 of the DDA 1991;
- extension of section 3 of the DDA 1991 to cover private property;
- introduction of compulsory microchipping;
- introduction of compulsory third-party insurance;
- provision of increased powers for the police and local authorities to address dangerous dogs through dog control notices;
- removal of exemption rules that allow people to keep banned dogs or proposals to improve the working of the IED.

The consultation ran from 9 March 2010 to 1 June 2010, with the responses published in 2010. There were 4,250 responses, including the following curious feedback:[2]

- 63% of respondents answered 'No' to the question, 'Do you think that the Dangerous Dogs Act 1991 should be extended to cover all places, including private property where a dog is permitted to be?'
- 88% did not think that breed-specific legislation (BSL) was effective in protecting the public but only 71% thought it should be repealed. The Association of Chief Police Officers, the Metropolitan Police Service and West Midlands Police thought current legislation effectively protected the public from dangerous dogs and (alongside the Greater London Authority) suggested that BSL should not be repealed.
- 62% answered 'No' to the question, 'Do you think that the exemption introduced by the 1997 amendment should be removed?'
- 68% thought dog control notices might be an effective measure, but 54% did not think they should apply on private property.
- 41% thought third-party insurance should be compulsory for all dog owners, and 84% thought all dogs should be microchipped.

- 78% thought all legislation regarding dogs should be consolidated into a single piece of legislation.
- 53% thought more effective enforcement of current legislation might improve the situation regarding dangerous dogs and 63% thought further training for police officers to become dog legislation officers might help improve the situation regarding dangerous dogs.
- 29% thought BSL should be extended to include other breeds of dog.
- 72% thought the government could do more to raise public awareness of existing legislation and 81% thought there were better ways for the government to communicate with the public, dog owners and owners of 'status dogs'.

Notes

[1] www.defra.gov.uk/corporate/consult/dangerous-dogs/100309-dangerous-dogs-condoc.pdf

[2] www.defra.gov.uk/news/2010/11/25/dangerous-dogs/

Index

Page references for notes are followed by n

Y